SHAPING THE FUTURES OF WORK

Shaping the Futures of Work

Proactive Governance and Millennials

NILANJAN RAGHUNATH

McGill-Queen's University Press
Montreal & Kingston · London · Chicago

© McGill-Queen's University Press 2021

ISBN 978-0-2280-0880-4 (cloth)
ISBN 978-0-2280-1005-0 (ePDF)
ISBN 978-0-2280-1006-7 (ePUB)

Legal deposit third quarter 2021
Bibliothèque nationale du Québec

Printed in Canada on acid-free paper that is 100% ancient forest free
(100% post-consumer recycled), processed chlorine free

Library and Archives Canada Cataloguing in Publication

Title: Shaping the futures of work : proactive governance and millennials
   / Nilanjan Raghunath.
Names: Raghunath, Nilanjan, author.
Description: Includes bibliographical references and index.
Identifiers: Canadiana (print) 20210217782 | Canadiana (ebook) 20210218002
   | ISBN 9780228008804 (cloth) | ISBN 9780228010050 (ePDF) | ISBN 9780228010067
   (ePUB)
Subjects: LCSH: Generation—Effect of technological innovations on—Singapore.
   | LCSH: Generation—Employment—Singapore.
Classification: LCC HQ799.8.S56 R34 2021 | DDC 305.242095957—dc23

This book was typeset by True to Type in 10.5/13 Sabon

To my dearest father

Contents

Preface

In 2020 we saw a pandemic spread quickly around the world. This has thrown not only a curveball but a wrecking ball at many jobs and livelihoods and brought to light the gross levels of inequalities across the world. While the research for this book was carried out before the start of the pandemic, the points I make about millennials and future generations being exposed to technological vulnerabilities are even more valid than ever. Unprecedented changes will mark employment opportunities and the way we work, and that future is now. From the sharing economy to the new-normal economy of the post-pandemic world ridden with trade disputes, debts, and nationalist protectionism, we are staring at flux. Flux refers to an uncertain and anxiety-driven new-normal world with fast automation and technological disruptions, failures for some and incredible opportunities for innovation and success for others. It is a world where we both fear and welcome innovative opportunities. The need for automation and remote work has sped up faster than ever before, making jobs insecure for all ages and professions. Hence, flux or rapid change, shown in a new skills divide, is what most countries are grappling with. Each country needs to work with all its peoples and institutions for economic opportunities rooted in merit, fairness, and equality, and provide avenues for current and future generations to thrive in a flux society.

The flux society is driven by the rise of the algorithm economy, which has changed the way we live our lives.[1] Our social and economic lives are shaped by algorithms (rules) that drive computer hardware, software, Internet browsers, and search engines. Giant organizations such as Google are powerful because of their proprietary rights over sophisticated algorithms for emerging technologies, such as Fintech, driverless cars, surgical robots, Internet of Things (IoT), and many other tech products and services. More recently, technology companies have begun experimenting with algorithms to program machines to perform socially intelligent tasks designed to replace many conventional jobs. The potential for what algorithms can power and change seems limitless, although views about how fast this will happen are both optimistic and pessimistic (Autor, Katz, and Kearney 2006; Autor, Mindell, and Reynolds 2019; Frey 2019; Frey and Osborne 2017). This leads to several questions: Will countries be able to keep up with these technological advancements and the resulting social complexities that arise for current and future generations of workers? Who controls the future of work and future economies? Where does such progress leave the rest of society? Will technologically savvy people be safe from job losses?

During my research, I came to realize that there were no definitive answers about how the future of work was going to evolve. As new anxieties emerge, we need to adapt our individual networks and resources. Changemakers in the present and coming generations will be individuals who can create opportunities for themselves, while being heavily invested in expanding their core expertise, along with multidisciplinary and nuanced skills subject to continuous upgrades. In other words, career paths and skills will no longer last a lifetime, even for digital natives. All of us must be prepared for a life of continuous change, for this is the future of work.

Right now, we are in the fourth industrial revolution. In the third industrial revolution, starting in the 1950s, information technology and knowledge-based services became the norm. The fourth industrial revolution is an upgrade of the third. In this current revolution, there is a blurring of boundaries between the digital, physical, and biological due to the rise of artificial intelligence, machine learning, biotechnology, and other innovations (Schwab 2016).

Adapting to those rapid technological changes, and staying economically and socially competitive, causes instability, or flux, as many existing skills become redundant. Flux is thus theorized as a new normal, where a state of constant change or upgrading is required to manage disruptions and remain competitive (see Bauman 2000; 2007).[2]

Allison Pugh discusses how employees today are entering an "age of insecurity" (Pugh 2015a). She focuses on the American economy, and how the changing nature of work and the volatile economic climate has led to job insecurity for most employees. This has created different levels of anxiety for workers, ranging from reconciling changing workplace expectations to managing personal relationships, where stress is then brought home and spills over. Pugh (2017) argues that the anxieties tied to job insecurities faced by younger workers are a cause for concern. People's inability to cope with these forces often has ramifications for their emotional health and family life (Pugh 2017). Most scholars are certain that insecure employment conditions are now a norm that cannot be challenged. The problem is global, and the discussion doesn't end there. Besides employees, companies and states are also facing increasing anxiety about the uncertainty of the future of work. How do they continue to perform in the midst of these uncertainties?

This book offers, as one solution, proactive governance, a form of collaboration between various economic and social actors. Although I discuss the example of Singapore, every nation-state should have its own version to co-create new jobs and new skills so that people can adapt to changing technology. Technology, in other words, should complement and empower human skills and create new jobs in the process of upgrading old jobs. Nonetheless, jobs as we know them today will be very different in the future. Mariana Mazzucato emphasizes the pivotal role of nation-states in furthering infrastructure and investments in innovation and argues that the private sector should follow suit. She also urges smart and inclusive economic growth, that nation-states not fall back on progress (Mazzucato 2013). The idea behind proactive governance is to urge states to update with the latest innovations that affect jobs and skills, make employers more responsible yet allow them to remain competitive, and help populations cope with the changing employment landscape, by providing them with more opportunities to re-skill. Furthermore, states should proactively lead the effort in creating opportunities for the current and next generation workforces and create policies with good feedback systems (Agar 2019).

This book also focuses on educated millennials because they are the bridge to the future of work. Why millennials, when all countries are very concerned about keeping all generations employed? I argue that millennials are highly vulnerable, because there is no longer a social contract that jobs and skills will last a lifetime even if one is tech-savvy, educated, and employed in white-collar professions, or as entrepreneurs and contractors participating in the sharing economy. Different generations across different countries face different kinds of job vulnerabilities, but educated millennials in developed countries, or those who work in white-collar jobs in multinational firms in developing countries, are not spared either, because, despite being technologically savvy, they face enormous challenges of redundancy (see Kochan 2015). I use the term millennials to describe those born between 1980 and 2000 (Howe and Strauss 2000). They are a pioneering group, having come of age not only in the advent of digital technology, but also in the time of the Great Recession from the late 2000s to the early 2010s. This has created a group of people who have both high expectations of the affordances and effects of technology, yet are cautious about taking risks (Bakhshi et al. 2017).

While the book has primary data on Singaporean millennials, it also looks at global studies of millennials conducted by corporations to debunk popular stereotypes of that generation's expectations and tech savviness. I have found some of my own popular conceptions of millennials to be mostly debunked. From commentaries and interactions with many managers, I used to think that millennials were entitled, lazy job-hoppers who love shared office spaces, remote work, collaboration, and innovation. I found many of the millennials that I interacted with neither entitled nor lazy, just anxious about success. Many of them are putting considerable effort into staying ahead of the game, whether they know it or not. They are hardworking and remain deeply committed to a set of core values imbued in them through their education and the Singapore government's efforts at nation-building. The Singapore story also serves as an important example, because it contains comprehensive policies that aim to help citizens cope with fast-paced local and global economic changes and innovations. These interviews and perspectives provide the substance for my analyses on how the tech-savvy individual responds to anxieties about automation when they are equipped with the resources to access education, continuous training, and job opportunities from the state.

Growing up in a climate of fast-paced change inevitably affects millennials' work ethic, which has been shaped by their education and socialization (Ter Bogt, Raaijmakers, and Van Wel 2005). I find that, like previous generations, millennials still desire stability and are pragmatic. But what sets them apart is the fast-paced environment in which they grew up and their relative comfort with technological tools. Surprisingly, that does not make them any less susceptible to becoming outdated. In fact, many employers assume too much about millennials' attitudes and skills, as shown in the data in chapter 2. The balance of power has also shifted, from those who have the most experience to those who have the most creative breakthroughs. Millennials grew up hearing success stories, for example how Mark Zuckerberg became one of the youngest ever billionaires. As a result, millennial workers are constantly fed the narrative that being young is not an obstacle to making a difference and that experience is a thing of the past. How should they then approach the changing future of work?

Automation also brought anxiety in earlier generations, in the nineteenth and twentieth centuries, because they feared losing their jobs. However, there is a lesson to be learned from twenty-first-century millennials and Gen Z. Some literature claims that the millennial and future generations are worse off than previous generations (Kochan 2015; Thierer 2012).[3] This book attempts to celebrate millennials who are taking on the daunting task of adapting to working in insecure times. They are constantly evolving. Some are taking on stopgap jobs, not simply to fill up time, but with a measured idealism, to achieve the career objectives they have set for themselves. Some contradict the claim that they have unrealistic job expectations. Underpinning these responses is a deep commitment to a larger cause of upward mobility that keeps them inspired. I am optimistic that there is much to learn from this generation about how to handle uncertainties in their careers.

The first contribution I want to make to the existing literature is to provide the perspective of how millennials (as well as those on the cusp of Gen Z) from different backgrounds are responding to change; to weed through all the talk about technology and make some sociological sense of the flux society that I theorize in chapter 1. Millennials are often regarded as being experts on technology and the ones best positioned for the flux society. Nevertheless, their expertise does not exempt them from the anxieties of the changing work environment. I want to offer a better qualitative understanding of millennials that brings their voices to this phenomenon. On the one hand, the millennials that I interviewed and observed were smart, technologically empowered, entrepreneurial, and had a drive to excel. On the other hand, the resources available to them to find and keep jobs had some information gaps. They are often told to network and communicate offline but have little confidence in their abilities to do so. How are their prospects compared with older professionals who face losing their jobs due to financial downturns, globalization, trade wars, pandemic disruptions, or their skills becoming redundant? Millennials will likely go through the same anxieties or more, because unpredictability is on the rise. How do they view their own careers and life chances? How are they coping? To find out, I embarked on a series of in-depth interviews with millennials from diverse backgrounds, including entrepreneurs and professionals at various stages of their careers. I also want to consider how non-millennials view millennials, especially their work ethic. I thus interviewed experts from various industries, including banking, academia, service and manufacturing industries, to understand how non-millennials are experiencing the flux society.

The second contribution I want to make is the role that the state plays in ushering in or being a catalyst for promoting fast-paced automation. A theoretical and empirical understanding of the white-collar workforce is incomplete without discussing how a proactive nation-state will serve as a catalyst for collaboration between citizens, the state, and private enterprise. The state must facilitate a continuous meritocracy, provide feedback about its services, and use various means to engage citizens on the effects of automation. They must carry these out alongside efforts to promote opportunities and legal safeguards for those who prefer entrepreneurship and freelancing, as well as retraining programs that align with the needs of the algorithm economy. Debates on the future of work are heavily invested in the fields of business, economics, and public policy, even if sociologists are the ones studying them. This book therefore attempts to steer the debate within a qualitative sociological lens: I will put myself in the position of millennials so I can understand their views about automation, since their careers are most at risk as it evolves.

Acknowledgments

The writing of this book was supported by a Singapore University of Technology and Design start-up grant. I would like to thank all my interview participants. Their experiences have been pivotal in transforming the way I think about the new work ethic of millennials and Generation Z. I want to thank my research assistants Linda, Jean, and Tony for their help at various stages and the anonymous reviewers for their time and commitment. I thank my late father N.S. Raghunath, mother Vijaya, brother Madhusudhan, sister-in-law Phoebe, and nephews Krishna and Keshava for their love, patience, friendship, and unwavering support. I love you all. Finally, a big thanks to McGill-Queen's University Press and Ms Khadija Coxon for their fantastic support in the successful publishing of this book.

SHAPING THE FUTURES OF WORK

Introduction

Technological anxieties are not new (Mokyr, Vickers, and Ziebarth 2015). David Ricardo (1821/1951, chapter 31) stated, "[T]he substitution of machinery for human labour is often very injurious to the interests of the class of labourers ... [it] may ... render the population redundant and deteriorate the condition of the labourer." Little over a century later, John Maynard Keynes (1930/1963, 358) identified a similar predicament: "Technological unemployment ... [is an issue born of] our discovery of means of economising the use of labour outrunning the pace at which we can find new uses of labour." Automation is imminent in most of the industrialized world and is most likely to affect middle- and lower-level jobs (Autor, Katz, and Kearney 2006; Frey and Osborne 2017). This means that we might see more class polarization (Mühleisen 2018). Polarized or segmented automation across different industries and at varying paces in different countries could worsen the digital divide, unless governments, industry, and academia collaborate with one another to provide training and retraining opportunities for their citizens (Mühleisen 2018).

Due to the rise of machine learning and sophisticated algorithms, those with education capital who have value in the current job market, and *skills updating capital*, have a clear advantage over those who are less educated and have poor access to credentials. The term skills updating capital builds on previous ideas by social-network and social-capital theorists, such as Pierre Bourdieu (1986), Robert Putnam (2000, 2001), and James Coleman (1988), who have contributed extensively to ideas on how people form networks and benefit from social, cultural, and symbolic capital, such as honour, prestige, and recognition, from the resources they can access (Bourdieu 1986). I argue that while networks and social capital are invaluable resources for accessing social mobility, it is now likely that the efficacy of credentials could potentially diminish in the fourth industrial revolution, because technological disruptions are reshaping business models and hiring strategies (Hirst 2015).

Millennial employees are perceived as collaborators, changemakers, and innovators. At the same time, they are sometimes typecast as being hard to manage. In an interview by Chris Myers (2016), one manager said, "As a millennial myself, I found accusations of our sensitivity, narcissism, and sense of entitlement in the workplace to be personally offensive and dismissed them as wholly unfounded. However, after managing a millennial workforce at [my company], I've come to realize just how hard it can be." It becomes imperative, therefore, for governments to do more to encourage entrepreneurship and to create jobs that foster skills suitable for the digital economy (OECD 2012).

The sharing economy, where individuals are able to borrow, rent, and share resources, is one major disruption, and means that jobs no longer consist of steady work and rising pay (Cohen 2017). Companies also face the ever-present challenges of innovation. Artificial intelligence and automation have developed so rapidly in the past decade that many things we considered science fiction have started to become reality today. Holograms, augmented reality, robots, virtual reality, and driverless vehicles in cities are just some of the exciting developments that could change our jobs in the future. However, change may not always be good. That is even truer now, as the Covid-19 pandemic raises many more concerns about the future of jobs and how much automation should be incorporated (Raghunath and Tan 2020a).[1] Although automation has not reached the level of development of displacing every job, it has already brought anxiety to workers globally, worried that machines may soon be able to do some or all of their job functions.

Today, we can enter a restaurant and be greeted by the sight of robots taking on the roles of waiters and chefs. At the same time, self-ordering kiosks and even unmanned convenience stores have increased around the world, all the more relevant now due to the needs of social distancing and contactless transactions. Although fascinating as technological advancements, the effects of this automation on people's lives are real and they have displaced the need for some jobs that are mostly repetitive. Automation's effect on work has been widely researched by scholars in the fields of business management, economics, and the sociology of work (Arntz, Gregory, and Zierahn 2016; Autor, Katz, and Kearney 2006; Frey 2019; Frey and Osborne 2017; Shestakofsky 2017; Vallas and Hill 2018; Vallas and Prener 2012) and others. With innovation comes the consequences of de-skilling as skills get outdated. Frey and Osborne (2017) argue that recent developments in machine learning will put a substantial number of occupations at risk unless they involve human creativity and heuristics.

Moreover, as technology becomes more advanced, the types of jobs that come under threat of replacement by automation may increase. In 2018, Google demonstrated its virtual assistant, Google Duplex, which can make realistic human-like phone calls on behalf of users to make appointments. However, the assistant has not fully replaced humans. In an interview, Google admitted that "about 25 percent of calls placed through Duplex started with a human, and that about 15 percent of those that began with an automated system had a human intervene at some point" (Chen and Metz 2019). Nevertheless, experts in artificial intelligence and automation have asserted that as the technology improves, it is likely that the process could become entirely automated (Moreno 2019). This example shows how humans can continuously be co-opted or phased out as automation technology improves, thus the need to manage the changes that come with the rise of automation in the workplace.

Who is, therefore, responsible for, and accountable for, the changes that are happening to the future of work? Whether competing or complementary, the increase in automation requires a discussion on the new power brokers of the future. Because automation can threaten employment in the future, it is important to consider the role of the state, businesses, and citizens in negotiating the future of work. For example, Singapore plans to roll out sophisticated technology such as AI in the coming years to improve the economy and the quality of life of its populace. Deputy Prime Minister Heng Swee Keat (2019) stated the following in a longer speech.

> Countries will need to keep pace with technology, and harness it to tackle common challenges and national priorities. Singapore has placed a strong emphasis on technology and innovation. Five years ago, we announced our vision to be a Smart Nation, using digital technology to transform our Government, economy, and society. Today, we are taking the next step in our Smart Nation

journey, by launching Singapore's National Artificial Intelligence Strategy. Artificial Intelligence, or AI, is one of the new frontiers in technology, and we can already see its applications in our daily lives. AI chatbots, which mimic natural language, are now widespread. Robo-advisors, powered by AI, can provide financial advice to clients and optimise their assets based on their preferences.

This shows that technology and innovation can and should be harnessed for social good, which is possible, though it will require countries to have much collaboration, foresight, infrastructure, planning, and resources. The above needs buy-in by citizens and businesses in order to work.

THE POWER OF COLLABORATION

Managing the future of work requires collaboration. But what is collaboration and what does it bring to the table? When there is so much uncertainty about the future of work, Sheila Jasanoff argues for a collaborative approach to establish a scientific understanding of the process. In her words, "capacity-building in the face of uncertainty has to be a multidisciplinary exercise, engaging history, moral philosophy, political theory and social studies of science, in addition to the sciences themselves." (Jasanoff 2007, 33). While the context that she speaks of is largely a scientific one, the same principle of co-constructing understanding can be applied here. Multiple disciplines from STEM, social sciences, and humanities need to come together to understand workforce and innovation challenges to formulate policy. Academics look at human resource and work policy as parts of the policy-makers' realm, whereas companies need more exposure to and understanding about the relevance of academic and policy research. At the same time, corporations are worried mainly about their bottom line and how to deal with competitors while trying to grapple with corporate social responsibility and their public image. Ideally, policy-makers, corporations, and academics ought to communicate more about the human resources challenges they each face and work collectively towards a holistic understanding of those challenges. Jasanoff also argues that collaboration is not a merely a matter of participation but should be "a standard operating procedure of democracy" and one of promoting "more meaningful interaction among policy-makers, scientific experts, corporate producers, and the public"

(Jasanoff 2003, 238, 243). Governments should thus do more to link businesses with academic consultancies.

The idea that collaboration brings benefits is also seen in the idea of "collective intelligence," the ability of a group to perform a wide variety of tasks (Woolley, Aggarwal, and Malone 2015). Instead of focusing on the abilities of individuals in a group, this idea suggests that a group possesses a different level of ability to perform tasks that may exceed the capability of any individual in the group. Anita Woolley, Ishani Aggarwal, and Thomas Malone (2015) suggest that the collective intelligence of a group is highly dependent on the ability of the individuals in the group to collaborate effectively, offering diverse perspectives on the issue. Although their research explores individuals and groups, the findings can be extended to higher levels of collective intelligence between various stakeholders such as citizens, businesses, and the government. By obtaining perspectives from stakeholders, the state might be able to offer solutions that individual groups cannot.

In discussing collaborative efforts, it is important to take note of differences between segments of the population. Millennial and Gen Z professionals will make up most of the workforce in the coming decades, and several studies conducted by Deloitte (2017, 2018, 2020), Gallup (2016), Oxford Economics (2015a, 2015b), and the Pew Research Center (2010, 2014, 2016) show that millennials present a major challenge to institutions and policy-makers, who seem to worry about their shifting attitudes in just about everything, including work patterns. Millennials are seen as the leapfrogging innovators who are ready to embrace connectivity in almost every aspect of their lives. Gen Z will likely face similar issues in the future as they join the workforce (Gilchrist 2019).

Even for those equipped with digital competencies and qualifications, there is no finish line on the road to success. Even people with tertiary (university) education are likely to face a skills gap over the course of their lives due to fast-paced technological and societal changes. Countries need a new education model that will prepare their workforce for lifelong employability fused with adaptability and creativity (see McGowan, Adelet, and Andrews 2015).

My conversations across different interest groups show that it has become commonplace among corporations, governments, and some academics to talk about millennials and Gen Z. While they all have different needs, the underlying theme seems to be one of anxiety. Concerns include how to hire millennials, retain them, sell to them, increase their creativity, and improve social integration with team members and communication with them. Overall, corporations and governments still seem to see the millennial generation as an enigma, as institutions try to compete for customers and for new ideas that improve their business and social inclusivity.

AIMS AND OUTLINE

The book is structured as follows: chapter 1 will introduce the reader to the changing work environment and the theory of the flux society. By examining current trends in the future of work, this chapter highlights several types of anxiety that individuals, corporations, and states face due to unprecedented competition, and the need for workers to be self-disrupters in the market. Here, the book argues that these anxieties have an impact on how work evolves.

Chapter 2 further explores one specific segment of the population experiencing the flux environment, the millennial professional, and looks at organizations as creators of flux. In this context, I examine the millennial literature and business reports to explore global perceptions of millennials. I argue that the anxieties and resultant flux explored in chapter 1 arose due to millennials' entrance into the workplace, alongside technological advancements and global professional concerns. Fast-paced technological changes have altered the millennial work ethic, and consequently made it difficult for corporations and states to manage the future of work, despite millennials' perceived tech savviness. By exploring various stereotypes about millennials, I aim to create a clearer understanding of their work cultures.

Chapter 3 introduces readers to the concepts of proactive governance and a proactive state. Proactive states are those that actively engage their citizens in innovation while collaborating with all stakeholders. I argue that proactive governance is a kind of collaborative approach that states can adopt to espouse millennials' co-operative nature. By anticipating changes in the work environment, states can prepare their citizens for the future by equipping them with relevant skills upgrading programs. By collaborating with people and private enterprises, states can instill in citizens a sense of ownership in the regulations that are created, allowing their policies to be more effective. This book emphasizes the notion that everyone plays equally important roles in the proactive governance model. However, the experiences of millennials offer unique insights on the flux society. When states anticipate changes and enact policies, they contribute to shaping current and future generations' work opportunities. Therefore, as states, corporations, and millennials collaborate, anxieties arising from the flux society can be better tackled. Different versions of this can be adapted by different countries according to their varying political systems.

Chapter 4 turns its focus to a case study and example of a proactive state, Singapore, which is also a global Smart City – a city that is technologically resilient, innovative, and safe (Juniper Research 2016). The chapter first briefly introduces the economic history of Singapore, before discussing how the state fulfills the four components of proactive governance. It looks at how Singapore's policies are shaping the future of work and a national vision of continuous meritocracy in this island nation. The latter half of the chapter explores various policies in depth, including the Smart Nation Initiative and the SkillsFuture Initiative, which are aimed at re-skilling the adult population and creating an innovative and future-ready society. The chapter analyzes how the country has adopted a governance style that focuses on constructing a meritocratic work ethic built around pragmatism, proactive and collaborative engagement, self-reliance, and respecting the rule of law as ways of creating both competitive citizens and infrastructure in a continuous remaking of the flux society. The chapter also discusses some of the challenges Singapore faces in fostering creativity and risk-taking, because of millennials' fear of failure, in the fight to remain competitive (Sinniah 2017).

Chapter 5 further examines Singapore's proactive governance by analyzing Singaporean millennials' career and mobility goals. This chapter uses interview data of Singaporean millennials born between 1980 and 2000. The purpose of these interviews is to provide firsthand accounts of their education and career aspirations, their motivations, their fears, and the factors they consider when making important decisions. The chapter analyzes various anxieties that pervade their career choices, and explores issues such as the paradox of choice, their experience with flux, and the choices they made in the process of being socialized by the Singapore education system. In this chapter, the stories of the millennials I interviewed will shed light on how Singapore's model of proactive governance has affected the decisions and work trajectories of these adults, offering a more localized understanding of Mills's theory that "public issues" often manifest as "personal troubles" in individuals' lives (Mills 1959). This chapter also highlights how Singaporean millennials partly fit the labels that businesses tend to have of millennials. Through Singapore's efforts as a proactive state, Singaporean millennials are encouraged to develop opportunities and skills to be more future-ready.

The final chapter, the conclusion, serves several purposes. First, it calls for further research in the areas of work and the changing roles of individual advocacy in various institutions, using multidisciplinary assessments. Next, it questions the lack of human agency and elitism in the debates on the future of work and the algorithm economy. It argues that while institutions mainly focus on the human-capital needs of employees, corporate restructuring, the future of jobs and of cities, and the innovative capacities of nations, they have not placed enough emphasis on understanding non-technological issues, such as changes in social class arising from disruptive innovation, and how technology has become democratized in the algorithm economy.[2] Finally, the conclusion suggests that, along with lifelong learning, stereotypes about age and abilities need to be broken in technologically disrupted societies. The chapter also looks at the forms of capital required in digital economies, such as symbolic capital acquired from one's digital footprint, and the re-organization of work and professions (see Bourdieu 1984). Considering how little discourse there is on the effect of technological changes on women and minorities in millennial studies, and changes in the Anthropocene, where machines and humans might interact more and in newer ways, this book suggests that the future of work clearly needs more thought, not only about its effects, but on how humans collectively shape their global futures.

METHODOLOGY

To explore the connections between millennials and emerging work cultures to tackle the future of work, and the possible opportunities that might arise from proactive governance, this book uses three types of data: first, qualitative interviews of employees, entrepreneurs, and managers; second, secondary data from numerous studies on millennials; and third, the case study of Singapore and its economic and education policies, as one example of proactive governance. The idea is to examine the Singaporean millennial within the larger context of proactive governance and corporations' global white-collar concerns. I therefore conducted interviews with forty college-educated Singaporean millennials and ten Gen X and baby boomer professionals (males and females) from a diverse range of industries.[3] The millennial interviewees included entrepreneurs, non-entrepreneurs, mid-career professionals, and early- or pre-career individuals. All had either obtained a bachelor's or master's degree or had almost completed their degrees, ranging across fields in engineering, the social sciences, and the humanities. I wanted to observe if any underlying patterns featured across these variations.

The methodological emphasis in this book is on educated millennials from developed economies who can afford to go to college and, to a large extent, find white-collar jobs. Researching young people with, at minimum, a bachelor's degree and above is timely, as many white-collar professionals in developed countries are likely to at least have a tertiary qualification such as an undergraduate degree (Graf 2017). Research on advanced economies has largely focused on the adverse effects that globalization has created for less-educated, low-skilled workers (Manyika 2017). The twin developments of the inflating cost of college degrees and worsening economic prospects have caused middle-income graduates to feel more vulnerable than their parents about their economic future. This book attempts to build on the research of these developments and to anticipate the new class of workers who will be affected by the increasing flux caused by automation. Highly educated millennials who have matured with the onset of new technologies are equally affected by its economic consequences, a paradox I seek to investigate with the following question: why has this generation's relative comfort in a digitally connected world afforded them less stability in navigating the rapid pace of automation in the workplace? I therefore examine several data sources that represent multiple narratives of the millennial experience and their perspectives on the future of work. My aim is to provide a sociological framework for understanding millennials in an environment of change and to categorize the volumes of data and literature published on this generation. In addition, the book focuses on understanding proactive governance as a collaborative approach to tackling the future of work. Thus, I have chosen the interviewees so I can gather a wide range of perspectives, including millennials at various stages of their careers, to derive a diversity of insights on the kinds of anxieties they face, and to observe the extent to which their educational training and backgrounds have assuaged some of their career concerns.

Besides engaging directly with millennials, I also conducted interviews with ten Gen X and baby boomer professionals to understand the diverse perspectives towards millennials in the workplace, with my focus once again on obtaining a diversity of views. Thus, the interviewees were selected to reflect a range of industries and professions, including individuals from software consultancies, academia, research foundations, career consultancies, and human resource departments. The professionals provided an important dimension to my research; the educators I spoke to worked in higher education and helped me glean perspectives on the future of work in their areas of expertise and the skills they deemed necessary for new entrants in the economy. The senior managers offered insights on intergenerational collaboration in the workplace. In addition, career coaches from universities provided observations of millennials in their job search process and the relationship between industries and universities. By including non-millennial interviewees who manage millennials, I aimed to obtain an intergenerational perspective on the prevalent issues in the workplace. I also conducted participant observations in company recruitment events in five multinational firms, where I networked extensively with employees across different generations to understand the challenges they face in response to automation in the workplace.

The millennial employment question and the future of work are being studied from several angles by governments, academics, corporations, prominent business literature, and from popular fiction around the world. The millennial employment question is also a term commonly used in the news media by anchors and analysts who try to unravel earnings, consumption, and millennials' voting behaviours. Therefore, I included relevant secondary data to compare them with the Singaporean millennials interviewed. This helped to contrast the local with the global to point out some of the shared concerns of white-collar college-educated professionals.

I relied on several different information sources to better understand the debates surrounding the future of work: 1) a broad selection of industry and government reports, surveys, and trade articles; and 2) professional workshops and talks on the latest trends in the tech industry. I analyzed millennial surveys, including those conducted globally by management consultancy firms such as Gallup, Deloitte, the McKinsey Global Institute, PricewaterhouseCoopers, the Boston Consulting Group, Ernst and Young, the Nielsen Corporation, and Kearney, and reviewed articles in global media companies such as *Forbes* and the *Harvard Business Review*. These sources provided a global context to understand the reasons why Singapore is trying to make its future workforce more competitive. I also analyzed research reports from the Pew Research Center and Oxford Economics, and studied research reports from technology firms, such as IBM and Microsoft. Some prominent business school reports, from the UNC Kenan-Flagler Business School, Stanford University, London Business School, and the Wharton School, provided good sources of information about management practices concerning millennials. To get a sense of what government agencies are saying about this generation of workers, I studied government reports on millennials, such as the White House Council of Economic Advisors, policy information from the Prime Minister's Office of Singapore, Singapore's Ministry of Manpower, Ministry of Education, Ministry of Social and Family Development, Ministry of Trade and Industry, the Housing and Development Board, SkillsFuture Singapore, Workforce Singapore, OECD, the International Labour Organization (ILO), and many other public sectors and organizations. I also attended several seminars on the future of work in Singapore and the United States, learning about some of the policies about the future of work. During my research, I spoke to millennials outside of Singapore to learn about their perspectives on the future of work. Their experiences have also informed my views on the issue. This book will compare global data on millennials and millennials from Singapore. It will show what concerns they might share about the future of work, and what might be different due to specific policy decisions and outcomes in Singapore.

My analysis shows that there could be more data sharing between key stakeholders, and more ethnographic studies on millennials if we are to embrace and build realistic work futures for millennials and the generations to come. The above sources of data were chosen because they comprise comprehensive surveys conducted on millennials in the workplace in the United States and Singapore, and globally. I situate the above literature in the sociological debates on work, and, to a lesser extent, I discuss the effect of policies on the future of work.

CASE STUDY

The future economy brings with it many social and economic challenges (Gunnion 2017). I chose to focus on Singapore to offer a sociological analysis on how these challenges are being handled by policies and national values. Although the unique history of Singapore might not make its specific idea of proactive governance generalizable globally, I hope that the analysis will provide insights for academics and policy-makers to consider proactive governance as adaptable to different social-economic, historical, and political contexts. The choice of Singapore as a case study is particularly relevant, because Singapore has always engaged in proactive governance to encourage economic progress; a unique form of multiculturalism, which is evolving with the times; national security; and strong ties with its neighbours, allies, and the international community (H.C. Chan et al. 2019). In particular, millennials who grew up in a more well-established Singapore from the 1980s onwards have had access to a good education and are entering the rapid automation phase of the Smart Nation initiative. Thus, examining millennials in Singapore offers deep insights into the long-term effects of proactive governance (Goh and Gopinathan 2008; ManpowerGroup 2016). Also, I analyze how the proactive state has affected the millennials' choices and trajectories. I build on C. Wright Mills's "sociological imagination" (Mills 1959) by analyzing how millennials navigate the structures they are placed within, by making sense of their station in society and by considering their individual histories and biographies (see Crouch and McKenzie 2006).

1

Theorizing the Flux Society

The best way to predict the future is to create it.

Unknown source

FLUX IS THE NEW NORMAL

The fourth industrial revolution brings with it the constant need to innovate and upgrade to stay competitive. This chapter discusses in more detail the theoretical premise of this proposition. Furthermore, this theory provides a bridge to understanding that millennials are more vulnerable than previous generations and, therefore, need more opportunities to withstand the many uncertainties they encounter in the job market (see Kochan 2015).

In the flux society, rapid technological changes become the underlying norm of how societal values develop and progress in the fourth industrial revolution. Such a society is created on the foundations of institutions and individuals adapting technological surveillance, integrating big data, simplifying communication, and increasing innovation. These define social and economic progress. At the helm of this change are hackers, innovators, start-ups, and big corporations that create, maintain, and augment algorithms, machine learning, 3D printing, nano materials, and hardware, which define mass capitalist culture. Figure 1.1 is a model of the characteristics of the flux society.

At its core, the flux society embodies innovation and entrepreneurialism. The power brokers of the flux society are thus corporations, governments, and some powerful individuals, who decide the course of capitalism in terms of production and consumption. However, while the flux society celebrates and rewards entrepreneurship

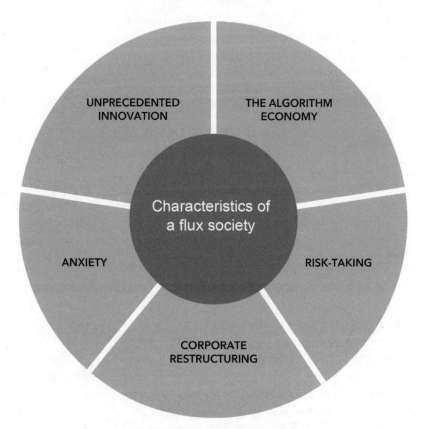

Figure 1.1 The five characteristics of a flux society

and innovation, the cost of failure is very high for those who are unable to adapt (due to the digital divide or lack of opportunities), or who choose not to adapt to the fast-paced changes driven by the state and private enterprise. The institutions and people in the flux society are pushing capitalism to its limits as they digitize most aspects of the economy, and create a workforce that is constantly able to adapt to technological changes.

Ernest Mandel (1975) hypothesized that automation would ultimately push the capitalist mode of production to its limits, and labelled automation the main perpetrator of all future disruptions to the economy. This notion of humans versus the machine implies that humankind is dependent on machines in the face of innovation. Bernard Stiegler (2016, 60) foresees that the "functional integration [of automation] leads on the side of production to a total robotization that disintegrates not just public power, social and educational systems, intergenerational relations and consequently psychic structures: it is the industrial economy itself." That is, automation would be expected to change the very nature of work and society. Yet, there is human agency behind every piece of technology. Automation is a social construct, because human actors shape economic and social progress. For example, machine-learning algorithms are created and facilitated by humans, who program robots with their own social values and biases (Shestakofsky 2017). Today's complex algorithms are increasingly value-laden because of how they are configured for autonomous decision-making. This has led to growing discussions on the ethics of algorithms and automation (Haftor 2009; Mittelstadt et al. 2016; Ramaswamy and Joshi 2009). Since the creators of algorithm codes control what the inputs and outputs should be, tech entrepreneurs and computer scientists are suddenly thrown into new positions of power to mould the future of work, positions for which they never asked to be accountable.

The pace of technological advancement and the exponential growth of workplace automation leave us questioning whether public institutions are losing control over the regulation of job markets. The United Nations Department of Economic and Social Affairs (UNDESA) also points to institutions and policy-makers as the key stakeholders responsible for managing the changes brought about by automation. "The sooner we start re-thinking and re-designing labour market policies, social security schemes and taxation systems, the better we will adapt to the future that is already happening" (UNDESA 2017). There is no doubt that the state plays a critical role in managing the effects of automation despite some governments' seeming lack of knowledge of the issue.

However, should governments be the only actors working towards managing the effects of flux caused by automation? Earlier studies by economists such as Carl Frey and Michael Osborne, and Maarten Goos, Alan Manning, and Anna Salomons, suggest that algorithm-driven automation will result in job losses and the restructuring of the labour market (Frey and Osborne 2017; Goos, Manning, and Salomons 2014). In the case of automation in the workplace, these economists suggest that corporations adopt more automation to increase economic efficiency. The state's role is therefore to facilitate the rapid incorporation of technology for increased efficiency in the economy. In more recent works, many economists, including Carl Frey, Maarten Goos, and David Autor, have taken on a less economically deterministic stance, suggesting that a technology-driven future still requires states, businesses, and people to integrate the technology into their lives for maximum efficiency (Autor, Mindell, and Reynolds 2019; Frey 2019; Goos et al. 2019). Although some economic sectors may stagnate from lack of automation, global economies are driven by the need for rapid digitization to remain competitive.

The flux society also embraces changing networks of people and ideas that are constantly shifting. This includes organizations and governments, which face persistent challenges to keep up. At the heart of this society lies the constant tension of being outdated and left behind. It is bound up in multiculturalism and cosmopolitanism and embedded in all social classes, which need to have access to upward mobility through education and digitalization.

Ulrich Beck and Martin Chalmers discussed the risk society as "an inescapable structural condition of advanced industrialization" (Beck and Chalmers 1996, 28), where the whole world becomes a testing ground for ideas. They contend that technology, which has been responsible for transforming modern societies, will also introduce new risks. In an earlier work, Beck defines risk as "a systematic way of dealing with hazards and insecurities induced and introduced by modernization itself" and as "politically reflexive" (Beck 1992, 21). By risk, Beck does not mean the commonly understood synonym of catastrophe, but the anticipation of catastrophe (Beck 2006). In addition, instead of the world progressing into a postmodern age, it is progressing into a "second modernity," where the first modernity is transformed and changed, often in undesirable or unanticipated ways (Beck and Lau 2000). Beck suggests that unforeseen outcomes of modernity will end up backfiring on their initial advocates (Wimmer and Quandt 2006). In particular, he suggests that the risk society poses global consequences, of generating nuclear technology, nanotechnology, and genetically modified products, which produce risks that threaten all classes. However, Beck acknowledges that some classes are more vulnerable to such risks due to inequalities in social class positions (Beck 1992; Beck, Giddens, and Lash 1994). Beck's ideas of risk also include the human obsession with continuous change and upgrading through science and technology.[1] These ideas gained trac-

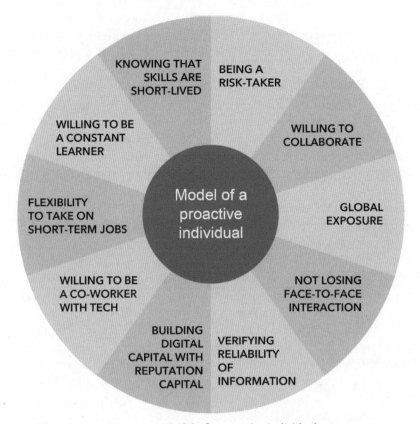

KNOWING THAT SKILLS ARE SHORT-LIVED

BEING A RISK-TAKER

WILLING TO BE A CONSTANT LEARNER

WILLING TO COLLABORATE

Model of a proactive individual

FLEXIBILITY TO TAKE ON SHORT-TERM JOBS

GLOBAL EXPOSURE

WILLING TO BE A CO-WORKER WITH TECH

NOT LOSING FACE-TO-FACE INTERACTION

BUILDING DIGITAL CAPITAL WITH REPUTATION CAPITAL

VERIFYING RELIABILITY OF INFORMATION

Figure 1.2 Model of a proactive individual

tion in the mid-1980s because they coincided with the occurrence of man-made risks like the Chernobyl disaster of 1986. When the distribution and anticipation of risks begin to spread at a supra-national level, the risk society becomes a global phenomenon (Beck 1992).

In a similar but more optimistic approach, Anthony Giddens associates the risk society with modernization, but, despite its name, does not consider it necessarily negative. He and Christopher Pierson aptly define the risk society as "a society increasingly preoccupied with the future (and also with safety), which generates the notion of risk" (Giddens and Pierson 1998, 209). Risk can be positively viewed as "the taking of bold initiatives in the face of a problematic future" (ibid.). The two ideas of risk and the risk society are both key in today's flux society; in Beck's words, "where risks are believed to be real, the foundations of business, politics, science and everyday life are in flux" (Beck 2000, 214). Beck argues that "being at risk is the way of being and ruling in the world of modernity; being at global risk is the human condition at the beginning of the twenty-first century" (Beck 2006, 330). It is with an understanding of these ideas and concepts that this book attempts to make the argument that adapting to change is necessary to thrive in the flux society, not just at the beginning of the twenty-first century, but beyond. The model in figure 1.2 summarizes the ten qualities that I predict will be most essential for workforces and future generations in the flux society.

Given that the face of work is rapidly changing, workforces will *need to be risk-takers* and willing to embark on unconventional endeavours since their *skills will be short-lived*. Instead of banking on one set of qualifications or degrees, workforces must be *willing to be constant learners* and embrace continuous meritocracy by updating their skills. Changes in their organizations and careers will be inevitable, so employees and entrepreneurs must be *flexible in taking on shorter-term job contracts* in the interim, entering new sectors where they feel uncomfortable, with open minds to learn. Is there an alternative to this? In the current pace of innovation, and how states and firms are embracing the same thing, probably not. In the age of fast-emerging technologies, workforces will also have to be *willing to be co-workers with technology,* and actively seek to *build their digital capital along with reputation capital* (Bourdieu 1989; Bughin and Manyika 2013).[2] Given that huge amounts of information are being disseminated through online media, workers will also need to be conscientious and proactive in *verifying the credibility and reliability of information.* Even though they will be expected to work with technology, employees should *not ignore face-to-face interaction* to build social capital and strengthen their existing ties. To remain relevant across transboundary economies, employees should not limit their ties to the local sphere but should actively seek to gain *global exposure*. In all these interpersonal interactions, what remains essential is that the employees be *willing to collaborate.*

When talking about millennials and other generations, a lot of emphasis is also placed on the effect of technology on their jobs, which is blamed for possible current and future job losses. There is also the question of millennials and their impact on work and the economy. Opinions are split on this issue. While some are cautious, or even wary of the future of work that this generation of workers will shape, others are positive about the kind of lifestyle that will come to be defined by millennials. For example, it has been argued that the millennial priority of living a particular, desired lifestyle that contrasts with the materialistic aspirations of former generations will herald an era of "late materialism," where technology and social innovation are deemed key ingredients for its flourishing (Taylor 2018). This combination of fearing the unknown (innovation from competitors and the impact of millennials) and getting ahead with innovation creates anxieties for corporations, governments, employees, entrepreneurs, freelance contractors, and other individuals trying to navigate uncertainty in the flux society.

THE FLUX SOCIETY AND ANXIETY

The flux society is riddled with anxiety about the future. The fast pace of automation provides grounds for many anxieties that centre on fears of collaboration, being outdated, trailing behind the competition, and not having the next innovative idea fast enough. This has generated anxiety among businesses. For example, instead of a dogged adherence to traditional, outdated models of organizational design, organizations are under pressure to quickly redesign themselves to facilitate faster adaptations and learning and be ready to accept the career demands of their employees, as well as the demands of the competitive global business environment. Moreover, smaller teams, rather than hierarchical structures, have been found to be more conducive to adapting to new economic environments; hence, the new work model needs agile formations and disbanding of teams made up of members who are mobile and can work in new projects (Bersin et al. 2017). Furthermore, the push to use the Internet and smart devices to create new work arrangements and IoT, with little understanding of how regulation and training might be effective for creators and consumers, is generating concern.

A conversation with business leaders Chin et al. (2017) in their McKinsey analytics report found that anxiety is felt by company leaders who are unsure what to make of the opportunities and disruption brought about by data and advanced analytics. They are uncertain about what value there is in applying analytics to yield business solutions deemed superior to existing ones, as well as how they can potentially use analytics to generate more sources of income. As a result, they struggle to make a case for analytics and to communicate its benefits in their organization. Even when they have successfully obtained data, the task of generating consensus on analytic methods and the types of data used for competitive advantages may prove difficult for business leaders to overcome. Access to analytics is also largely restricted to business leaders in most companies, which can make decision-making about analytics myopic and limited. Business leaders also face pressures to look for employees who are not only good at either business or technology, but are adept at both (Chin et al. 2017). Change anxiety is also highlighted in organizational perceptions of millennial attitudes towards work and organizational responses to changes in government policies. According to a biannual global risk report by Aon, companies fear changes that are uninsurable, such as failure to innovate and business interruption; failure to attract top talent; damage to reputation; increase in competition; and regulatory changes, among others (Rapoza 2013).

Companies are also concerned about deficiencies in their corporate cultures, which can become obstacles to company success. The 2016 McKinsey Digital survey found a clear correlation between cultural barriers and poor economic performance (Goran, LaBerge, and Srinivasan 2017).[3] If companies lack initiative in proactively changing their organizational culture, they may be unable to catch up with the growth of digital penetration. The onus is therefore on executives to be proactive in how they view and handle their culture, in very much the same way they manage other organizational transformations.

In the area of risk-taking, it might be too simplistic to think of risk and failure as a straightforward equation, where experimentation, in addition to an absence of punishment for failure, would always lead to positive results. Time is a crucial factor too, in that risks can take a long time to present themselves and capital markets are often reluctant to take on investments that take a long time to bear fruit. In today's digital age, risk-taking has become even more frightening because of the high cost of failure. Leaders must make sure that all ranks of the organization are free to take risks and innovate and take bold steps in the process of changing their own mindsets about risk. This may mean two things: they have to trust their employees without putting in place too many obstacles that might stifle the latter's liberty to take risks, and they must take on the responsibility of making bold decisions. For employees, the changing attitudes towards risk and failure will help encourage a similar spirit of willingness to take risks without undue fear of failure, while being equipped at the same time with skills, mindsets, and information access, upon which they can draw. Alternatively, companies can engage the expertise of outside start-ups or digital natives to provide fresh and innovative ideas, as Target has done (Knowledge@Wharton 2015; Target 2018).

Business leaders must be ready to work on goals that reflect how fast disruption is moving within their industry. For example, retail stores have had to rethink the role of physical stores because of the disruptive impact e-commerce has had on sales. Central to any company's survival is adopting a customer-centric organizational model that leverages consumer collaboration; it requires abolishing barriers that prevent information sharing and garners innovative input through customers' opinions and perspectives. LEGO is one company that has been successful in using this model. In doing so, the relationship between company and customer is also tightened. In short, technological changes will always move faster than companies can change their organizational cultures. This means that leaders will have to be more proactive in anticipating and acting on potential cultural issues they identify. To respond quickly and efficiently to technological changes, business leaders need to ensure that their organizational cultures are able to not only perform in terms of business functions and business units but are open to taking risks and focusing on customer satisfaction (Goran, LaBerge, and Srinivasan 2017).

White-collar professionals are also anxious about the changing nature of work. Ilana Gershon (2017) argues that the nature of work and career trajectories have changed in the past decades to involve a stronger sense of personal branding. To find jobs and be promoted, workers must manage their public image. Gershon adds that technology is facilitating this change in the nature of work. For example, recruiters can gather more information on job applicants by accessing their social media accounts. Moreover, because the shift towards the sharing economy and other forms of gig work has inevitably made jobs more precarious (Kalleberg 2011; Vallas and Prener 2012), workers are paying more attention to personal branding (Vallas and Hill 2018). Although there are differences among this population on the necessity of personal branding due to occupational differences, it is undeniable that personal branding has become ubiquitous in the contemporary economy (ibid.). The need for employees to not only excel at their jobs, but to present a brand of themselves creates a sense of resistance and anxiety among some millennials (ibid.).

Another anxiety experienced by professionals stems from their perceptions about practical approaches to effective social networking. This anxiety is created by the need to form and upgrade diverse networks across generations for local and global collaborative teams, clients, etc. Target's and other similar firms' emphasis on reverse mentoring signals their interest in ensuring their employees bridge both formal and informal ties between generations (Alcorn 2016). Companies like Target view the cohesion of different generations across the workforce as an important bonding ritual, and consequently organize numerous bonding events to forge these ties. As Elizabeth, a career coach, pointed out, reverse mentoring may be more visible in newer technology firms than in larger corporations with formal hierarchies. Although the younger generation entering these technology firms may have skills that the older generation lacks, the role of experience and relationships is more important in larger corporations (Kwoh 2011).

The organizational push to make employees super networkers and super collaborators clearly shows that there is no end to new opportunities and ideas. Networking is often treated as a social event or a form of organizational recreation time for employees to mingle. Luke, a millennial early career employee at a technology firm, remarked to me, "I am not sure I am a good networker. Can I improve that? What are the exact steps?" Employers benefit from harnessing the informal networks of their employees (Bryan, Matson, and Weiss 2007). It is easier when networks occur in a natural state, as information flows in non-hierarchical and informal settings, especially when people share interests. Employees urge corporations to boost these informal networks, rather than force-fit people into collaborative teams (Bryan, Matson, and Weiss 2007).

The sociological literature on networks is enormously rich, and tells us everything from the importance of structure, position, and quality of ties to time analysis and influence.[4] However, we still know little about the personality, social positioning, and influential characteristics of a person either with strong ties within a group, or weak ties to other groups. Organizations use social media extensively to get employee suggestions for various organizational needs such as how to improve sales targets, generate innovation, etc. Nonetheless, what millennials lack are the skills for conversations, both offline and on social media.[5]

Talent and performance anxieties arise due to the emergence of newer arrangements of work such as remote work and contract work. Performance is no longer just about being a compliant and efficient employee. It requires flexibility, creativity, social bonding, etc. Lucas, a millennial manager from a major software giant, mentioned to me that his company measures performance from reports of subordinates by project managers, and then compares it across the cohort of employees in the same grade. Other firms use a scale from 1 to 5 and rank their employees according to a curve. The performance report is a mixture of qualitative and quantitative feedback and ratings. Interestingly, I heard, from conversations between millennial employees at a technology firm, that they were unclear about how their individual contributions were measured as opposed to their contributions as a team. Performance varies depending on the function of an employee, department, etc. Therefore, greater transparency is required.

The *New York Times* called gruelling competition the defining feature of the modern workplace after it surveyed many technology and law firms (Steinhage, Cable, and Wardley 2017). In Deloitte's 2019 Global Human Capital Trends survey, it was found that 86 per cent of the respondents believed that they had to reinvent their ability to learn. The study also states that technological implementation will create a new breed of "super jobs," which will need workers to constantly reinvent their skills and work attitudes (Deloitte 2019). Deloitte believes that the gap between technological advances and actual work performed can be closed by understanding how technology, employees, businesses, and public policy play a role in managing employees (Bersin et al. 2017).[6]

Of note is the pressure that companies are feeling to provide "always on and always available" learning experiences, so that their employees can obtain skills quickly, easily, and on their own terms (Bersin et al. 2017, 29). This recognizes the reality of longer lifespans and their impact on the world of work, among other concerns, claim Lynda Gratton and Andrew Scott (2016). Gratton and Scott contend that working into one's seventies or eighties will be the norm because of longer lifespans, and because skills obtained in one's youth are unlikely to remain relevant over one's lifetime. Therefore, re-skilling is of paramount importance (Gratton and Scott 2016). Also, to identify, attract, and recruit the right people for jobs in a constantly evolving employment market, talent acquisition is becoming one of companies' key concerns. How employees are evaluated as well as what business leaders are needed will also change. Digitalization is poised to continuously revolutionize workplaces. Words associated with automation, such as robotics and AI, as well as those associated with the open-talent economy, such as sharing economy and freelancers, have infiltrated work rhetoric, reflecting the impact that technology is having on the changing face of work (Bersin et al. 2017). Susan Lund, partner at the McKinsey Global Institute (MGI), observes that the decline of traditional 9-to-5 jobs will continue. In addition, freelancers and sharing-economy contractors are on the rise, which is only possible through technology, according to Michael Chui, an MGI partner (Camden et al. 2017).

The sharing economy, enabled by technology, is one key reason for the job insecurity that engenders anxieties in the flux society. The definition of the sharing economy remains unclear. It has been described as a working environment that offers flexibility in employment hours and, more cynically, as a form of exploitation with very little protection (Wilson 2017). The sharing economy is also defined by Juliet Schor as a new system comprising peer-to-peer transactions, enabled by digital platforms (Schor et al. 2015). In more neutral terms, the sharing economy is commonly characterized by gigs, or short-term and freelance work without the permanence associated with traditional jobs, where the remuneration for work done is on a task-by-task basis. This is arguably not a new phenomenon despite only recently becoming a byword for technologically mediated economies. It has been pointed out that before the first Industrial Revolution, most types of economic exchanges were community-based and peer-to-peer and were made possible because of the trust based on social ties (Chandler 1993). The flexibility that comes with the on-demand work model has often been hailed as one of the biggest benefits to employers and workers alike. However, as independent contractors, with no access to employee welfare, such as sick pay and minimum wage, sharing-economy workers are also more vulnerable to exploitation and have no recourse if they are treated unfairly (Wilson 2017). Because sharing-economy workers are paid per task, their income is directly dependent on the availability of jobs. In the example of a 2014 case against Uber classifying the people who work for the company as contractors rather than employees, Arun Sundararajan points out that the traditional notions of employment may no longer apply in this age of the sharing economy (Sundararajan 2016). The insecurity arising from the sharing economy has led advocates, including Robert Reich, labour secretary under the Clinton administration, to push governments to consider ways to hedge their workers against job losses arising from technological disruption. Specifically, he suggested that developed economies should provide assistance in the form of a universal basic income (M.H. Chua 2018). Despite the prominence of the sharing economy, the lack of policies providing social safety nets has generated great anxiety among these workers (Sundararajan 2016).

Talent and performance anxiety might also become a concern as automation enters the workplace, with its potential for worker displacement. The Robotic Industries Association estimated that in 2015, more than 260,000 robots were operating in the United States, primarily in the automotive, semiconductor, and electronics industries. This figure, which ranks third to Japan and China, is projected to increase, with no signs of slowing down (Robotic Industries Association 2016). This means that the demand for low-skilled labour will continue to decrease. Additionally, robots in the form of cognitive computing assistants, or virtual assistants, capable of fulfilling human duties such as auto-correspondence, appointment scheduling, and other office functions are also slowly changing employment in white-collar workplaces (Miscovich 2017).

So far, I have explored the ways that various groups have experienced anxieties due to the flux society and examined what actions they've taken in attempting to tackle these anxieties. Flux is the new-normal high-speed change that is here to stay. As the face of work continues to evolve, with developments in automation, states, and businesses, people must constantly upgrade their skills and welcome the changing future. However, this might not be possible for everyone. Many of the anxieties discussed have been associated with the introduction of automation into the workforce and the entrance of millennials as the latest part of the workforce. However, millennials (and soon Gen Z), as the new entrants to the workforce, have often been poorly understood. Corporations often perceive them as a problematic generation of workers that needs to be managed appropriately.

In the next chapter, I will examine the global literature about millennials and dispel some myths that have shaped millennial stereotypes. By understanding this group more deeply, we will be able to better appreciate how they can contribute to tackling the rapidly changing future of work in a flux society.

2

Corporations as Agents of the Flux Society

In this chapter, I will examine the global literature from corporations and research institutions and seek to debunk some myths to more clearly understand millennials and their vulnerabilities. Corporations are major agents of flux, because of their constant push for innovation. This destabilizes work environments because requirements for employees are constantly changing. Because millennials are tech savvy, they are expected to adapt easily, but this also means expectations for them are high (Deloitte 2017; ManpowerGroup 2016).

THE RISE OF THE FLUX SOCIETY
AND CHANGING ORGANIZATIONAL CULTURES

Classical sociological theory provides us with a basis for understanding macro-level social changes such as industrialization, work ethic, and division of labour. The works of Max Weber (1904/1998) and Emile Durkheim (1893/2014) help us to frame the fundamental questions that have continued from their time to ours. How do attitudes towards work and the organization of work shape society? What these theorists predicted is relevant even today, such as the important role of bureaucratic rules and structures and their interplay with conceptions of science, individualism, and capitalist practices for profit-making. Weber and Durkheim correctly predicted the kinds of social anxieties caused by technological innovation. When Karl Marx talked about the industrial worker of the nineteenth century, he was referring to disenchanted, underpaid people economically exploited by the elites who ruled them, since the latter controlled both knowledge flows and the means of production (Marx 1859/1904). The early sociologists and economists focused on specialization, and, with it, the division of labour, but they could not predict the unprecedented innovation that would result from the magnitude of personal and corporate ambition and scientific achievements of digital technology. The changes in bureaucracy in firms, as Max Weber envisioned, are very different now with the rise of flexible organizations. Catherine Turco aptly describes them as "conversational firms," which attract young people to innovate in what seem to be flat hierarchies that encourage their employees to voice their opinions about everything (Turco 2016). Richard Sennett sees a decline in organizational trust and the value of employees (Sennett 2007). The flux society is steeped in dichotomies: on the one hand individualism is on the rise; on the other hand, nothing happens without teamwork or a network.

One of the main social agents of the flux society is corporations because of fierce competition amid massive insecurities and anxieties about the future. Companies, from fledging start-ups to big and established firms, are plagued by a pressing issue: the failure to implement creative ideas generated by employees, because of time limitations and resource difficulties or failed "intrapreneurship" (Altringer 2013). Even when outsourced to consultancy firms, the ever-present uncertainty underlying the making and delivery of the product means that the anxiety felt by the client company is never fully assuaged (Kwoh 2011). The correlation between creative ideas and anxiety also goes beyond dollars and cents; the lack of initiative to implement innovative ideas can also be socio-political, stemming from management's desire to avoid conflict and disruption (Baer 2012). Furthermore, never in history have risk-taking, flexibility, and innovation been pushed and celebrated in every aspect of organizational culture and individual goal-setting. As Anthony Giddens aptly summarizes, "The risk climate of modernity is thus unsettling for everyone: no one escapes" (Giddens 1991, 124). Innovation is no longer just the priority of scientists in laboratories; it is now expected from any techie, leader, or entrepreneur who wants a progressive firm. Volumes of literature have emerged from companies, such as Deloitte, on the numerous types of innovation, such as product, process, marketing, organic, and enhancement. This clearly indicates that companies want to overhaul their processes and find ways to invigorate new ideas into their organizations (Keeley et al. 2013). This poses a lot of interesting questions. How do the pressures to innovate affect employers' and employees' sense of commitment to their firms? Countless research studies show that millennials are less committed to their firms, but few studies have really tried to understand the opportunities and obstacles being presented to this generation (Brack and Kelly 2012).

Millennial employees are under pressure to innovate (in whichever way the organization defines that). In other words, innovation has grown beyond the research and development departments of organizations, as other departments, such as legal teams, human resources, marketing, and finance, all hope to be effective team players within an organization (Hamel 2006). Hence, expectations of millennials and younger generations to confront rapid technological change by embracing risk and failure as lessons for growth are increasing. Millennials are thus forced not only to build their personal brand, but to be part of a larger conversation with organizational teams and networks for rapid and financially rewarding innovation. This theory of a flux society is pushing for an ideal type of millennial employee, a techie stereotype with a college degree; a big dream; and social, economic, or environmental sustainability at heart. This image in turn puts a lot of social expectations on millennials within corporations and makes them vulnerable to constant technological upgrades with little in the way of long-term secure jobs.

Businesses see millennials partly as assets walking in and out of a revolving door, replaceable contingent resources, in effect, who are largely valued in the way they affect the bottom line of innovation and profits, even though much is being done to create flat hierarchies and open cultures, as Turco's (2016) study suggests, particularly in tech firms. Employers can no longer promise lifetime employment, so they need a continuous and uninterrupted supply of well-trained recruits whom they can retrain. Millennials have been socialized to think that career insecurities are the norm and that networks are the answer to a successful career. The helicopter parents of this generation urged their children on to make them more competitive in stressful economic times. Hence, millennials are often depicted as demanding quicker promotions, training, and developmental opportunities (PwC 2018). From the organizational viewpoint, companies want profits and an image of social inclusivity and social responsibility. While some scholars like Turco (2016) correctly attribute the rise of the flexible organization to the empowerment of employees, more could be said about how millennials leverage their networks and take on risks in disruptive forms of capitalism (see Sennett 2007). Lifetime commitment is clearly a thing of the past in most organizations. Millennial employees are likely to be more committed to their network than the current organizations they work for, as mentioned by some of the interviewees. Perhaps both employees and organizations are aware of this estranged sense of commitment, especially non-tenured professionals, including managerial and senior management jobs that are prone to the chopping block. So how do both employers and employees play the human resource function in a competitive world of flux? Employees need to hone their skills and constantly retrain and have plenty of what Mark Granovetter (1973) called the "strength of weak ties," i.e., establishing a lot of connections to a lot of people. In the banking industry, it is already possible to witness the strength of these ties. When an investment banker is poached by another investment bank or a hedge fund, it is not surprising for the hiring firm to subsequently hire many of their contacts as well (Hanlon 2004). Similarly, Ronald, a millennial founder of a virtual reality company, used his ties to find employees for his start-up:

> I think my team, some of them, I met them from meetups that we do during when we were just starting out. Before I started the company, we had a lot of meetups and organized meetups and through that platform, we managed to find some people who are like minded and believe in the same vision. So, we got them. I also roped in some of my friends who are looking for a job, and, like, free. So, I managed to get them on board and teach them the ropes and ask them to help me out when we were just starting out.

Organizations in highly competitive markets benefit from hiring a group of networked individuals. As organizations become more answerable to regulators, and numerous internal and external stakeholders, changes in organizational culture that foster inclusivity among various generations have become the norm. When I attended technology firms' recruitment drives for undergraduate engineering students, the message from recruiters was clear. They wanted employees who could network, innovate, and grow beyond their job scope. Students' main concerns, however, centred on training, on-the-job learning opportunities, and a short timespan for promotions. Both sides appeared to be concerned about stagnation, hence the push for constant change (see Bauman 2000; 2007).

In an age where security and material successes are highly valued, employees are constantly under pressure to perform. Their work ethic is driven by the constant push to take risks rather than any commitment to long-term organizational goals. Ulrich Beck argues that risks and how society conducts its technologically intensive constituents are closely related (Beck 1992). Advanced modernity in the twentieth century has seen accelerated changes in the number of risks and their rapid spread (Rosa, Renn, and McCright 2013). In light of new threats to humanity, the focus is now on preventing, and anticipating, future risks (Beck 2006; Ewald 2002). The changing nature of risks and difficulty in predicting these risks cause businesses to feel a great sense of anxiety. While they like to mitigate and plan for avoiding the types of big economic, environmental, and political risks that Beck (2006) envisioned, they also want to be reflexive and flexible in their organizational cultures in order to innovate and race their competitors, which can potentially pose further financial risks (Gans 2020).

THE TECH-SAVVY GENERATION
AND ITS STEREOTYPES

Indeed, in the course of my research, most of the millennials I spoke to had differing motivations for pursuing careers as varied as entrepreneurs and as professionals in banks, the civil service, logistics, manufacturing, and technology firms. Some of them were motivated by a combination of encouragement from close friends and family, as well as personal interest, whereas for others it was simply identifying an up-and-coming trend from which they would benefit. One similarity I observed is that these millennials are all aware of what their interests are, even if their ability to pursue them as a career may depend on other factors, such as opportunities and financial resources.

During a trip to the United States in 2016, I spoke to several millennials to better understand the phenomenon of automation and work. Among these individuals were ten students at a premier research university in the Boston area who shared their plans post-university. One of them said she was unsure about the type of company she wanted to work for, but she was sure that she did not want to be in trapped in a big firm. She wanted the freedom to think and play, but had several financial concerns, which she said would influence her final choices. Another member of a design team told me that he could not work in a firm where he did not have the freedom to think, where his ideas would not be valued. Six others were very confident that the status of their degree would get them a job anywhere and in any firm. Two graduates of an elite business school were clear that being a founding member of or joining a start-up is trendy for millennials and has mostly taken over the keen interest to join investment banks and consulting firms of a decade ago. These conversations highlighted the types of jobs these American millennials want in the future. Though they were ready to embrace risk to maintain their individuality, they were also worried about the future.

Risk can also be appropriated to create wealth for organizations and need not always be negative in the flux society. Paired with the promotion of entrepreneurship and innovation spearheaded by governments, younger employees are often seen as technologically savvy game-changers. However, technological savviness comes at a cost: the need to constantly upgrade and adapt, and many millennials are reporting burnout from overwork (Gilchrist 2019). In that sense, millennials are just as, if not more, vulnerable than older generations to disruptions. As a result, numerous studies are carried out each year to try and understand how to bring out the best in this generation (Deloitte 2020) and play an important role in the general population's views of generational differences. Some examples of such studies include Simon Sinek's Inside IQ Quest talk on millennials in the workplace. Sinek talks about millennials' lack of physical interactions and problems of instant gratification, placing them at a disadvantage in the workplace, because they feel entitled and impatient (Gregory 2016). Sinek blames this on failed parenting strategies and superficial relationships. Millennials are good at putting filters on things due to social media but are unable to cope with the real world (Ochen 2017). Many of these studies have heavily influenced corporate perceptions of millennials, making them vulnerable to stereotypes.

Almost every major company has surveyed their employees because they believe it is beneficial for human resource teams to make informed decisions, and enable organizations to empower employees through flat hierarchies, validation, and constructive feedback. These surveys and other reports have revealed several recurring themes about millennials: a desire for flexible work arrangements, an ability to harness technology for work, and relative optimism about employment despite bleaker economic conditions, as well as the importance they place on intrinsic motivators, such as a company's purpose. Often, these themes come with associated stereotypes and myths about the millennial work ethic, which largely depict millennials as a problematic group of workers that must be managed by firms. Within corporate cultures, these stereotypes dominate the conversation. By imagining the work ethic of millennials through stereotypes, corporations inevitably shape the work ethic of their employees. The image of millennials perpetuated by these stereotypes subsequently affects how firms choose to manage them and their careers. It is not unusual for big corporations to intervene in the socialization of their employees by training them continuously, giving them both soft skills and technical skills, as well as teaching them how to talk and act (Kunda 1992). By aligning millennials with company values and the image of the ideal employee, firms can benefit from greater employee loyalty and work commitment. Jason Wingard from the Wharton School found that millennials who developed a clear understanding of the company's goals tended to work harder (Knowledge@Wharton 2015). In fact, some employers are so pervasive in individual private spaces that they are everywhere in the lives of millennials and other generations. They have taken over non-business activities such as sports and family outings and made these avenues of bonding and bridging ties between employees and clients.[1]

MODERN WORK ETHIC

Contemporary studies on work values or work ethic focus on generational characteristics. A generation can be defined as a group of individuals who not only share birth years that roughly correspond to the passage from youth to adulthood but also experience and share significant life experiences (Buonocore, Russo, and Ferrara 2015; Howe and Strauss 2000; Kowske, Rasch, and Wiley 2010; Krahn and Galambos 2014; Mannheim 1952). Neil Howe and William Strauss also argue that this shared experience forms part of what they call a "generational persona," which also includes perceived membership in a common generation, common beliefs, and behavioural patterns (Howe and Strauss 2000). Because of this shared experience, unique to each generation, variations in ideas, values, and behaviour can be expected to arise between generations (Callahan 2008). A study by Michael Laskawy (2004) found that young adults' career planning in the 1970s differed from that of young adults today, despite similarities in their levels of education and ambition. The differences lay in how the 1970s group had more long-term strategic gains, could articulate their goals better, and had clearer desires.

However, the findings of another study done by Raymond Van Ness et al. (2010), seem to disagree with Laskawy (2004). The study set out to investigate possible differences between generations of workers, by comparing the work values of college students and workforce professionals. These college students were from a large northeastern university and a smaller northeastern college in the United States, and the workforce professionals were selected from businesses in a variety of industries, such as manufacturing, financial services, and medical supplies. Using the Multidimensional Work Ethic Profile, a measure of seven dimensions of work ethic developed by Michael Miller, David Woehr, and Natasha Hudspeth based on Weber's work ethic construct, the authors found instead that there were no significant differences in the students' work ethic (Miller, Woehr, and Hudspeth 2002; Van Ness et al. 2010).

While the college students in this study were not referred to as a specific generation, their ages at the time of the study suggest that they belong to the millennial generation. Howe and Strauss argue that a new generation is defined when there are rapid and unexpected shifts in the perception of children, and millennials belong to the era of "wanted children," a notable shift from the 1970s and the 1980s when abortion rates in the United States were at their highest (Howe and Strauss 2000). This group of yearned-for individuals have thus received much attention not only from their parents and schools, but also from scholars, popular literature, and the press (Howe and Strauss 2000; Myers and Sadaghiani 2010). The sociologist Ruth Milkman also notes that this generation is highly educated but must fend for themselves in a stagnant labour market with limited options, a global phenomenon that observes them alternating between postsecondary education and unstable jobs, resulting in a prolonged transition to adulthood. This contrasts with the generation of baby boomers, characterized by people who came of age in a time of more abundant job opportunities (Duke 2016; Milkman 2017).

This economic set-up, in addition to others in areas of social, educational, and political significance, is unique to millennials and together may have given rise to popular, and negative, stereotypes (Thompson and Gregory 2012). Some of these stereotypes include a lack of loyalty, a sense of entitlement, and a casual attitude towards work-related codes of conduct, such as dress codes and office hours (Chatrakul Na Ayudhya and Smithson 2016; Marston 2019; Thompson and Gregory 2012).[2] These perceived weaknesses of millennials, nevertheless, can arguably be transformed into strengths that benefit the organization (Thompson and Gregory 2012). Karen Myers and Kamyab Sadaghiani (2010) suggest that the nonlinear route of pursuing advanced degrees, volunteering, and taking on internships – a perceived challenge – can be viewed positively, because such experiences can enable millennials to contribute more positively to the organizations they eventually decide to join. This is a sentiment shared by Catherine Turco, who notes that today's firms need to take into consideration the expectations, habits, and strengths of this generation to gain a competitive advantage (Turco 2016). In the following sections, I will examine some of these flux-related anxieties, discussed in chapter 1, because they contribute to creating unstable careers due to corporate responses to millennials and automation.

Alongside their technological competencies, an associated, and prevalent, stereotype, job entitlement, arises. This stereotype may have arisen because of the more open expression and dialogue millennials bring into the workplace (Turco 2016). Howe and Strauss (2000) had predicted that millennials would hold higher job-entitlement beliefs, such as better work-life balance, compared with their parents. Job entitlement beliefs and work-life balance are issues where differences between generations may arise. Findings from an online course by Thomas Kochan (2015) among 7,900 millennial students from all over the United States and the world in the spring of 2015 found that these students wanted to achieve work-life balance. Another study by Gillian Maxwell and Adelina Broadbridge (2016) set out to investigate the employment expectations of British undergraduate millennials, which also included their opinions on job entitlement.[3] What the authors found was a strong tendency for these undergraduates to expect both intrinsic and extrinsic rewards in their future employment. These rewards were found in three areas: enjoyment; opportunities for employment in an unstable labour market, as well as personal growth within the job; and progression along career paths (Maxwell and Broadbridge 2016). The authors also noted a focus on the self in all three areas, but this perceived self-centredness was not necessarily selfish (Maxwell and Broadbridge 2016). This observation reflects the argument made by Uracha Chatrakul Na Ayudhya and

Janet Smithson (2016), who hold that the concept of job entitlement in the literature on millennials' work values tends to be portrayed uncritically in a very negative light. A study by Sara De Hauw and Ans De Vos (2010) sheds further light on millennials' view of the issue of work-life balance. They looked specifically at their career expectations, surveying two groups of Belgian students from three universities in 2006 and 2009. The majority of them were pursuing master's degrees. Though both groups consisted of millennials who had grown up in a time of prosperity, in the '90s, those surveyed in 2006 also graduated at a time of prosperity, but those surveyed in 2009 graduated during a recession (De Hauw and De Vos 2010). De Hauw and De Vos found that expectations of job security, job content, financial rewards, career development, and training were consistent in both groups, suggesting that these expectations were a feature of the millennials' generation. However, expectations for work-life balance and social atmosphere were mostly influenced by contextual factors and were unlikely to be a result of generational influences (De Hauw and De Vos 2010). These findings thus contradict Howe and Strauss's prediction that millennials would demand better work-life balance, which their parents did not have (Howe and Strauss 2000).

Similarly, Karen Foster offers an alternative explanation to account for what is perceived as millennial entitlement. In her interactions with millennial managers, Gen Xers, and baby boomers in the workplace, she came away from her experience with a very negative impression of millennials as entitled, but argued that they had been very much maligned in this area and that such accusations of entitlement may have been a matter of hierarchy and power politics in the workplace rather than a flaw in the attitudes of millennials (Foster 2013).

The existence of generational differences has also been challenged by Jennifer Deal, David Altman, and Steven Rogelberg. Like De Hauw and De Vos (2010), they argue that any differences observed between generations are largely insignificant, and a natural result of contextual influences rather than generational factors (Deal, Altman, and Rogelberg 2010). The same authors also maintain that it is the life stage one is in that determines one's desire for work-life balance (ibid.). Although Brenda Kowske, Rena Rasch, and Jack Wiley did find significant differences in job satisfaction, satisfaction with pay, and turnover intentions between millennials and the two preceding generations (Gen Xers and baby boomers), they noted that the differences were negligible. They were therefore cautious in arriving at the conclusion that generational differences exist (Kowske, Rasch, and Wiley 2010).

Another issue linked to millennials' sense of entitlement is a lack of focus on learning at work. Companies use digital technology and e-learning in corporate training. This breaks away from the traditional model of conducting corporate training during working hours and caters to millennials' preferences for flexible learning and working styles, allowing them to access the training materials at their convenience (Erickson 2016). The RAND Corporation found that millennials have shorter attention spans, having become accustomed to interactive stimulation, and thus learn better in short bursts than in long lectures (Weinbaum, Girven, and Oberholtzer 2016).

It is often mentioned that the easy access to information afforded by an adept ability to harness technology can also lead to a lack of critical thinking and a penchant for taking accuracy and validity for granted (Hershatter and Epstein 2010). A conflicting view adopted by Deal, Altman, and Rogelberg suggests that millennials' perceived lower level of work commitment is caused by the pervasiveness and accessibility of technology, which means that there is no clear end to their work day, making them less receptive to the idea of committing more to the company (Deal, Altman, and Rogelberg 2010). This is probably what Catherine Turco refers to as "unpaid digital labour," work done using technology like social media outside of office hours but not paid (Turco 2016, 37).

Clearly, digital technology has altered the work culture and careers of millennials, and is harnessed by the appropriate corporate training culture, to maximize their effectiveness at work. As a result, technology can be viewed as more problematic for millennials than for previous generations, because it signals a changing approach to work and up-skilling that punctuates their entire careers.

MILLENNIALS AND WORK TURNOVER

A Gallup study found that slightly more than 21 per cent of millennials changed employers within the last year, more than three times as often as non-millennials (Gallup 2016). Similarly, only about half of the millennials studied expressed a willingness to remain with their current employers, compared with a higher proportion of non-millennials (60 per cent). The same trend is also seen in how open millennials and non-millennials are to new job opportunities: about 60 per cent of millennials express a willingness to explore other job opportunities whereas only 45 per cent of non-millennials feel the same. Millennials are also more likely to explore new job opportunities if the job market improves; 36 per cent expressed this sentiment compared with slightly more than 21 per cent non-millennials. Despite being the most educated generation, millennials come in second after Gen Xers in reporting the highest levels of unemployment (7 per cent) and underemployment (10 per cent). The millennials who fell within the underemployed category were typically employed part-time, but desired full-time work (Gallup 2016). This percentage has grown because the hardest thing millennials have found is to attain jobs they desire. To earn a living, millennials take on other available jobs if they are unable to obtain their desired occupations. As a result, some of them find themselves overqualified for the jobs they can find.

Authors have sought to explore generational differences in work attitudes, and they conceptualize them as intrinsic and extrinsic values. Extrinsic values refer to the material outcomes of work – whether as income and benefits, job security, or opportunities for advancement, or status symbols. Intrinsic values, in contrast, are defined by the rewards gained from the process of work – from its potential for learning and growth, opportunities to exercise creativity and innovation, to effect social change, and how interesting the work is to the worker (Krahn and Galambos 2014; Twenge et al. 2010). Harvey Krahn and Nancy Galambos sought to find out if values and beliefs changed in individuals from the age of eighteen to twenty-five, by comparing patterns of change in these variables between two cohorts of Gen X workers and millennials (Krahn and Galambos 2014). The Gen X participants were high school seniors from the class of 1985 chosen from six Canadian public high schools in Edmonton, and the millennials were high school seniors from the class of 1996 from eight Edmonton public high schools, five of which were also included in the 1985 study.[4] The study found that whereas millennials placed more importance on extrinsic work rewards as they aged than the Gen X workers, neither cohort had any significant differences in intrinsic work values.

Twenge et al. found that Gen X workers placed more importance on extrinsic values than millennials did (whom they also identified as "GenMe" in their study) (Twenge et al. 2010). A possible reason to account for this difference could be the fact that the study by Twenge et al. adopted a time lag approach, unlike Harvey Krahn and Nancy

Galambos, whose study was longitudinal (Krahn and Galambos 2014; Twenge et al. 2010). Another study on the work values of baby boomers and Gen Xers found that both groups of workers were less likely to emphasize intrinsic work values such as loyalty to one's company and the belief that work ought to be an integral part of one's life, and predicted a similar pattern in millennials (Smola and Sutton 2002). While the different approaches used could have affected the results obtained in these studies, the inconsistency of these sets of results could point to a lack of generational differences (Krahn and Galambos 2014).

One area recognized by Krahn and Galambos as having a bearing on millennials' intrinsic and extrinsic work values is unemployment. A distinctive feature of today's skills economy is the presence of many educated but unemployable young people (Krahn and Galambos 2014; Sennett 2007). According to Krahn and Galambos (2014), millennials who have been unemployed are likely to have higher work commitment and emphasize extrinsic work values such as job security. A related study on the effects of unemployment on work commitment by Chau-kiu Cheung, Ngan-pun Ngai, and Steven Ngai (2012) investigated work commitment levels among unemployed millennials in Hong Kong, Shanghai, and Tianjin. In contrast to Krahn and Galambos (2014), Cheung, Ngai, and Ngai (2012) found that experiencing unemployment lowers work commitment levels. However, they noted that the effects of unemployment on work commitment might differ under different social structures and beliefs about work skills.

Job insecurity affects one's commitment to work, which Sennett (2007) recognizes is part and parcel of today's institutional model. Filomena Buonocore, Marcello Russo, and Maria Ferrara recognized that work-family conflict also contributes to shaping work attitudes (Buonocore, Russo, and Ferrara 2015; Sennett 2007). In their study, which sought to investigate how work-family conflict and job security influenced the work attitudes of millennials, Gen Xers, and baby boomers, they surveyed 48 Italian millennial graduates, as well as 214 employees of an Italian company that processed and marketed tomato-based and related products. Of the 214 company employees, 48 were millennials with an average of 12.44 years of schooling, and a majority of them were employed temporarily (ibid.). The study observed that millennials perceived they had higher job insecurity, possibly due to economic uncertainties that contributed to a sense of pessimism (ibid.). This contrasts with what Kowske, Rasch, and Wiley (2010) found, that millennials reported a higher sense of job security. However, working on the same premise of economic instability that millennials experience, they suggested that lower expectations of job security, or even redefining what job security should be, helped to account for the higher levels of confidence in job security. Despite the perception of job insecurity found in the Buonocore, Russo, and Ferrara study, it was not found to influence millennials' affective commitment and job satisfaction as much as it influenced that of Gen Xers and baby boomers (Buonocore, Russo, and Ferrara 2015). Thus, it is only partly true that millennials are necessarily job-hopping to tackle their sense of job insecurity in an era of economic uncertainties and high levels of automation.

Instead, a deeper look at these observations reveals that the job-hopping syndrome could be a manifestation of millennials' desire to find a job that is meaningful and in line with their values. They appear to job-hop, because they are willing to give up existing opportunities until they find a job that better aligns with their interests. However, like older workers, the jobs they prefer might also face a high risk of automation (Paquette 2017). While differences between the generations at work might be a matter of perceptions rather than actual reality, stereotypes about generational differences do persist, despite the lack of evidence (King et al. 2019).

Another study shows that millennials tend to choose to stay with companies that focus on their development and prefer to work for bosses who are more like coaches that give them regular feedback on their work. However, one notable difference between millennial workers and their non-millennial counterparts lies in millennials' preference for positive feedback from their superiors. Millennials generally prefer more frequent recognition or rewards for their work. Of millennials, 41 per cent would like that frequency to be at least monthly compared with less than a third of non-millennials (30 per cent) wanting the same (Finn and Donovan 2013). A survey by Oxford Economics showed that millennials valued feedback and career progression as more important than non-millennials (Oxford Economics 2015a, 2015b). Steven, director of an entrepreneurship centre, suggests a similar phenomenon in Singapore:

> [Entrepreneurship] requires a lot of self-starting ... to deal with rejection. When you pitch to VCs, you're not going to get funding

straight away. [Entrepreneurs] [must] be very persistent with [getting funding]. For some reason [here], they are still not thinking globally. They are still very focused on Singapore. It's good to use Singapore as a base to test the ideas, but they [must] be global, or at least regional from the start. To be honest, I'm not sure. Not enough exposure maybe. It's very important that they think beyond Singapore. The market size here is too small.

Thomas, a senior policy expert on education policies and a professor at a local university, concurs and suggests that it is not unreasonable for millennials to want greater flexibility at work.

I don't think so as long as they're productive and the deliverables are met. If somebody says, Prof, I have to do this project for you, but I'm not going to come into the office. I will submit it at the end of the week if you find it acceptable. Where I choose to work, when I choose to work, as long as you specify your deliverables and the timelines of delivery. So why should you say I should see you in the office at your computer. We should not be fixated on these time-honoured practices in the workplaces.

A Gallup study (2016) found several examples of intrinsic values: In addition to prioritizing interest in their work (58 per cent), millennials seek opportunities for learning and growth (59 per cent) and career progression (50 per cent), good managers and management (58 per cent) (Gallup 2016). The key to engaging and retaining millennial talent also seems to hinge heavily on the types of managers under which millennials work. Millennials place strong emphasis on working for someone they consider a good superior, a boss who views them as both an employee and a person, who is keen to take on the role of a coach to support and engage them at work and is able to set well-defined expectations and goals on top of giving regular feedback on their progress. They value conversations that touch on both personal and professional issues with their managers. Millennials who feel more connected and appreciated by their managers trust the latter more and are therefore more likely to be loyal to the company. It was also found that millennials who receive affirmations about their strengths at work and are held accountable by their managers are likely to be more engaged, thus increasing their likelihood of staying longer at the same organization (Gallup 2016). In my interview with Beatrice, a human resources manager, she shed light on some of the strategies that she had adopted to gain the buy-in of her younger workers. When she first took over the department, she let her younger workers "take on projects and run with them," and consistently noticed that they tended to go the extra mile when empowered with such ownership. As part of their exposure, she also invites younger employees to join her when she goes on recruitment trips abroad because this exposure and new environment excites them. As a result, she has found that her firm tends to have a very high retention of millennial workers. From my interviews, 70 per cent of millennials remarked that work cultures and interpersonal relationships are the most important factors influencing their decisions to stay in a company.

Millennials consistently look for firms that pledge a social cause or articulate a strong sense of social consciousness. The emphasis on a socially minded organization was clear, given that a significant percentage of millennials (88 per cent) would choose a company based on its values and mission, with planet-saving goals as a priority (Bates 2017; Brandon 2015). Among millennials' top goals are making a positive impact on their companies (25 per cent) and taking on initiatives to address social and environmental challenges (22 per cent), in addition to working with a diverse group of people (22 per cent) (Baird 2015). On the organization front, millennials look for companies that are trustworthy and have clear direction and purpose (Gallup 2016). About three in four millennials express optimism, feeling that businesses exert a positive effect on society, with active and heavy users of social media the strongest proponents of businesses (Deloitte 2017). The Boston Consulting Group has also observed this positive evaluation of businesses and that it can be seen across all demographic sectors. One study shows a decrease in respondents who feel that businesses focus too much on their own agendas (Baron 2004). Doing good in society and working for causes seem to be important factors for millennials. Strong evidence for this may be seen in how congruent their beliefs and practices are. Millennials are more likely to reject the status quo, and pursue change at home, in the marketplace, and in the workplace. This idealism is most apparent in their strong belief in purpose, not just in the work they do, but also in their choice of companies (Gallup 2016). With this emphasis on making a difference in the world, it is no surprise that millennials would be willing to leave their jobs for other opportunities until they find a more suitable fit. Unfortunately, such behaviour has commonly led to generalizations about millennial workers as uncommitted job-hoppers, even though Gen Xers and baby boomers also cite these same reasons for wanting to leave their jobs. However, millennials are more likely than previous generations to change jobs (Gallup 2016). A high proportion of millennials (86 per cent) feel that the measure of a business's success should go beyond mere financial performance, and most of them are employed by companies involved in social initiatives and matters of personal concern to millennials (Deloitte 2017). This could reflect a tendency for millennials to leverage the resources of large organizations, such as companies and governments, to make a difference in the world (Barton, Fromm, and Egan 2012). However, when the spotlight is focused on large enterprises, views tend to be less favourable. While most participants (74 per cent) feel that big organizations have the power to make a positive impact on society, only slightly more than half (59 per cent) believe that they have done so. Also, millennials express more skepticism about the motivations of large multinational companies in engaging in social initiatives (Deloitte 2017).

The Deloitte (2017) findings suggest that instead of the one-way relationship of job seekers trying to appeal to potential hirers, it is now companies that are also expected to actively engage with and court their potential employees. The findings further propose that larger businesses can improve their standing with millennials by engaging in more social initiatives, and that the benefit of involving millennial employees in such activities is three-fold: they have been shown to display a greater level of loyalty to the firm, and they have a more positive view of organizational behaviour when they are empowered to make a positive difference in society. The study found that such initiatives, when done at the individual level, give millennials a greater sense of social influence. The collective effect of this influence can be large enough to create a ripple effect in the organization. Millennials see the workplace, then, as somewhere they can build a sense of purpose, and establish a sense of influence and accountability.

By perceiving millennials as self-absorbed, companies are treating them as problematic workers who are unwilling to work within firms' existing frameworks. However, if companies shift their perspective to understanding that millennials are seeking out firms that fight for social causes, it is they who are instead seen as problematic for not promoting social causes. Take the case of labour rights, for example. In the 1990s, the use of sweatshops in supply chains of multinational corporations such as Nike and Walmart sparked strong anti-sweatshop social movements. This pressured companies into adopting changes in their practices to improve labour standards (Bartley and Child 2011). However, companies began subsuming corporate social responsibility under their business strategies instead of it being part of genuine concern for promoting social causes (Nijhof and Jeurissen 2010; Shamir 2004). Rather than being seen as problematic workers, millennials would be more accurately depicted as drivers of social causes who can be engaged by firms. Shamir (2004, 683) suggests that corporate social responsibility can be used as a "normative control apparatus over its [companies] own employees." Employees in firms that are more socially responsible tend to have stronger levels of work commitment (Shamir 2004). The need to attract millennials to firms and retain them can therefore serve to promote social responsibility in companies.

MILLENNIALS AND WORK ARRANGEMENTS

Millennials' preference for flexible work arrangements has often led to the generalization that they have high expectations of career progression in innovative firms. However, several studies have found that there are specific reasons underlying their preference for flexibility rather than a general resistance to putting in longer hours at work. With technology facilitating the effectiveness and increasing the popularity of telecommuting tools, alternative working arrangements may soon become a mainstay of millennials' work culture, shifting away from traditional arrangements of fixed working hours and offices. In a 2017 Deloitte report, a high percentage of millennials reported that they desired some degree of flexibility in work arrangements (84 per cent), and almost (39 per cent) millennials currently work in organizations that give them a highly flexible working environment (Deloitte 2017). In a PwC survey of its employees, more than half of their millennial employees desired more flexible work arrangements. If given the option, 64 per cent millennials would choose to work from home from time to time, and 66 per cent prefer to adjust their work hours (Finn and Donovan 2013). For them, the work they produce is more important than their physical presence, and they believe that the measure of one's productivity should be defined in terms of work output rather than the hours put in at the office (Finn and Donovan 2013).

While there is a fear that productivity might suffer due to such arrangements, the findings show that the willingness to make such concessions can result in several beneficial outcomes. For example, companies that have such arrangements tend to have higher employee loyalty, greater productivity, and employee engagement, while also increasing employees' personal well-being, health, and happiness. This may be explained by how flexible work positively correlates with accountability and trust. In the same survey by Deloitte (2017), 73 per cent of millennials say that they trust their colleagues to be accountable and responsible, even though the abuse of such privileges is a reality they recognize. The preference for flexible working arrangements may also be linked to a desire to achieve work-life balance. This appears to be another area of concern on which millennials are reluctant to compromise, even if they are promised compensation. Regarded as a major issue faced by workforces today, the lack of a work-life balance can cause workplace stress (Low and Chua 2019). While millennials all over the world aim to achieve work-life balance, this sentiment is more keenly felt in North America, Europe, and Asia, where the economies are more mature and where work-life balance is closely linked to turnover, commitment, and job satisfaction compared with other parts of the world. Differences are also observed between millennials and older generations. Compared with non-millennials (63 per cent), slightly more than 71 per cent of millennial employees feel that their work commitments disrupt their personal lives (Finn and Donovan 2013). Non-millennials value transactional needs more than millennials, such as having more control over their work, developmental opportunities, and pay satisfaction.

In an employee survey by Randstad (2016), flexible work schedules were found to be part of the top employee benefits desired by millennials. These preferences for some degree of flexibility also emerged in my own conversations with millennials, particularly those working in technology firms and start-ups. Even if they did not explicitly state that they were looking for flexibility as a criterion, the flexible arrangements and "Google-y" culture of these start-ups convinced them to join the company. In my own interviews, Thomas, a professor, attributed this to a change in the meaning of work across generations.[5] As a baby boomer, he recalled how the 8 to 5 (9 to 5 in North America) workday was internalized in his generation, regardless of the kind of work that his cohort chose to pursue. Today, younger people operate on a twenty-four-hour cycle instead, and prefer to have autonomy in controlling when they work. It is not so much a desire to work less as a desire to balance work with all the other endeavours they want to pursue concurrently. In another survey, by Morar Consulting in 2017,[6] it was found that up to 71 per cent of millennials' employers offered flexi-work arrangements, but only 25 per cent of millennials took them up on these arrangements out of fear that they would be seen as not hard-working if they were not in the office (Mock 2017).

Even though work-life balance is much sought after, it is not always easy to achieve. A study by The Harris Poll on behalf of Ernst and Young was conducted online in the United States from 20 November 2014 to 14 January 2015.[7] It found that work-life balance was harder to achieve for one-third of the respondents, with almost half of the group surveyed citing increased expenses, wage stagnation, and increased workloads. Other reasons cited included increased responsibilities at home (39 per cent), longer working hours (36 per cent), and parenthood (23 per cent). In terms of generational differences globally, millennials (35 per cent), along with Gen Xers (34 per cent), find it more difficult to achieve work-life balance compared with baby boomers (30 per cent) (Ernst & Young 2015).

Not surprisingly, the quest for work-life balance influences what millennials consider when looking for a job. They want flexibility without excessive work hours for full-time employees, on top of competitive pay and benefits. Flexibility seems to be a concern for full-time workers, with 74 per cent wanting to work flexibly, but not at the expense of promotional opportunities, mirroring Deloitte's finding that millennials want to develop both personally and professionally without having to sacrifice their work-life balance (Deloitte 2017). Other preferences include working with bosses and co-workers who support their flexible work arrangements and paid parental leave (Ernst & Young 2015). However, Helen Russell, Philip O'Connell, and Frances McGinnity (2009) highlight the difficulties in achieving work-life balance through flexible work arrangements. Their study examined employees in Ireland in 2003 and found that flexible work arrangements such as flexi-hours and working from home can result in longer working hours in certain firms or institutional contexts. For the latter, it can also intensify the intrusion of work into personal lives. Unlike the stereotype, millennials seem willing to work slightly longer hours in exchange for greater flexibility in their work lives.

MILLENNIALS AND AUTOMATION

Millennials are often purported to be tech savvy and spend much of their time interacting with technological devices and tools. They have become comfortable with using the Internet on their phones in their everyday lives. Gallup found that most millennials using their phones to access the Internet (85 per cent) were also constantly plugged in, with much of their daily lives conducted online, such as maintaining relationships, consuming media, and researching online (Gallup 2016). In addition to growing up in an era of ICT-enabled technologies (information and communications technology), millennials have also grown up in an environment of extensive discourse about automation. Despite their relative comfort with technological devices and tools, studies thus far have concluded that millennials hold divided views about automation.

Millennials who are heavy users of social media hold a more favourable view of their future job prospects despite the introduction of automation. Most of them report being optimistic that automation would not affect the number of available job openings (85 per cent) and increased job opportunities (64 per cent) (Deloitte 2017). On the other hand, some fear that the intrusion of automation will pose a threat to their employment (40 per cent). A similar proportion (44 per cent) believes that their skills will be in less demand, and slightly more than half (51 per cent) feel that retraining is necessary to keep up (Deloitte 2017).

While it may be true that technology and automation threaten traditional work, some studies suggest that millennials should not be overly pessimistic. In fact, technology can also create new areas of work. Some of these new areas include app creation, IT development, hardware manufacturing, and IT systems management and security. The effects of new technologies on work can thus be very positive, as a McKinsey survey found. In that study, 2.4 jobs were created for every job replaced by technology, resulting in a net increase in jobs (Manyika 2017). Millennials and employees of other age groups felt the importance of using the latest technology for better success in their firms (Baird 2015). Nevertheless, to assuage some of their anxiety about being replaced or lacking the appropriate skills, millennials should ideally look for jobs that provide opportunities to obtain new skills. Technology is not only beneficial in allowing for greater productivity and economic growth, but also in creating opportunities for millennials to take on more creative and value-added activities that include learning new skills. Technology has also enabled millennials to take on work that fulfills their income and flexibility needs (Manyika 2017). Flexibility and decent pay make part-time jobs with companies that use technology (including Uber, Lyft, and web-developing companies) very attractive to millennials; one-third of those surveyed by employment site FlexJobs expressed a preference for freelance work together with some part-time jobs (Dowdy 2016). Ajay Agrawal, Joshua Gans, and Avi Goldfarb (2018) support the idea that combining technology with humans is often more effective than humans or robots working alone.

How millennials see the effects of automation largely depends on the industry type or size of business. For example, at least 50 per cent of the millennials in technology- and media-related fields, manufacturing, finance, and energy and resource industries feel that their employers have at least put in a fair amount of effort not to reduce human involvement via automation. They also view automation less as a threat in education and in the industries listed above, partly because these industries have included automation early (Deloitte 2017). This sentiment is also more prevalent in larger enterprises of more than 1,000 employees, compared with smaller workforces of fewer than 100 employees (51 per cent and 42 per cent respectively). However, everyone else will face some risks. In that sense, it is difficult to provide a general answer to the question of whether millennials are worried about automation (Deloitte 2017). Rather, considering how automation affects occupations differently, it is expected that millennials with different skill levels will experience differing levels of anxieties about automation.

MILLENNIALS AND EMPLOYMENT PROSPECTS

The White House Council of Economic Advisors released a study that found that it would be challenging for millennials to begin their careers during a climate of economic turmoil (The White House Council of Economic Advisors 2014). If millennials start their careers in a time of economic instability, they are expected to suffer significant income losses, of at least 2.5 per cent and up to 9 per cent, a trend that can persist for more than a decade. Millennials with a college degree are hit harder by early career choices in an unstable economy, even though their level of education will help them to offset those initial losses in the long run (The White House Council of Economic Advisors 2014). This is especially true in light of the disparities between millennials with differing educational levels. Whereas the unemployment rate of millennials in the twenty-five to thirty-four age bracket with a college degree was 3.7 per cent in 2013, this rate is almost four times higher for millennials with less than a high school education (13.5 per cent) (The White House Council of Economic Advisors 2014). These findings seem to suggest that millennials who have just entered the workforce with a tertiary degree ought to be concerned about their prospects in an unstable economy. As of 2018, millennials make up 35 per cent of the labour force in the United States (Fry 2018). Martin Reeves, Kevin Whitaker, and Christian Ketels (2019) suggested that many economists are forecasting an economic downturn or even an economic recession in the next one to two years. Thus, it is particularly salient to consider how optimistic millennials are about their job prospects, especially now during the pandemic and in the post-pandemic era.

Various studies since 2014 suggest that millennials have a general sense of optimism about their employment prospects. Despite bleak economic conditions in 2014, lower personal incomes compared with earlier generations, debt from student loans, poverty, and unemployment, millennials were more positive about the future than preceding generations (Pew Research Center 2014). However, a newer study by Pew shows that millennials are now less optimistic than in 2014 about the future, especially in the United States (Fry 2018).

A 2016 global report by ManpowerGroup, which also included Singapore millennials, reveals a similar sense of optimism about job prospects. Of the millennials surveyed in eighteen countries in their study, 62 per cent felt confident in finding an equally good or better job within three months if they lost their current jobs (Manpower-Group 2016). However, a more recent report by Deloitte (2018) reveals that millennials' optimism about social progress has decreased, whereas economic outlooks remain the same, with 45 per cent thinking that the economy in their own countries would improve over the next year. However, millennials' optimism about the economy is still largely dependent on economic stability. With economists predicting a possible recession (Reeves, Whitaker, and Ketels 2019), it is not surprising that the level of optimism fell, showing that millennials are not necessarily more pessimistic about the future than previous generations.

Thus far, we have found that the rhetoric about millennials being self-entitled, job-hoppers, unwilling to work long hours, not worried about automation, and being pessimistic about their employment prospects are partial myths and present an incomplete picture of what the millennial worker is like. Instead, the picture shows that millennials desire flexibility and seek jobs that align with their values and purpose, as well as companies that are socially conscious. Furthermore, while they benefit from innovation and automation, they are also vulnerable to technological and economic disruptions (flux) and have unstable futures due to their exposure to volatility in their careers, because employers no longer hire for a lifetime (Kochan 2015). Millennials therefore need to harness their skills with technology to complement their learning process and remain optimistic about their careers despite the bleak economic conditions that they are experiencing now, more so with a global pandemic wreaking havoc on jobs (El-Taliawi and van der Wal 2020; World Economic Forum and Futurity 2020).

THE MILLENNIAL EXPERIENCE DIFFERS GLOBALLY

While the literature on millennials has sought to investigate if generational differences exist, the picture remains murky, and findings in various areas by different groups of sociologists and psychologists are conflicting. One limitation of most of these studies is the narrow demographic of the samples studied. The studies primarily examined millennials who received tertiary education and at least a high school diploma and are literate. However, this sample only represents an educated demographic. It is hardly representative of all millennials. Furthermore, the literature is skewed towards a Western context and Asian nations are underrepresented. My focus on Singapore in the later chapters serves as one example of millennial cultures. Despite the cultural and education differences, I argue that educated millennials in developed countries are highly vulnerable to career insecurities due to global, technological, and economic uncertainties and the nationalism and protectionism that arise as a response (Raghunath 2019).

Karl Mannheim argues that to be considered a member of a generation, one must participate in certain common experiences as part of an integrated group (Mannheim 1952). Following this argument, if a generation is defined as one that shares significant life experiences, it follows that different countries can have different definitions of generations depending on the events they go through as an integrated group (Mannheim 1952). Deal, Altman, and Rogelberg (2010) argue that the concept and definition of a generation varies from culture to culture. Therefore, generalizing what millennials are like globally is likely to be faulty. For example, Japan has a set of generational labels that do not fall neatly in line with persons living and working in a Western context, and the definition of each generation tends to fall within a much shorter time span – five to ten years – compared with the Western definition of between twenty and thirty years. For example, what the Western world recognizes as Gen X corresponds roughly to Japan's second generation of baby boomers, people born in the first half of the 1970s who came of age in the early 1990s (Coulmas 2007). The life events and experiences of these two sets of individuals, Gen X and the second generation of baby boomers, are also different, and issuing the blanket label of Gen X to everyone born in the 1970s to the 1980s would neglect this factor. Hence, more studies must be done in different cultural and national contexts to form informed and objective conclusions about generations that more accurately represent how the future of work affects them.

One caveat that must be recognized in the analysis thus far is that the millennials studied belong to a population that grew up in developed economies. For one thing, millennials have contrasting attitudes towards the overall prospects of economic improvement (Deloitte 2017).[8] Whereas millennials in developed markets (with the exception of the United States) feel that their economic and social situations have stagnated, and express anxiety, their counterparts in emerging economies hold much more positive views about the economy of the future, possibly reflecting how differently developed and developing economies experience flux. Another commonality shared by more than half the millennial population globally is their concern over political conflict and other tensions in the world (Deloitte 2017).

Considering that 27 per cent of the world's population consisted of millennials in 2015 (the numbers are growing in many parts of the world), it is important to not only consider the absolute numbers, but also the proportion of the millennial population to the country's overall population when thinking about issues of country-specific economic prospects and business opportunity assessments. This is because millennials have become the most important generation in terms of economic growth, consumerism, and employment, as older generations start to retire (Kearney n.d.). Kearney identified eight countries that have both large absolute millennial populations and a large proportion of millennials: Bangladesh, Egypt, India, Iran, Pakistan, the Philippines, South Africa, and Vietnam. All these countries are either Asian or African emerging markets and are termed the "millennial majors" in the company's study (Kearney n.d.). China and the United States, the nations with the world's largest population and the largest consumer market, respectively, are not "millennial majors" because they have relatively low proportions of millennials, 27 per cent and 23 per cent, respectively (Kearney n.d.).

Of the eight "millennial majors," three are poised to advance economically: Bangladesh, the Philippines, and Vietnam. They have low youth unemployment rates and rapid economic growth projected over the next five years, two factors, which, if they continue to generate economic opportunities for millennials, could mean sustainable economic stability and growth. Though India and Pakistan have higher youth unemployment rates than those three countries, their situation is still manageable. Although both nations appear to be experiencing an economic slowdown, they are some of the fastest growing economies in the world now and are projected to have strong GDP growth over the next five years. The remaining three countries, Egypt, Iran, and South Africa, have more issues to tackle, such as their high youth employment rates and lower medium-term growth prospects. Creating adequate employment opportunities may be a big challenge for them (Kearney n.d.). Nonetheless, educated professionals from developed and developing countries with jobs in multinational firms are much more likely to experience similar career anxieties because of the global connectivity and risk exposure of the corporations they work for particularly now during the pandemic (International Monetary Fund 2019; Raghunath 2019).

For the most part, millennials in developing countries will still be met with a worsening labour market. The International Labour Office reports that the hardest-hit regions are Latin America and the Caribbean, with a projected rise of 0.3 per cent in the unemployment rate. Vulnerable employment will also remain a problem globally, especially in regions like Southern Asia and sub-Saharan Africa, with a projected growth of 11 million and a rise in precarious forms of employment per year worldwide (International Labor Organization 2017).

These projections of millennials in developing economies say several things. First, the global economic climate remains bleak for most millennials. Not only those in developed economies, but also those in developing economies face precarity when it comes to finding jobs. Second, the unfavourable employment conditions in these countries might put greater pressure on all governments to maintain a strong labour force. The studies also show that the responses to workers have increasingly become technologically driven in anticipating, with trepidation, the rise of innovation and flux (Kearney n.d.; Deloitte 2017). Clearly, the fourth industrial revolution will require jobs and human resources to be reorganized (Autor, Mindell, and Reynolds 2019; Frey and Osborne 2017; Goos, Manning, and Salomons 2014). However, the focus should not be on the hindrances that machines (or robots) bring to the workforce. Instead, the phenomena of innovation and automation should be discussed alongside people's potential to adapt in the workplace.

Humans will still need to compete with other humans for jobs, and human skill sets will become the defining feature of who gets ahead and who stays ahead (Sawhney 2018; Walsh 2017). Instead of worrying about machines taking over our jobs, organizations need to think proactively about how they can retrain their workers, and society needs to collectively talk about how intelligent we want these machines to be. If we want bright futures for millennials and older generations of workers, there need to be more conversations about how to become co-workers and co-creators of technology.

OPTIMISM AND PESSIMISM FOR THE FUTURE

Although the image painted of millennials seems conflicted and contradictory, Howe and Strauss seem to take a rather positive view. They posit that each generation does three things: it solves a problem that the previous youth generation was facing, corrects for any behavioural excess perceived in the current middle-aged generation, and fills the social roles vacated by the departing older generation (Howe and Strauss 2000).

Based on this generational theory, Howe and Strauss predict that millennials will fulfill three goals. First, they will tackle the problems of civic decay and social splintering experienced by the previous generation of youth, Gen X, by setting high standards for carrying out community responsibilities. Second, they will correct for the problem of talk over action of baby boomers. Third, they will step into the role of civic and team players previously played by the departing generation (Howe and Strauss 2000). However, the cyclical pattern of generations that Howe and Strauss hypothesized seems a little too neat, and some of the predictions they made of millennials conflicts with what research has found. The market of today is radically different from what the "Greatest Generation" (or the G.I. Generation as it is called in the United States) experienced.[9] This may have a significant effect not only on millennials but on all the preceding generations who are still in the workforce today. Although Howe and Strauss (2000) looked at the characteristics of millennials and the generations before them in the United States, they neglected to look in detail at the kind of uncertain market climate caused by automation that they would have to face.

In contrast to Howe and Strauss's optimistic view of millennials and the world they are predicted to usher in, the sociologist Richard Sennett focused on the new business model that millennials would find themselves using and found a less-than-ideal picture. Sennett observes that businesses today are eschewing the traditional bureaucratic model in favour of decentralized control to promote a sense of community, but he argues that they have not achieved this sense of togetherness. Instead, dismantling the bureaucratic structure, despite bringing in more wealth and enabling technology to flourish, has resulted in more socially fragmented lives than before (Sennett 2007). Today's economy is marked by instability, constant change, and inequality (see Bauman 2000; 2007). Inequality, Sennett argues, is a vulnerable area of the modern economy. It comes in the form of widening gaps in wealth and in social distance, which indicate the extent of the differences between different social groups in areas like education, income, gender, and race. In the new flexible firm of today, due to the fragmented company structure, there is little interaction along the chain of command. Hence, the social distance between people within the firm is a lot larger than that in a traditional bureaucratic company, where, despite the gap between management and employees, the social distance between them is not as large, because they feel connected to each other through the organizational structure. Therefore, while power may still be concentrated at the top in today's firms, Sennett (2007) argues that that authority may not necessarily increase as a result of fragmentation.

Authority can be either charismatic (charisma of popular leaders) or bureaucratic (long established cultural norms and legal rules), and Sennett notes that the firms of today may invoke charismatic authority but that they fail to impose a sense of bureaucratic authority (Sennett 2007; Weber 1920/1947). Another quality is trust, which can be either formal, by virtue of contracts signed, or informal, an implicit knowledge of who and who not to rely on. Again, in a fragmented working arrangement where work teams are temporary, cultivating informal trust can be greatly hampered. In firms where conditions are volatile, such deficits of informal trust can cause anxiety in employees, resulting in networks that are fragile and come apart easily.

Taken together, low institutional loyalty, diminished trust between employees, and weakening institutional power are related to lower social capital, which refers to how much employees participate and are involved in social groups (Portes 1998; Sennett 2007). Sennett's definition of social capital differs from Putnam's, which defines social capital as people's willingness to engage in social and civic organizations (Putnam 2000). Sennett's definition is more about the judgment people make of these engagements. The higher people's evaluation of the quality of the social engagement, the higher the social capital invested (Sennett 2007). Sennett argues that loyalty is a litmus test of social capital, and in this sense, the fragmented structure of organizations today commands very little loyalty from employees. And due to employers' perceived lack of loyalty, employees today also command very little social capital from their employers.

Sennett's (2007) observations come from Weber's idea of civil society, which is one shaped by militarization, where structure is key, and everyone has a defined place and function to fulfill within this structure (Weber 1922/1978). Weber argues that this model, when applied to businesses, sought to lower the likelihood of revolts, thus forming the foundations for social capitalism (Weber 1904/1998). According to Weber, a well-designed and strict hierarchical structure must be in place for businesses to survive uncertain market conditions and busts (Weber 1904/1998). However, the structure of today's institutions has deviated from the traditional pyramid-like organization, where tasks are performed in a chain-like sequence, to one that is more like a machine, where the number of functions invoked is flexible. Not only that, the sequence of these functions can also be varied. This enables what is known as "delayering" to take place, such as having the flexibility to add on or shed layers within the organization in response to the demands of the tasks at hand. What this implies for the modern institution is that the "casualization" of the labour force takes place both externally and internally. Sennett (2007) observes that this phenomenon of burgeoning temporary employment can be seen in the United States and the United Kingdom and, I would add, more globally. Delayering, non-linear sequences, and casualization of labour enable emphasis to be put on immediate and small tasks, thus reducing the likelihood that employees will have long-term careers. Such disruption is the defining feature of the flux society.

While modern institutions have not eroded the social identities derived from work, they have disturbed the moral prestige of work stability. Stability is seen to lack moral prestige and is hence eschewed by many young people, who instead go for jobs in which risk-taking is emphasized, as in the private sector. However, as Sennett observes, risk-taking is not as attractive in the long run for young people. They express a preference for more permanent conditions after working in floating labour markets for some time (Sennett 2007).[10] Even though entrepreneurship and risk-tasking are lauded as great goals and mentalities, the fact is that millennials still prefer a stable lifestyle. Thus, the types of skills that millennials need to survive in the new economy must be considered, not only as risk-taking entrepreneurs, but also as employees in firms.

The new economy has implications not only for millennials, but also for the generations before them. As workers get older, their skills become more irrelevant in an evolving economy, or what is called "skills extinction" (Sennett 2007, 98).[11] It is estimated that the average blue-collar worker must relearn skills three times during a working lifetime. Nor are white-collar workers spared this fate. Hence, an employer's choice boils down to retraining the older worker or hiring a young worker already equipped with the latest skills. But the idea of having the latest skills is a mirage, because they do not last (Kasriel 2017). Firms tend to do the latter due to the younger worker's lower wages, the higher costs of retraining programs, and the perception that the older worker is expensive to hire and is less digitally skilled. The choice to hire younger workers is probably true of modern companies whereas companies that prefer to retrain their older workers tend to be more traditional. Albert Hirschmann (1970) argued that companies that invest in their employees' skills over the long term are also likely to value employee loyalty more (see Schneider 1978). Despite that, the trend and the tendency are for companies to acquire fresh skills. Sennett observes that this, together with skills extinction and the insignificance of experience in the face of automation, marks today's economy (Sennett 2007).[12]

In an institution where quick results are expected, time-demanding processes are frowned upon, and the emphasis is less on ability than on the future. One example is craftsmanship, or the mastery of one skill, a time-consuming endeavour requiring trial and error to perfect. In an age of automation, craftsmanship is valued even less. For sociologists, the advent of automation used to imply freeing up human hands to do mechanical work, and led to an increase in white-collar and human-service jobs. These days, however, automation can replace even human-service jobs, and job insecurity is even more pronounced (Frey and Osborne 2017). Sennett thus suggests that to thrive in such unstable and fragmentary conditions, workers need to address the challenges of managing short-term relationships and nomadic working styles, constantly upgrading and retraining themselves to keep up with a new culture of work that no longer values craftsmanship, and being able to let go of the past so they can move on (Sennett 2007).[13]

David Weil shares a similar view of today's changing face of employment. He observes that the concept of employment has changed, from that of the traditional employer-employee relationship to one where the responsibility of supervising, managing, or paying the employees is no longer the singular task of the employer. Some responsibilities of managing employees are shared with other organizations, such as labour brokers and third-party management firms (Weil 2014).

This remodelled concept of businesses involving other organizations brings about a variety of effects that are often negative. There is less clarity in determining who is responsible for work conditions, a downward pressure on wages and work benefits, and increased chances of basic labour standards being violated. Not only that, there tends to be a widening gap between those at the top and those at the bottom, while working conditions become increasingly unfavourable for workers at the bottom levels. Also, the blurring of responsibility brought about by franchising, management outsourcing , and labour subcontracting can lead to multiple issues, such as fewer safety laws and violation of minimum wage laws. In such "fissured workplaces," lead companies have the advantage of being able to impose strict standards and guidelines, and yet be free from the responsibility of employment obligations such as fair wages and protection against workplace hazards (Weil 2014, 94). This also results in employment that is more precarious, because risk is no longer tied to one employer, but has become the responsibility of individual workers and smaller employers. Some of the other consequences of the fissured workplace, Weil notes, are a gradual decrease in the amount of work that once provided decent wages, benefits, and job stability (Weil 2014). Depressed salaries can come about as a result of significant pressure exerted on employee wages and benefits, which happens as competition among employers increases, and affects most industries.

In such a tense and unpredictable business environment, millennials armed with technology may have a work ethic that differs significantly from that of previous generations. This may be a result of social media influence, which has created new customer and employee expectations in the market, and may mean that a radical overhaul of the traditional concept of a company is needed, as Catherine Turco argues (2016). As the economy continues to be transformed by technological and social factors, it has become even more important to understand how economies can advance smoothly in the fourth industrial revolution and create better employment for current and future generations.

A COLLABORATIVE FUTURE

Catherine Turco suggests that the answer to this may be found in the "conversational firm," a type of company that seeks to implement openness in all operational areas of the company. In her book, *The Conversational Firm*, Turco studied a technology firm in an urban area of the United States that adopted the conversational model, and noted its potential, as well as the challenges that come with it (Turco 2016).[14] Like Sennett (2007), Turco also noted the organizational structure envisioned by Weber in the narrative of today's worker. Weber believed the organizational form of the bureaucratic firm to be structurally and technically superior to other forms by its adherence to strict vertical, hierarchical, clearly defined divisions of labour, rules and regulations, the promotion of staff based on technical competence, and the clear demarcation between corporate and personal affairs (Turco 2016; Weber 1922/1978).[15] Weber recognized that this structure was dehumanizing, but while predicting an eventual attempt to look for alternatives, he concluded that the structure would ultimately prove impossible to discard. While evidence contrary to Weber's idea of an efficient and rational bureaucratic structure has been established, earlier academics, like Merton (1940), had also argued for the indispensability of this structure (Turco 2016).[16]

Turco likens this rigid bureaucratic structure to Weber's "iron cage" and suggests that its indestructibility can be explained by two theories. First, the labour process theory in the 1970s hypothesized that the goal of the bureaucratic firm was not efficiency, but capital control and the exploitation of workers (Braverman 1974; Burawoy 1979; Edwards 1979; Turco 2016).[17] Second, the institutionalist school of organizational theory from the late 1970s to the early 1980s, which is still popular today, postulates a less sinister aim, conforming to long-standing beliefs of what efficient and rational organizations are like, but failing to put into practice what they purport to subscribe to in real life (Meyer and Rowan 1977; Turco 2016).[18] Despite the seeming impossibility of escaping from this iron cage, Turco argues that the conversational firm is a new organizational form that does not entirely abandon bureaucracy, but that deconstructs traditional hierarchical structures (Turco 2016). This deconstruction can be seen in how the conversational firm separates processes of communication and decision-making authority that are traditionally parallel and allow the voices of the lowest-level employees to be heard. In this way, there is a radical level of transparency not seen in traditional mainstream companies: a top-down approach of disseminating detailed and often confidential information with the entire workforce, followed by a web-like flow of communication of ideas and opinions between employees and executives (Turco 2016).[19] The desire to keep this interlinked web of communication open has resulted in no formal organizational chart in the conversational firm that Turco studied (Turco 2016). In other words, the conversational firm is one that promotes employee voices, even allowing employees lower on the corporate rungs to weigh in on business decisions that in a mainstream firm would have been restricted largely to higher-level management. This concept of openness has been adopted by various industries and is the corporate revolution of today. It is a complex idea most associated with freedom of expression and democratic practices, but also linked to surveillance and a loss of privacy. (Turco 2016).

This openness can be a double-edged sword, as seen in this conversational firm's use of a wiki as a platform for expressing, sharing, and openly discussing ideas within the company. While employee voices are ostensibly encouraged on this platform, this freedom of expression can border on aggression and inappropriateness. Not only can backlash from colleagues as a result of sharing an idea become a distraction from the topic at hand, it can also serve as a deterrent to others to share their ideas. In addition, the sheer deluge of ideas and opinions can reduce employees' desire to participate (Turco 2016). Employees have also noted the tendency for some to use the wiki to promote themselves or to impress others. The wiki also serves to legitimize possession of intellectual property; employees have on occasion exercised some form of self-censorship and refrained from sharing good ideas with each other until they have posted the same idea on the wiki under their name, out of fear of having their idea appropriated on the wiki by someone else (Turco 2016). Issues that stem from freedom of speech, such as aggression, inappropriateness, distraction, self-promotion, a sheer deluge of ideas and opinions, and self-censorship have undermined the efforts to encourage employee voices on this platform. Self-censorship was also observed in employees who hold somewhat precarious positions in the firm because of poor performance (Turco 2016). This, and other areas of tension associated with the wiki, illustrate the difficulty of maintaining a truly open atmosphere.

A solution offered by management was to administer an anonymous survey to obtain employees' opinions and comments that might otherwise have been suppressed on the wiki. Turco notes that this is remarkable, albeit imperfect, considering how mainstream companies have a vested interest in preventing a collective consciousness from developing among their workers. The conversational firm goes out of its way to harness the use of technology and communication platforms to make employees' private sentiments, which criticize the company's policies and practices, accessible to all in the firm (Turco 2016).

The challenges of maintaining openness are also seen in the company's decision-making. In the quest to push for sharing ideas, no real constructive feedback was given. That lack of direction from management made the employees feel that certain decisions and directions were being withheld from them, leading to frustration (Turco 2016). They therefore eschewed the unpleasant task of expressing doubts about a certain project, and as a result, gave no real constructive feedback on how to proceed with the project. Employees thus called for greater hierarchical control and direction. Turco notes that this does not contradict the aversion to corporate control that is commonly associated with millennials, but it also does not completely negate the regard that they have for hierarchy (Turco 2016). Incidentally, the call for higher hierarchical control by employees is also linked to the lack of an organizational chart, which is an attempt to treat all staff as equals. However, this sentiment was repudiated by many of the employees, with many of them agreeing that while a hierarchy was undeniably present, having an organizational chart did not eliminate the atmosphere of equality pursued by the company.

This desire for structure may have been a result of the highly structured patterns of education millennials have experienced. While the need for openness and the need for hierarchy and structure seem to conflict, Turco argues that what might be more important for millennials is being able to have their voices heard, even if, ultimately, they do not have any control over the decision. Communicative empowerment, Turco holds, is distinct from decision-making empowerment (Turco 2016). What Turco discusses is not too different from the observations of Beatrice, a human resources manager I interviewed. She noticed that millennials' preferences for flatter organizational structures over traditional hierarchies does not mean that there is an erosion of respect in the workplace. Instead, what she observes is that this generation of workers wants to feel a sense of empowerment. Instead of being told what to do, they seek the challenge of using their knowledge and resources to complete tasks creatively. The challenge then is to find out how experienced workers can coach the younger generation to translate their ideas and solutions into more feasible, implementable steps.

Considering this understanding, it was agreed among employees that some decision rights could be distributed throughout the company. The *use good judgment* policy then came into play at TechCo, allowing employees to exercise informed and considered freedom in using company resources, working hours, and staying within their job scope (Turco 2016). While this has been well-received by most, some executives and employees have expressed concern that the concept of exercising freedom was more difficult to grasp when practised. For instance, flexible working hours, which had been advertised in the firm's recruitment advertisements, was a major draw for many millennials who ended up applying to the company. However, these benefits do not apply to all positions in the company (Turco 2016). This perceived inequality can have an effect on employees' morale, not only those who do not get to enjoy these privileges, but also those who do, and, as a result, feel bad. Turco notes that in a company like the conversational firm that she studied, where most of the employees were similar in age, the disparity can be especially incongruous (ibid.). Also, judgment is subjective, and what is done using what one employee considers good judgment may not be considered so by another employee. This is more significant in a growing workforce where the sheer number and types of opinions expressed make it difficult to come to a common agreement on what good judgment is all about (ibid.). It is also thought that the ambiguity of using one's good judgment absolves firms of one of their responsibilities, namely, to define instructions clearly (ibid.).

While the freedom given to employees may seem like a disaster waiting to happen, conversational firms' belief is that the freedom given will yield trustworthiness, which in turn ensures more genuine freedom. This policy of freedom of speech seems to go against what sociologist Ezra Zuckerman (2010) argues as the need for firms to confine voice rights to those at the top of the management hierarchy.[20] However, Turco points out that there is still some level of control both by the management and by the self-discipline imposed by social media. The kind of freedom granted to employees is, therefore, one bound by what can be said on social media, according to the rules set by the company, which are valued and understood by the employees (Turco 2016).

Another area of openness that the conversational firm strives for is how the company's image and values are presented externally. A strategy, observed by the organizational scholar James Baron, is then used in recruitment to draw talented workers that fit the company's environment and social needs, and are hence more likely to behave in a manner that is in line with the requirements of the firm (Baron 2004; Turco 2016).[21] This would then minimize the necessity for hierarchical control, contributing to the overall openness of the firm.

However, as with the issue of freedom of speech, some employees found the divide between what was marketed and what was practised in real life disconcerting. Turco found that employees agreed with what was marketed to the outside world but felt strongly that the firm's culture should be practised rather than exist merely as a list of ideals (Turco 2016). These two sets of beliefs and practices rooted in culture are what Orlando Patterson calls "cultural knowledge" and "cultural pragmatics." Turco argues that a firm can define its cultural knowledge well without being able to do the same for its pragmatic culture (Patterson 2014, 3, 6).[22] Having TechCo spell out its culture was also perceived as a top-down control of employees' voices, and the resultant unhappiness was conveyed to management, as part of employees' openness and freedom of speech. The "culture deck," a set of slides that TechCo uses for marketing, was subsequently modified, and became something to which both management and employees were held accountable (Turco 2016). While the concept of the culture deck brings to mind Gideon Kunda's argument that companies in the early 1990s were "engineering" particular company cultures to implement some form of workplace control to get their employees to behave in a certain desired manner, Turco found that the approach taken by this conversational firm was different (Kunda 1992; Turco 2016).[23]

The physical workplace is another feature of the conversational firm where the ideal of openness is pursued. Research shows that employee happiness is generally lower in offices with open layouts because of a lack of privacy, interruptions, and noise, the last of which caused the most unhappiness among employees about their workspace in this conversational firm (Turco 2016). [24] This was also validated in my visits to firms, where I spoke to employees, who preferred dedicated and private working spaces. However, these same factors were viewed positively as well; the lack of privacy gave rise to opportunities for valuable feedback and learning, the interruptions contributed to the overall spirit of togetherness and provided opportunities for connection and collaborative learning, while the noise was also a "buzz," which employees saw as a symbol of the company's collective spirit (ibid.). The lack of privacy was hardly an issue for most of the employees, since the managers were seldom at their desks. Turco found out that these managers were often at one-on-one meetings with their staff, a common strategy when working with millennials, whom studies have found to be accustomed to personal feedback and attention (Howe and Strauss 2000; Turco 2016).[25] Turco believes that the modern workplace is a very different reality from the workplace of Weber's time (Turco 2016). Weber believed that the power of bureaucratic authorities came from their expert knowledge and their position in the hierarchical structure (Turco 2016; Weber 1922/1978). To maintain the structural integrity of the organization, careful restrictions of conversations had to be implemented within and beyond the company. However, Turco holds that in today's world, attempts to control conversations in this way have increasingly proved impossible. The modern conversational firm has kept the structure of authority intact, while redefining its structure of communication (Turco 2016).

Despite some bureaucratic practices still in place today, Turco argues that the emergence of a new definition of communication means that the concept of the conventional bureaucratic firm can also be revisited (Turco 2016). Even though Weber believed that managerial knowledge and wisdom are the basis for authority, there is a growing acknowledgement of the limitations of managerial expertise and the distribution of knowledge throughout the organizational structure (Turco 2016; Weber 1922/1978). The conversational firm's policy of open dialogue thus means that managers and employees have opportunities to learn from each other without forfeiting their authority. Weber (1920/1947) argues that having a position of authority may not legitimize that authority. Thus, there may be problems of insubordination even in companies that retain a highly hierarchical structure. A conversational firm is possibly a solution to what Weber saw as a problem in his time. With conversation flowing between managers and employees, even if the final decision is not in the hands of the employees, the knowledge that they have contributed, Turco argues, legitimizes it more in their eyes (Turco 2016). Turco concludes that rethinking communication can help build a conversational firm, but this does not come easily. It requires cooperation, a commitment to the concept of open dialogue, and a variety of perspectives and voices. One of the key benefits to be reaped is that companies become more self-reflective in the process of engaging in open dialogue (ibid.). Notably, my interview with Matthew, a director of a software consultancy firm, revealed an important caveat to establishing a conversational firm:

> I think that there is a common misconception that open floor plans naturally generate collaboration. It is provable not true, as I have seen many open floor plans. They are a metre apart, but it might as well be a kilometre because the social structures and the organizational structure did not encourage or force communication.

Although Turco has envisioned various features to a conversational firm, Matthew held the view that encouraging collaboration relies on the company culture. It is only when firms seek to encourage collaboration and communication between employees and managers that these goals can be achieved. Interestingly, Matthew highlighted that this culture may not necessarily be suitable for all firms. It depends on the goals of the firms themselves.

The essential lesson to be learnt from Turco's illustration of the conversational firm is that while such organizational arrangements already exist, they cannot merely exist within a single technology firm. The process of fostering open dialogue for collaborative learning is an important tool for any hierarchical structures introducing feedback and openness. Thus, it cannot only be technology firms implementing this; the conversational firm has to be implemented on a larger scale in the private and public spheres to encourage collaboration and innovation.

The ideals of open dialogue have become the norm of firms that want to be characterized as progressive. They believe that such an approach will increase innovation and provide early warning signs of problems within the corporate structure. It is also a way for senior management to tap into informal networks within an organization and find out what employees really want and think. However, it also shows that companies that adopt the style of conversational firms are, in a way, trying to shape the work ethic of their employees by using feedback to manage their expectations and weed out those who either do not contribute much or are complainers. It is unclear whether there are any safety mechanisms for millennials and other generations who might make mistakes, misjudge, or take risks when providing feedback. It is also not clear how the individual is ranked by their boss vis-à-vis their team. The conversational firm clearly needs much more study and in many other contexts and cultures. For example, do conversational firms increase inter-organizational trust? Do more conversations between employees mean more innovation for the firm? While collaboration and flexibility have been identified as the new values needed for organizations to succeed, there is still much more collaboration needed between employees and management to brainstorm what exactly the future organization should look like.

These questions need further exploration. One thing is for certain: Technology companies have been looking towards collaborative approaches, between higher management and employees, and between different employees. Collaboration has become the pathway to the future of work. However, despite the substantial research done on millennials and the emerging work culture centred on beliefs of the millennial work ethic, academics, business leaders and policy-makers have yet to come to a consensus on how to collaborate effectively.

Perhaps this is where governments, public institutions, and policy-makers can learn a lesson from the conversational firm that Turco

(2016) talks about. Governments need to consult younger citizens a lot more and plan for innovation with various groups and create fair opportunities. One way is through proactive governance. The other is through tripartite agreements. I look at these in detail in the next two chapters, where I take the example of Singapore's approach to the economy, allocation of resources, and meritocracy and how they shape the lives of its younger citizens.

3

Proactive Governance as a Response to Flux

This chapter proposes a global model of a proactive state, where the government has been actively involved in "proactive governance," a collaborative effort between the state, the media, intellectuals, businesses, and policy-makers. In some sense, it could be a much bigger and scaled up version of Turco's conversational firm (2016). However, we do know that governments play hugely complicated roles, much more than firms.

I conceptualize a proactive state as one that anticipates, enables, regulates, and co-creates policies. To remain future-ready and hedge itself against unprecedented developments, a proactive state is necessary to support its citizens for the future due to the challenges of job losses and re-skilling brought about by automation and the resultant flux. While the state has to provide employment opportunities for all generations, the focus here is on millennials to build a resilient future economy through innovation and alleviate some concerns expressed by firms and employees discussed in the previous chapters. This type of governance, with effective communication to all parties, is also needed to handle unprecedented risks and disruptions, such as the current pandemic, resourcefully and pragmatically, focused on safeguarding both the current and future health and livelihoods of all its citizens (El-Taliawi and van der Wal 2020; World Economic Forum and Futurity 2020).

SOCIETAL AND GOVERNMENTAL ANXIETIES

One of the many challenges for the flux society will be the process of phasing in technology upgrades, which will have major infrastructure costs. Technology will clearly be the major driving force behind most jobs, and new upgrades will phase out older technologies (ILO 2017). Countries that are left behind in the technology race will face severe challenges to catch up with those at the forefront (Mazzucato 2013). Hence, they will have to combat the digital divide, as they and individuals try to compete. One example of this is the proliferation of mobile networks across the globe. Some countries are still struggling with 2G networks, with their populations too poor to afford higher upgrades, and other countries have phased out 2G networks completely and are already using 5G networks. This also includes data storage devices where citizens and companies of richer countries can access cloud storage, and the majority of the poor or lower middle classes are left with outdated hardware dumped into their markets. Significant global policy sharing will be required to combat some of these problems faster. Newer business models will also have to be incorporated to keep sections of the global market up to date with others to avoid economic stagnation (ILO 2018).

The entry of digitalization means that governments need to understand the implications that arise, and in the process also share resources and learn from each other. However, two factors hamper this process. The first is citizens' loss of confidence in governmental institutions, which are unable to keep pace with digital transformation. This leads to concerns among citizens about the government's capability to craft a roadmap for the future. The other difficulty is in the areas of data storage, privacy, access, and stewardship, to which some governments have been slow to react. Specifically, few governments have successfully implemented digital tools to improve policy design, implementation, and assessment. Governments also need to do forward planning to build human capital and *skills updating capital* by providing opportunities for people to pick up the necessary skills and to upgrade quickly. Transition policies with support plans will be needed to handle the challenges and difficulties that will come along with the changes. It has been argued that the crux of the digital transformation is more than just considering policies related to technology; it needs to address issues of distribution and equality, making sure that opportunities are inclusive and available to all (Wyckoff 2017). I argue that the purpose of proactive governance is to foster social inclusivity. Different countries should create their own versions based on their political will and apparatus.

Matthew Bidwell, management professor at the Wharton School, feels that the changes to the future of work due to the entry of automation technology will not just affect the economy, but will also affect society politically. For example, Bidwell predicts that one of the political implications that may arise from a small number of organizations controlling technology is "the massive concentration of power" that these companies will continue to acquire (Knowledge@Wharton 2016). The fear is also that social inequality will ensue because of automation replacing humans, and that some governments are not adequately equipped to prepare for the possible repercussions of automation, such as lower-paid jobs and even permanent unemployment. While Bidwell believes that government intervention is crucial to restore balance, he feels that current political sentiment, particularly in the United States, does not favour it (Knowledge@Wharton 2016).

Interestingly, when I spoke to Matthew, a senior director of a software firm, about his views on how work is changing in the software industry, I found that there is an increasing emphasis on having soft skills, such as creativity and design skills, which are more difficult to automate:

> What we are seeing at the cutting edge … Over the past … half a decade, maybe 7–8 years. There is a realization that it is not enough to just build things … There … were new methodologies and … development [that] came out of a desire to build software better. I think there has been an increased focus. It started from about 2010 and probably accelerated since then, about building the right thing. And that means changing the way that you do design and product management and the way you … talk to your customers. Because if you have … software capability, where you can deliver things really fast, that allows you to go talk to your customers more frequently and get feedback and respond to that feedback a lot faster.

At the same time, Matthew remarked that "the rate of change in industry, the rate of change in company has accelerated. Any job that has a repetitive nature to it is at extreme risk of being disrupted by automation." According to him, demand will be for individuals with "highly in demand skills and having proven to give good results with those skills."

Colleen LaRose, the president and CEO of the North East Regional Employment and Training Association, points out that there is a lack of communication and collaboration between the workforce and the economic development institutions. This means that each party is holding on to valuable information that, if shared, could potentially facilitate the creation of new jobs (Knowledge@Wharton 2016). According to Ed Husic, an Australian politician, governments are still suffering from inertia when it comes to the many government reports that call for a change in how education and training are done. Husic feels that while the issue has not been ignored, it should be urgently considered. He is also of the opinion that when it comes to planning for the future of work, the Australian government needs to consider two groups of people: those who are still in the workforce, and those who have reached the traditional retirement age but are keen to work longer (Lane 2017). For example, Mark Warner and Mitch Daniels point out that for governments to be able to help people face the new economy, credible data needs to be collected (Warner and Daniels 2015).

The second Dell Future-Ready Economies Model was released in 2016 and ranked fifty cities according to attributes that enhance their future-readiness, such as the capacity for access to new tools and ideas, which in turn results in better connectivity, economic performance, and the ability to attract talent. Evaluated by employee skill sets, infrastructure, and commerce, the top three cities are San Jose, San Francisco, and Singapore (Business Wire 2016). Common features of future-ready communities include environment-friendly transportation such as bike paths, a high percentage of voting citizens, a high proportion of college-degree holders, and an infrastructure that supports open-data initiatives and Internet accessibility.

Other cities not on the list are also doing their part to prepare their people for future-readiness. The Canadian province of Alberta, with its eighteen cities, is one example. The Government of Alberta launched Future Ready in 2016, which aims for "a long-term focus on integrating education and training from kindergarten to work, so all Albertans have the knowledge and skills they need to succeed in the changing Alberta and global economy" (Alberta Government 2016; CBC News 2016). It comes as no surprise that the initiative is a collaborative effort involving not only government ministries, but also industry and labour professionals. Teachers and parents have a say as well; one of the first steps in the Future Ready endeavour is an online survey to obtain the opinions of parents and other Albertans about the K–12 curriculum (ibid.). Future Ready is also looking into employment skills, such as adult learning programs, apprentice training awards, temporary summer employment programs, bridge-to-teacher certifications, and training programs that equip industry professionals to teach in schools, thus bringing together industry and education (ibid.).

Policy-makers will have to balance objectives between different interest groups and the objectives of individuality and nations bound together by their communities, privacy, security, as well as aging populations in richer countries, and millennial and post-millennial youth in poorer countries, who may have less access to technology than the shrinking number of millennials and Gen Z in richer countries. National borders will not necessarily coincide with digital borders set by Internet traffic lanes and global corporate firewalls. The Internet will continue to produce more virtual communities organized along the lines of social interests and skills rather than only national identities. States will have to become more flexible and transparent, yet even stronger, as physical borders will be more and more supplanted by virtual threats and, perhaps, future pandemics. Technology is, however, not something that runs by itself. Proactive governance ensures that the vested parties and the affected parties communicate to build better resilience and infrastructure. A sense of readiness for constant change is something that all stakeholders can agree upon and take steps to do in the here and now (ILO 2018; Mazzucato 2013; Raghunath 2019).

In a discussion between partners, experts from industry, and academia on the policy implications of automation, worries about the potential of automation to reduce jobs were often cited as a major concern (McKinsey & Company 2017). However, Katy George, a senior partner at McKinsey, argues that the issue with automation is less about unemployment and more about automating quickly to benefit from higher productivity and a higher standard of living. Another concern she raises is the need to help employees transition quickly from their current job positions in response to the changing face of work, a sentiment echoed by James Manyika, McKinsey Global Institute's chairman and director. This is where policy-makers are under pressure to step in to facilitate the transition and deal with an emerging class of people who are "unemployed, permanently unemployed, and unemployable," according to Tom Siebel, founder, chairman and CEO of C3 IoT (Manyika 2017, 2). Thus, rigorous discussions about developing policies and regulations will need to take place between policy-makers, lawyers, and governments on a global scale.

Policy-makers, however, tend to be more reactive than proactive when confronting problems and crises. To better anticipate the challenges of automation and worker dislocation, policy-makers need to

plan around worker benefits and invest in their education and training, namely policy measures that foster their adaptability in an ever-
changing work environment. For example, Finland's education
system, and Singapore's adult retraining and re-skilling programs,
have been hailed as examples of best practices where the very same
technologies that caused disruptions are used to solve the problems
they brought about. By adopting policies that aim to integrate new
technologies into the workforce, states can avoid a future where
automation heralds the end of employment for both skilled and low-
skilled workers. On the contrary, when used properly, technology can
make it possible for low-skilled workers to take on work that previously required more training, and it can make work more efficient
and reliable (Agrawal, Gans, and Goldfarb 2018). The pressure for
policy-makers, then, is to first understand the future of work, to anticipate its impact on workers, and then craft policies that will benefit
as much of the population as possible (McKinsey Global Institute
2017a). This will require the work of a visionary, committed leadership. In my interview with Thomas, a professor, he said:

> No responsible politician and all of society will expect their politi-
> cians to say, "We don't know about tomorrow." We still have to
> plan, we still have to direct a lot of information out there. So, the
> judgment call will be to decide which set of trends are going to be
> important for us ... And for this, I think highly educated, talented
> leadership is important.

One of the ways policy-makers can do this is to tap into the population itself. One example is the Pakistan government's pilot proactive governance system, set up in 2011, which obtains feedback on services
delivery directly from citizens. By making it mandatory for service
providers to use smartphones, and then following up with customers
through robocalls and sms messages, the system bypasses the traditional
model of customers filing complaints in favour of service providers taking the proactive step of making sure that services were delivered. The
Pakistan model extends the initial conception of proactive governance
by incorporating the elements of anticipating and enabling. These two
elements are especially important for a proactive state to be able to effectively function within the flux society, where changes are rapid. In other
words, "the citizen is not coming to the state; the state is coming to the
citizen" (Bhatti, Kusek, and Verheijen 2015, 19).

MODEL OF A PROACTIVE STATE

The World Economic Forum recently published a white paper on the need to reimagine traditional governance into "agile governance" in light of the fourth industrial revolution (World Economic Forum 2018). With the emergence of more technologies and disruptions to the economy, the private sector's influence is growing and governments will need to involve it in policy-making. What the Forum's paper proposes is a position of agility, defined as "an action or method of nimbleness, fluidity, flexibility or adaptiveness," that will allow states to keep up with the rapid developments in society (ibid., 6). More specifically, it offers a new framework to consider how "policies are generated, deliberated, enacted and enforced" (ibid.). Some examples include designing thinking methods through policy labs that allow for quick testing and iteration, and regulatory sandboxes that encourage innovation and provide a platform for companies to test new products (World Economic Forum 2018).

In some ways, proactive governance shares similarities with agile governance. They both regulate and create conditions that are conducive to innovation, as well as encouraging co-creation, which aims to give citizens and non-state actors a say in the process. However, I argue that proactive governance goes a step further than agile governance because it does not just stop at regulating, but uses this information to enable people to deal with technological changes as empowered individuals, by equipping them with the skills. Using the model in figure 3.1, I will illustrate and describe each component of proactive governance in greater depth.

The first step in proactive governance involves *anticipating* or understanding the source for the latest available information about aspects of people's lives and preferences, for example, via surveys. This anticipation also includes getting up-to-date information from businesses for job opportunities, not just locally but globally as well. This helps economies manage disruptions in a timely manner and look for new opportunities to mitigate problems.

Enabling comes next. This step consists of equipping people with the skills that are in demand in the job market. This requires the state to have extensive knowledge of innovation and automation. This form of enabling also maintains a certain degree of minimalism, fostering a spirit of self-reliance that differentiates it from conventional welfare expenditure. However, I also argue for a view of the state's ini-

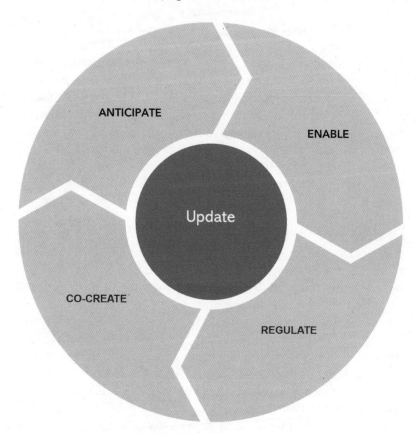

Figure 3.1 Model of proactive governance

tiatives that are more proactive than minimalist, due to the extensive infrastructure and policy work that the state needs to do to prepare its citizens (see Calder 2016; Lee and Qian 2017).

Next, *regulation* allows innovations to develop safely without being stifled. Regulating also means creating and updating legal infrastructure, either physical or social, to provide ample jobs and opportunities for people. A proactive state does not spoon-feed its people but provides favourable conditions and access to opportunities.

This brings forth the need for *co-creation*, to allow citizens to have a stake in their community and economy. Providing opportunities to develop a sense of ownership can establish the grounds for social cohesion, which is arguably a prerequisite to economic well-being. This is rooted in functionalism, which argues that different components of a much larger social body work in harmony to allow the overall system to function efficiently, not unlike how individual human organs work to enable the body to function as a whole (Urry 2000).[1] Durkheim's idea of organic solidarity in more advanced societies reflects the interdependence of human relationships. For example, the Singapore pledge also reflects this belief in the need for social cohesion (Durkheim 1893/2014; National Heritage Board 2019; Zhi and Saparudin 2014).[2]

Furthermore, it is important to note that if any of the four components fail, the system will not work. Thus, there is a need for strong feedback and for corrective mechanisms so that policies can be constantly updated and any failure to deliver promises will be tackled directly by the state. For example, Dennis Linders (2012) argues that citizens can easily provide feedback to the government and co-produce policies through information and communications technology. In this way, citizens can play a more active role in shaping policies. Similarly, Catherine Bochel and Hugh Bochel (2017) suggest that petitions and e-petitions are possible ways for citizens to effectively provide feedback to local governments, allowing citizens to take part in the decision-making process. Besides these innovative methods, which use technology, citizens are also able to provide feedback by meeting with their political representatives or using opinion polls (Fishkin 1997). Through these various means, citizens and corporations are able to provide timely updates on the successes and limitations of any policies. The state can use this information to make appropriate policy changes, thereby improving their effectiveness.

Furthermore, the proactive state should be comfortable viewing the economy as consisting of tasks, not jobs. Due to technologies such as digitalization, globalization and disruption have atomized work into smaller tasks (Poon et al. 2017). Hence, to tackle the issue of the future of work on the scale of the city, company, and citizen, the focus should be on tasks rather than jobs. The government's role in this, at the city level, could involve a task-based study of the city's economy by looking into the effects of digital technology on work, as well as tailoring work and tasks in existing sectors in ways that complement the strengths of their people (Bakhshi et al. 2017).[3] This move is meant to be inclusive too, as it seeks to build on the strengths of some demographics that are often overlooked in the discussion of work, such as the elderly and those with special needs. Moreover, the line between work and school will have to be erased, so that matching work to workers can start from within education systems, rather than after they get a job. This will help to foster a collaborative partnership between the state and companies and nurture a mutually beneficial relationship in which the two parties share resources. In particular, there is a need to start these policies at a younger age, to shape the work ethic of the next generation of workers. Gavin, a senior manager of a multinational bank, highlighted to me that while there may be subsidies for skills upgrading courses, "it is not natural for folks to want to take on these courses unless their attitudes are already shaped." Thus, a proactive approach by the state that anticipates future needs is crucial to enable the flux society to flourish.

On the other side of the equation, companies, especially citizens, have a crucial part to play as well. Companies can play a part by taking the initiative to assist their employees in transitioning to new job requirements, preparing themselves for disruption, and enabling new opportunities for technology to work with people, rather than against them. At the citizen level, the employee at risk of being displaced by automation can look at filling the gaps in their repertoire of skills, or matching their existing skills to opportunities in adjacent occupations (Poon et al. 2017). In a proactive state, everyone has a stake in the system. Hence, everyone has to be engaged in being future-ready. With various stakeholders collaborating, good policies can gain consensus and traction. Moreover, the literature on collective intelligence suggests that greater levels of collaboration will create policies that may exceed the capabilities of individual actors (Woolley et al. 2015). Through the efforts of the various parties, the state can move towards a collaborative vision of the future, while ensuring that citizens and corporations are well equipped to take on the changes.

Nevertheless, as discussed in chapter 2, millennials are important subjects of study in the flux society. Current literature explores their impact on the economy and how to engage them in the workplace. In addition, the global perceptions of harnessing a disruptive future have resulted in anxiety for millennials, corporations, and states. Proactive states can anticipate future changes and create appropriate regulations. In the following chapter, I will elaborate on Singapore as a case study of a proactive state. In chapter 5, I will shift my focus to millennials in Singapore and examine how the proactive state has shaped the work ethic and lives of millennials there to prepare them for the flux society.

4

The Proactive State
and the Rise of a Smart Nation

Singapore is one example of a country that is working hard to become future ready and the Covid-19 crisis has only strengthened its commitment to a sustainable and digitalized future for all its citizens. I use it as a case study to illustrate how a proactive state and a Smart Nation can work. Singapore is making many efforts to create new forms of employment for all ages, but I focus particularly on new graduates and younger professionals, because they face many challenges in an uncertain world of work where professions will be phased out at a much faster rate (Parker and Igielnik 2020). As the world faced a pandemic, Singapore, like many countries, introduced generous stimulus packages with a focus on (1) creating jobs and building skills for workers; (2) boosting resilience for businesses; and (3) strengthening inter-community bonds. While some of the above were a reaction to the economic and job losses of the pandemic, they also show Singapore's deep commitment to tackling economic issues head on, often with the foresight to avert future trouble by taking responsive measures (KPMG 2020).

I take a deeper look at meritocracy and tripartite agreements in Singapore, where everybody is encouraged to do their part for economic progress and social welfare (R. Chang 2015; Katz, Lee, and Lee 2004; Sheldon, Gan, and Morgan 2015). I mostly focus on the future readiness of the state, suggested by Mariana Mazzucato (2013), as being very important if countries want to progress. While this model may not be globally replicable due to different political, economic, and social conditions, it is nonetheless a prime example of why the state needs to keep up with corporations, innovations, disruptions, and future generations in a complex world of flux. All nations have their own policies and plans for future readiness. What Singapore already does well is planning ahead through economic pragmatism. What it can do more of is connect to the values of the younger and future generations through extensive conversations and feedback mechanisms.

Singapore, a small island nation, has embarked on a transformation to becoming a Smart Nation considering the needs and challenges of the fourth industrial revolution. The country's ideal of the Smart Nation is part of a larger trend by developed regions (including the United States, Europe, Scandinavian countries, and others) to build a technology-led urban utopia that is efficient, sustainable, and prosperous at the same time (Hollands 2015). I particularly focus on Singapore as an example because the nation has made efforts to respond quickly to flux caused by disruptive innovation and to set tangible targets to make sure that everyone, not just millennials, but all workers, will eventually be empowered by smart technology. For example, Singapore has rolled out a national strategy to develop artificial intelligence technology use in government, finance, and other sectors of society (Tang 2019). The end goal is to create a Smart Nation, where technology permeates most aspects of Singaporeans' lives. While these endeavours do not claim to solve every problem in society, the idea is to keep up with fast-paced global changes and to create a prosperous and harmonious local population and economy that is becoming increasingly more sensitized to closing existing socio-economic gaps (Chang 2015; Katz, Lee, and Lee 2004; Sheldon, Gan, and Morgan 2015). Furthermore, like most other countries, even Singapore needs to hear diverse younger voices when it comes to shaping futures as technological disruptions will have a more enduring effect than disruptions from the pandemic, both of which have millennials or PMET (professionals, managers, and technicians) very concerned about their jobs (H.C. Chan 2020).

This chapter will begin with the economic history of Singapore to explain how some of its historical developments have influenced the ideologies that remain deeply rooted in Singapore society. The story of Singapore's development cannot be seen in isolation from its continued emphasis on social cohesion and social policies, which were necessary to create an environment conducive to economic growth. This will help to contextualize certain ideologies and practices, as I turn to an analysis of present-day Singapore to show how it demonstrates a model of a well-functioning proactive state.

ECONOMIC HISTORY OF SINGAPORE

In the course of the last 17 years since 1945, no one has ever suggested that
Singapore should be independent by itself. It is a political, economic and
geographical absurdity.

Lee Kuan Yew, 1962

Singapore's economic history is closely linked to its political history.
Joining the Federation of Malaya, Sarawak and North Borneo to form
the Federation of Malaysia on 16 September 1963 was meant to help
the island leverage its neighbour's rich natural resources and bigger
market (*The Straits Times* 1963). By doing so, the plan was to create
more jobs, leading to economic development (T.Y. Tan 2008). However, the separation from Malaysia on 9 August 1965 and the withdraw-
al of the British military meant that Singapore was now on its own.
Not only did it have to solve the pressing problem of unemployment,
partially caused by the sudden loss of jobs for some 16 per cent of the
workforce previously employed by the British military, it also had to
get its economy off the ground (Young 1992). At that time, it was an
underdeveloped nation with a GNP per capita of less than US$320
(Iswaran 2015). Its economy was characterized by a lack of decent
infrastructure, limited capital, limited commerce, and hardly any
opportunities for foreign direct investments, because the very small
number of industries only produced goods for domestic consumption (Pek 2017). Singapore's lack of human and land resources also
meant that it was necessary to open the country to trade and investment to develop its domestic economy (B.H. Chua 2011).

Thus, what Singapore had to do to create jobs was to remove the
barriers to its economic growth, by investing in infrastructure and
human resources to create conditions favourable to foreign investment (B.H. Chua 2011). Singapore's first step was to set up the Singapore Economic Development Board (EDB) as an entity that was
separate from politics, but intricately linked to markets (Pek 2017).
The EDB was responsible for marketing Singapore and parcels of
its land as ideal for investments, acting as a middleman between
foreign and local firms (Calder 2016; B.H. Chua 2011; Pek 2017).
Singapore developed its export manufacturing internationalization
by setting up EDB centres overseas to attract more foreign investors
(Pek 2017).

To adapt to contemporary priorities, in the 1960s the EDB shifted its strategy of developing labour-intensive industries towards training in capital- and technology-intensive industries and, later, knowledge-based work (Pek 2017).

At the same time, in 1965, a tripartite model was set up (National Trades Union Congress n.d.-b), a collaboration between the government, represented by the Ministry of Manpower (MOM); unions, represented by the National Trades Union Congress (NTUC); and employers, represented by the Singapore National Employers Federation (SNEF). In this model, the tripartite members "negotiate, aggregate and align their interests" towards fair labour policies that serve the economic and social development objectives of Singapore (Soh 2012, 11). The consultative nature of this engagement has enabled workers to develop trust in the government and establish a collaborative industrial relationship that has been pivotal in Singapore's economic growth and progress (Katz, Lee, and Lee 2004; Ministry of Manpower n.d.-a, b; Sheldon, Gan, and Morgan 2015). The tripartite model also exemplifies the value of achieving consensus in any situation for the larger purpose of achieving national interests.

Chua Beng Huat (2011) observes that the political situations that China, India, and Indonesia were facing in the 1960s resulted in these three countries having a lock on cheap labour. As a result, Singapore, along with the Asian Tigers – South Korea, Taiwan, and Hong Kong – faced very little competition for foreign direct investments, a period of growth and development that lasted some twenty years (B.H. Chua 2011). Singapore attracted many multinational firms with generous tax incentives in the 1970s to produce for global export markets. It was also during this time that a labour shortage arose. The government responded by starting an immigration program to bring both educated professionals, as well as unskilled and semi-skilled workers, into the country as well as giving scholarships to potential future citizens (V.T.H. Koh 2006). The Monetary Authority of Singapore was also set up at this time to establish Singapore as a financial hub (Young 1992).[1]

In the 1980s, the electronics and engineering sectors received a boost when institutions of technology were co-established with Germany, Japan, and France to provide the highly specialized expertise needed in high-technology industries. In addition, the Skills Development Fund made it possible for Singaporeans to receive training for such specialized jobs. However, at that time Singapore started to move away from labour-intensive industries, implementing a high-wage policy with increases of more than 40 per cent, coupled with a trend towards high-technology industries. In the process, it forced out low-end, labour-intensive manufacturing industries that did not adopt higher technology (B.H. Chua 2011). Recognizing the importance of promoting local enterprises as well, the EDB established the Small Enterprise Bureau in 1986 to offer assistance that would encourage the growth of these smaller companies (Pek 2017).

In the late 1980s and the early 1990s, the services industry started to become one of the key pillars of the economy, and in the years that followed the focus shifted from manufacturing to the new key industries of chemicals, electronics, and engineering. The biomedical sciences, including pharmaceutical biotechnology and medical technology, were also developed, thus diversifying and balancing Singapore's economic structure. Beyond this, by leveraging the advantages afforded by the country's geographical location and time zone, the financial sector also underwent a transformation as part of Singapore's goal to poise itself as Asia's financial hub (B.H. Chua 2008; Huff 1995). Skilled talent from all over the world was brought in to enrich the local skill pool (Pek 2017).

From the year 2000 and beyond, the focus turned to knowledge and innovation-intensive activities, with R&D one of the key areas of the economy. In 2006, more than SG$13 billion was allocated to promote R&D, in line with the government's aim of increasing gross expenditure on R&D from 2.25 per cent to 3 per cent of GDP within a five-year period. The National Research Foundation (NRF) was set up under the national R&D agenda to develop, coordinate, and implement national research and innovation strategies (Pek 2017). Singapore is also a leader in intellectual property protection and enforcement policies, which supports its innovation and investment strategies and makes it a safe place for companies to pursue their R&D goals with confidence (Economic Development Board 2018).

From 2011 to 2015, under the Research, Innovation and Enterprise Council (RIEC) 2015 plan, the government pumped in a hefty investment of SG$16.1 billion (Agency for Science, Technology and Research 2015). The council's roots date back to late 2001, when an economic review committee was set up by former prime minister Goh Chok Tong. The aim of the committee was to review existing policies and lay the groundwork for policies that would encourage entrepreneurship in Singapore (H.L. Lee 2003). Singapore's efforts to promote acceptance and a spirit of entrepreneurship and risk-taking seem to have taken off, judging from the Global Entrepreneurship Monitor (GEM) 2014 Singapore Report, which found a slight increase in the 2014 total early-stage entrepreneurship (TEA) rate of 0.3 per cent compared with the rate in 2013 (11 per cent and 10.7 per cent, respectively) (Chernyshenko et al. 2015). Although there was a decrease in intent to start a business in 2014 compared with the years 2011 to 2013, Singaporeans are less deterred by failure than respondents from twenty other countries when it comes to taking risks in starting a business (ranked 21st out of twenty-seven selected economies) (Chernyshenko et al. 2015). Similarly, Singapore's former senior parliamentary secretary for education and current minister of state Low Yen Ling is of the opinion that young Singaporeans are less afraid of failure, and are also more likely to be open to the idea of entrepreneurship, risk-taking, and unconventional routes in life (Sin 2016). These findings bring to mind the words of the former minister of education Ong Ye Kung: "A new type of Singaporean hero must be the entrepreneur; someone who has a dream or passion, who took risks to do something about it, suffered setbacks and failures but picked himself up again" (M. Lee 2017). However, the relative confidence of aspiring young Singaporean entrepreneurs might be a testament of Singapore's economic stability, rather than evidence of a developed attitude towards risk-taking. In comparison with the aforementioned tolerance of the failure of current Singaporeans, the GEM Singapore report observes that the respondents with the highest rates of fear of failure mostly originated from regions of economic instability (Chernyshenko et al. 2015).

The local educational institutions are also doing their part to encourage and foster entrepreneurship. NUS (National University of Singapore) Enterprise has been assisting Singapore start-ups with their expansion efforts by partnering overseas incubators with countries such as Japan and China. In the pipeline are plans to partner more countries, in addition to setting up incubator spaces with select countries (Today 2016). One of the initiatives by NUS Enterprise is the NUS Overseas Colleges (NOC) program, where undergraduate students have the opportunity to be immersed in an overseas entrepreneurial environment, take classes at renowned universities, and interact with the start-up community. Both undergraduates and postgraduates also get to participate in short immersion programs in various locations around the world (National University of Singapore n.d.-b). The Nanyang Technological University (NTU) also runs a similar program with NTUitive, NTU's own innovation and enterprise company. NTUitive's Overseas Entrepreneurship Programme places students in various technological hubs, including New York City, Beijing, London, and Berlin, providing industry experience while allowing them to attend classes part-time at a partner university (NTUitive 2016). NTU also has a Nanyang Technopreneurship Center that offers undergraduate courses, minors, and graduate degrees in entrepreneurship, and is also conducting entrepreneurship development programs in both English and Chinese (Nanyang Technological University 2018). Similarly, the Institute of Innovation and Entrepreneurship at Singapore Management University (SMU) organizes a wide range of events and activities, such as workshops, competitions, training programs, and internships, which are geared towards encouraging entrepreneurship, in addition to an incubation program that assists aspiring entrepreneurs to realize their ideas and bring them to market (Institute of Innovation and Entrepreneurship n.d.). The Singapore University of Technology and Design (SUTD) has an Entrepreneurship Centre that aims to "spark the flame of entrepreneurial spirits and passion in SUTD community." It conducts a wide range of activities similar to those from the Institute of Innovation and Entrepreneurship at SMU, such as workshops, internships, and incubation programs. SUTD takes the goal of pushing for entrepreneurship even further with entrepreneurship capstone projects available for final year undergraduates. SUTD students have launched several successful start-ups as a result (Singapore University of Technology and Design n.d.-a).

Since the 2010s, the Singapore government has continued to anticipate the kinds of changes it will have to deal with, and the strategies it will need to adopt to prepare its workforce and citizens to be future ready. The Smart Nation Initiative, first announced in 2014, aims to improve the lives of Singaporeans through the use of technology (H.L. Lee 2014). This includes the use of technology within individual homes, to wider communities, and in public services. In 2018, the government released additional plans to move this initiative forward: The Digital Economy Framework for Action, Digital Government Blueprint, and Digital Readiness Blueprint. The SkillsFuture Initiative was launched in 2015 to enable Singaporeans to continue to be economically mobile by taking on new skills that will help them remain employable. The Future Economy Council (FEC), previously known as the Council for Skills, Innovation and Productivity (CSIP), oversees the plans and strategies necessary for industry growth, as well as develops initiatives like SkillsFuture to ensure that economic growth remains inclusive for all Singaporeans (Ministry of Trade and

Industry 2017a, 2017b). A future economy needs a future-ready society (M.H. Chua 2018).

Singapore has consistently been ranked as the most competitive economy in the world (IMD 2020). However, this comes at a price because it is dependent on international trade and sensitive to global financial flux. From trade wars to pandemics, despite intense and timely planning by the state, there are local consequences of job losses due to financial and health crises and automation. Hence, building continuous opportunities for its citizens through actionable policies and a strong social compact for social cohesiveness have become paramount for economic success. Singapore's serious commitment to race and religious harmony, and meritocracy means that the rule of law is highly efficient and exacting in making flouters accountable, and is applied equally to all citizens and institutions (see Ministry of Home Affairs 2021; Tan and Tan 2014).

SOCIAL COHESION AND ECONOMIC GROWTH

Singapore's economic success is not merely a result of planning with great foresight, it also shares a symbiotic relationship with the politics of the nation. This has been recognized by the People's Action Party (PAP) since its formation in 1954, and as the incumbent ruling party since 1959 (B.H. Chua 1999). The PAP arguably derives its legitimacy and continued political success from its ability to sustain economic prosperity (B.H. Chua 1999; Lauria 2014). A stable government provides the ideal conditions for implementing long-term economic growth (B.H. Chua 2011).

The importance of achieving and maintaining this harmony is underscored by a number of measures that the Singapore government has implemented; of note is the government's response to the nation's racial demographic make-up. Singapore's racial make-up consists of three major groups: Chinese, Malays, and Indians, and minority groups that include Eurasians and other ethnic groups (B.H. Chua 2011). Dispersing racial groups proportionally within the general population is important to help create a sense of shared identity with fellow Singaporeans and discourage the creation and segregation of racial enclaves. In light of the racially motivated riots before Singapore's independence, preventing racially charged feelings from fomenting is key to building a stable and harmonious nation (Han 2014; L. Tan 1997).[2]

The Singapore government has gone to great lengths to maintain racial and religious harmony. The country adopts a neutral, secular, and pragmatic position to maintain harmony. According to a 2014 Pew Research Center survey, Singapore ranks the highest globally on religious diversity, a feat that Prime Minister Lee Hsien Loong attributes to the state's firm stand on preserving religious and racial harmony (Cooperman and Lipka 2014; Y.L. Lim 2015). The government is known to take strong action against any behaviour or speech that offends religious or racial feelings and stays true to its conviction of maintaining social harmony at all costs (Heller 2015).

These policies are not just pragmatic for their own sake, but align closely with Singapore's core values, or shared values, which were conceptualized in 1991 to anchor the nation with a sense of common identity between individuals and society (Seng and Tan 2015). The five shared values are:

1) *Nation before community and society above self* emphasizes that communal interests that better society at large should always precede individual interests.
2) *Family as the basic unit of society* emphasizes the importance of the nuclear household in bringing up children and caring for the elderly.
3) *Community support and respect for the individual* emphasizes the community's obligation to support individuals and their rightful place in society.
4) *Consensus, not contention* emphasizes the desired goal of achieving agreement in any dispute in a constructive rather than confrontational manner.
5) *Racial and religious harmony* emphasizes the importance of respecting individuals who are racially and religiously different and seeks to preserve harmonious relationships for the sake of progress. (Seng and Tan 2015)

Other values permeate Singapore society. Meritocracy, for example, "dictates the establishment of systems of rewards and advancement at various levels" (Khan 2001, 4), emphasizing a Singaporean's right to equality in opportunity, but not equality in outcomes. In other words, the government will offer platforms that are accessible to everyone to get ahead and achieve socio-economic mobility, but it does not guarantee that everyone will obtain identical results. The ideals of meritocracy have created a high-performing education system in Singapore (Deng and Gopinathan 2016; Poon et al. 2017). It is world-class and highly subsidized by the government. At the end of every phase, students sit for nationwide standardized examinations. Since academic institutions assess their admissions based on students' performances in these exams, such a method of banding and streaming students has led to schools being ranked according to those results, with the top few schools branded as elite institutions. So, while all children are given equal opportunities to access primary-level education, their trajectories within the system for accessing secondary and tertiary education are heavily dependent on their individual merit and parental resources.

This does not come without concerns from a small number of citizens who worry about the growing social inequality and subsequent life chances for current and future generations who are born into humbler households (Y. Teo 2018). Chua et al. (2019) argue that rich children benefit from the social capital of their access to extra resources such as tuition, elite schools, and parental connections. So the skills divide might worsen for those who do not benefit from those resources. Teo argues that those with fewer resources find it hard to catch up in the education race and therefore have limited chances for social mobility in a highly competitive Singapore. The well-organized route to success comes at a heavy cost for those who lack the resources for academic performance (Y. Teo 2018). Nonetheless, the economic successes of the country, backed up by multiculturalism, tripartite agreements, and high rates of home ownership, the rule of law, world-class infrastructure, and many other factors have meant that there is a high level of trust and expectations from the state. The state is expected to work and perform well, and politicians and institutions are expected to have the highest of professional standards. In other words, there is high pressure on all parties – the state, citizens, and businesses – to deliver economic growth via compliance, efficiency, and innovation. However, research shows that despite huge amounts of input, Singapore could improve innovation, efficiency, and creativity (Cheng and Hong 2017).

The development of creative and critical thinking is crucial for increasing a country's capability and effectiveness to cope with the changes of a transient economy in light of globalization (Chiam et al. 2014). The Ministry of Education has made considerable progress in boosting creativity through various policies and interventions across all levels of education. One suggestion is plans to make both primary and secondary education more flexible and to scrap the streaming of students into different education paths (J. Lee 2019). However, parents feel some trepidation about the risk factors. They tend to look at creativity as a trade-off for rote learning to meet societal and family expectations (Averill, Chon, and Hahn 2001). With increased creativity comes a critical generation, which might not be as conformist as is expected of them (Kuah 2020). The recent election in Singapore showed that, though the long-standing PAP won the mandate, some younger voters voted for the opposition Workers Party, giving the latter more seats in parliament. Singapore's ambassador at large, Professor Chan Heng Chee, in her series of intellectually provocative IPS-Nathan lectures, said that the younger generation largely supports the ruling party, but expects diverse voices in parliament to look at aspects such as fairness, wider representation of diverse views, social inequality, and social justice (H.C. Chan 2020; Mahmud and Mohan 2020). This is arguably an outcome of a more discerning and creative generation that is thinking outside the box.

Tied closely to the idea of a meritocracy is the Confucian ethos of hard work and self-discipline (C. Tan 2012). In the early years of Singapore's independence, PAP espoused "hard work, thrift, and self-discipline," fearing that Singapore would become too westernized in the absence of its own Asian values (Mauzy and Milne 2002, 57). These values continue to be reiterated in the present day as a reminder to younger generations that the country's transformative progress has only been possible with this consensus on the need for prudence and a strict work ethic.

Self-reliance is another idea that resonates in many of Singapore's policies. Like shared values, it echoes the emphasis placed on upholding communal interests rather than individual interests. Along with its emphasis on Confucian values, the PAP was also known for its rejection of "welfarism in favour of volunteerism," which brought home the message that over-dependence on the community for personal gain was discouraged; instead, individuals should instead seek opportunities to uphold and contribute to larger community interests (Mauzy and Milne 2002, 57). The promotion of self-reliance is also evident in many social policies: from co-payment models in the MediSave Scheme, to the compulsory savings scheme through the Central Provident Fund (CPF), the government has sought to ensure that citizens and permanent residents and their employers have contributed to healthcare and retirement savings.[3]

There is a recurring tone of pragmatism in many national policies. This is not surprising given that Singapore's founding prime minister Lee Kuan Yew was known for emphasizing values like hard work and pragmatism, so that Singapore, as a young city-state of 2 million people in 1965, stood a chance of survival and success. These values took shape in the form of economic policies promoting an export-led economy, as well as educational policies that emphasized technical training to equip workers with skills needed for post-industrialization (see Bell 1973; Menon 2015). In a 1968 speech, Lee Kuan Yew remarked, "Poetry is a luxury we cannot afford," to students at the National University of Singapore, later elaborating that students need "a philosophy of life ... a value system" (Woo 2016).

The attitudes of pragmatism and hard work, prioritizing and lauding only what was necessary to survive and grow, characterized the early rhetoric of Singapore (Woo 2016). Its economic prosperity is a result of "a comprehensive package of inextricably linked ideological, political, and economic practices," but not one without costs (B.H. Chua 2011, 34). The state's almost omnipresent hand in the country's matters is instrumental in influencing and shaping the country's developmental model. The government not only intervenes in the areas of language, race, and religion, but also in labour market regulation, foreign direct investments, retirement savings, state-owned enterprises, macroeconomic stability, and international financial services development (Huff 1995).[4] This control, while credited for the development of Singapore's economic competitiveness, underscores Singapore's dependence on global market conditions for its survival. The costs in achieving harmony and multiculturalism are deeply rooted in pragmatism, and probably seen as necessary in the country's struggle for survival. The seventh president of Singapore, Tony Tan, once asserted that "for Singapore, racial and religious harmony is fundamental not only to our progress but to our very existence" (Seow 2016). Indeed, the prevailing national consciousness of Singaporeans has been one of *survival* and *vulnerability*. Former minister of foreign affairs George Yeo probably captured this sentiment best when he said this about Singapore's success: "Our success is the result of anxiety, and the anxiety is never fully assuaged by success" (B.H. Chua 2011, 35). It is this anxiety that keeps Singapore constantly on its toes. Notwithstanding its economic success in the years since its independence, Singapore continues to adopt the mindset that it cannot rest on its laurels.

Economic development, social cohesion, and pragmatism have been highlighted as some of the key values that underpin public policies in Singapore. It will be useful, then, to keep in mind how the government, through its policies, narratives, and institutions, has tried to outline and mould the ethos expected of the workforce. Having this contextual understanding of policies and values will create depth to the interviews and stories of Singaporean millennials featured in chapter 5 and shed light on some of the unspoken motivations behind their decisions and anxieties to stay competitive in the present and in the future.

SINGAPORE: A MODEL OF A PROACTIVE STATE

The Government cannot deal with the multi-faceted challenges of an ageing population alone. I am glad that the CAI Report had been a collaborative effort involving the people, private and public sectors. Together, we can make Singapore a home for all of us to enjoy productive and fulfilling lives in our golden years.

Prime Minister Lee Hsien Loong (2006)[5]

The above quote by Prime Minister Lee is about combatting the challenges of an aging population. However, it can also be applied to an overall concerted effort to involve the citizens of Singapore, government agencies, and corporations in preparing to be future-ready and proactive in predicting future trends and implementing measures to deal with any contingencies. As a small island nation, Singapore recognizes that the responsibility cannot rest entirely with the government. In short, Singapore continues to be a state where all citizens are encouraged to play a part in enabling social mobility.

One way the state does this is through proactive governance, a collaborative effort between the state, the media, intellectuals, businesses, and policy-makers. Singapore's example has been cited as a possible "policy laboratory of best practice," with global implications for today's unpredictable and disruptive economic climate (Calder 2016, 64).[6] In this way, it fulfills the four aspects of proactive governance: anticipating, enabling, regulating, and co-creating, which was discussed in the previous chapter.

In Singapore, citizens are expected to be self-sufficient and to work to provide for their housing, medical, education, and retirement needs. At the same time, they are not left to fend for themselves; the government puts in place measures to enable citizens to equip them-selves so they can stay employed in a changing economic environ-ment. This is all the more pertinent in current times, when Singapore is facing challenges that could severely handicap its economy and growth, i.e., a slowing economy caused by external factors and com-petition from neighbouring nations in the area of low-value-added sectors such as some types of mass manufacturing and agriculture, as well as domestic structural issues, such as an aging population. While the book focuses on millennials, it is important to note that other demographics in Singapore share these values. Chris, a Singaporean millennial, shared with me his own experiences and stories he has heard from elderly cab drivers about Uber and Grab:

> When Uber and Grab first came to Singapore and it became easy to become a taxi driver, my mother and brother tried to do so. I realize how difficult it was to make a living off Uber. I remember having to take over my brother's job and drive a few trips in order to help him hit the required trips for bonuses from Uber. This made me wonder how hard it is for the taxi drivers to survive. Whenever I asked them about it, they would tell me that they had to join Uber and Grab even though it pays less, because if you are stuck with being a "normal" taxi driver, you will not find any cus-tomers. Essentially, "if you can't beat them, join them."

Despite the disruption, these cab drivers have adapted to the changing norms of the sharing economy to stay economically productive, because the values of self-reliance prevail in Singapore society, even with the short-term economic challenges of technological disrup-tions. These attitudes are underpinned by future-ready policies made by the state and relevant institutions.

The following section looks at two major steps taken by Singapore to be future-ready, the SkillsFuture and Smart Nation initiatives, and how the government is anticipating, enabling, regulating, and co-creating amid automation anxiety while working towards economic viability, social participation, and cohesion. Through proactive gover-nance, Singapore has been able to be at the forefront of future-readiness to tackle AI disruption (Tham 2019). These steps consider the values of meritocracy and self-reliance as they offer opportunities to citizens but they do require the latter to take their own initiatives to become future-ready. Instead of providing full social security benefits, Singapore's approach involves putting in place social policy innovations to build assets to assist its citizens, such as the Central Provident Fund scheme, Edusave, Baby Bonus, and Child Development Account.[7]

In Singapore, ethnic integration is deeply tied to norms of meritocracy and this is achieved via the nation's public housing scheme, where an overwhelming majority of its population live in high-rise public housing (B.H. Chua 2005; Housing and Development Board 2020).[8] Singapore's housing policy is a citizen-, community-, and asset-building scheme that has been named as an example of successful social innovation by Michael Sherraden, the George Warren Brown Distinguished University Professor at Washington University in St Louis (WUSTL) and the S.R. Nathan Distinguished Professor of Social Work at the National University of Singapore (NUS). Sherraden identifies four main themes in Singapore's social innovation efforts: "[L]ook and plan ahead; build a multiracial society; house the nation; invest in human capital" (Miller 2015). It is the last theme, investing in human capital in the hope of encouraging the spirit of entrepreneurship that the SkillsFuture and Smart Nation initiatives are rooted in.

SkillsFuture Initiative

With the entry of automation and the increasing ubiquity of technology in the workplace, the chasm between those who have access to human-capital-building tools and those who do not will widen if nothing is done to bridge the gap. Add disruption to the picture, and the overall situation appears bleak for those who are unable to keep up. The former deputy prime minister Tharman Shanmugaratnam (currently senior minister) acknowledged this reality to some 550 student representatives from thirty pre-university institutions in the 2016 Pre-University Seminar, as he talked about the potential threat of higher unemployment in ten to twenty years (Shanmugaratnam, as cited in Intellasia 2016). He predicted that the job scene would look very different in the future, with traditional occupations such as lawyers, accountants, radiologists, financial planners, real estate agents, and insurance agents in low demand due to the ability of technology to deliver the same service at a lower cost. Senior Minister Shanmugaratnam also reiterated Singapore's global market advantage despite its size. He said that high unemployment rates could be avoided by responding quickly to and also by taking advantage of technological changes; the affordances of technology can also be harnessed to "enhance human abilities in every job and to create satisfying jobs." Mr Shanmugaratnam also discussed averting job losses in the future. "We can avoid that. First, because we have an advantage of being a small society but with a global market. And secondly, we can avoid that by responding in advance to what is coming – respond quickly to technologies, take advantage of technologies and make sure that we create better jobs for everyone." (Intellasia 2016). It is imperative that the government and companies collaborate to help workers equip themselves with the right skills to remain employable, a sentiment also expressed by Max Loh, the ASEAN (Association of Southeast Asian Nations) and Singapore managing partner of professional services firm EY (O. Ho 2016).

Recognizing that education and training have played an important role in developing human capital for Singapore's economic growth, SkillsFuture Singapore (SSG), a statutory board under the Ministry of Education (MOE) and the SkillsFuture initiative, was launched to equip the workforce with skills essential for a future-ready Singapore. To this end, the Ministry of Manpower, Ministry of Education, Workforce Singapore, and other governmental agencies aim to work collaboratively to develop an integrated and high-quality system of education and training that will not only meet the needs of industries, but also encourage lifelong learning (Ministry of Manpower n.d.-a, b).[9] In a report released in early 2017 by the Committee on the Future Economy (CFE), seven recommendations were proposed to help Singapore stay open and connected in challenging global conditions: deepen and diversify Singapore's international connections; acquire and use deep skills; strengthen enterprise capabilities to innovate and scale up; build strong digital capabilities; develop Singapore as a vibrant and connected city of opportunities; develop and implement industry transformation maps; and finally, partner one another to enable growth and innovation (CFE 2017).

The strategies are designed to help citizens acquire skills to prepare for future jobs and assist companies to innovate and transform their firms. The CFE (2017) report is an example of how collaboration between different stakeholders is necessary for tackling challenges. Prime Minister Lee Hsien Loong highlighted this fact in his speech.[10]

The report epitomizes how in Singapore, Government, businesses and workers tackle challenges and seize opportunities together. Its publication marks the beginning of another chapter of the Singapore story. Now the hard work begins, and every Singaporean has a role. (R. Sim 2017a)

The Future Economy Council is responsible for carrying out the proposals by The Committee on the Future Economy (CFE).[11] One of the main issues that the Council seeks to address is an expected rise in unemployment as well as implementing the Industry Transformation Maps. These maps that detail how the state, companies, and trade associations might work closer together to deal with issues in various industries (Ministry of Trade and Industry 2017a, 2017b). Other projects in the pipeline include looking into skills, productivity, innovation, and internationalization, as well as responding to the different needs and challenges faced by industries. Again, while this endeavour involves the participation of ministers from different ministries, the chair of the council, Deputy Prime Minister Heng Swee Keat (former finance minister and current coordinating minister of economic policies), made it clear that the collaboration between the government, employers, and workers is part of the plan (Channel News Asia 2019; Wong 2017).

Even though Singapore has made a conscientious effort to outline the future economic well-being of workers of all ages and levels of education, these strategies have their limitations; no government in the world can fully guarantee economic well-being for all during times of disruption. Chua Mui Hoong suggests exploring more social safety nets for those working in the gig economy and as industries transform and job insecurities increase (M.H. Chua 2018).[12] Despite the push towards innovation and entrepreneurship in Singapore, the lack of societal tolerance for failure might deter individuals from taking more risks. Steven remarked to me that young entrepreneurs in Singapore face pressure from parents and society, because they believe that taking the traditional role of working as an employee is the only way to ensure financial stability:

Pressure from parents. Some are very good and encourage them. Others are more realistic and tell them not to spend too much time on it. If it does not work in half year or one year, then they will ask them to get a proper job … Career is on hold until start-ups are a success. They also see contemporaries moving ahead, getting good salaries, going on holidays, buying a house and car. Those are real things.

Thus, there may be a need to further consider social safety nets in conjunction with the existing policies for Singapore to better motivate the younger generation to take risks and be creative in terms of a mindset change. There is clearly a need to alleviate career anxieties.

Another body that plays a role in the nation's efforts to upgrade its citizens' skills is the National Trades Union Congress (NTUC n.d.-c), a "national confederation of trade unions as well as a network of professional associations and partners across all sectors in Singapore." NTUC's vision is to help people regardless of their backgrounds to get better jobs and live better, with higher salaries. It is also concerned with maintaining Singapore's competitiveness and building "a strong, responsible and caring labour movement" (ibid.).[13] It carries out a wide range of programs, including career coaching, legal clinics, education, and training funds, that cater to a diversity of people, and provides an assortment of vouchers for education and daily necessities.

Like the NTUC, the SkillsFuture initiative does not discriminate and is meant for all Singaporeans in all stages of life and jobs, notably the SkillsFuture Credit Scheme, which is available to all Singaporeans 25 years and above (Y.K. Ong 2016b; SkillsFuture n.d.-a). Mr Shanmugaratnam called it the government's "broadest initiative" for this reason (Shanmugaratnam 2016a). The training programs it supports are all relevant to industry needs, and there are a wide range available, from creating a mobile application to obtaining a university degree (Y.K. Ong 2016b; Seow 2017). The inclusiveness of this initiative is also seen in the new SkillsFuture Study Awards launched in September 2016, with two award categories, one for people with disabilities, the other for disability employment professionals (Goy 2017). In fact, Mr Shanmugaratnam stressed that the drive to create an advanced economy is not merely about increasing productivity and wages, it is about creating an inclusive society, in which every individual is empowered to "build on their strengths, developing the skills that enable them to maximize their potential, earn their own success and contribute to society" (Shanmugaratnam 2014). A truly inclusive society can be made possible by equipping individuals to play their full role in society, respecting each individual's innate dignity, or sense of satisfaction that arises from the ability to do so (Shanmugaratnam 2014). An inclusive society can only be realized if everyone is able to find avenues to contribute to society at all stages of their lives. This will require reviewing the concept of meritocracy, which traditionally has meant academic performance achieved at a young age.

Thus, according to Mr Shanmugaratnam, the kind of meritocracy that Singapore needs to adopt is continuous: evaluating individuals throughout their lives, where one's educational experience and qualifications matter less than one's drive and potential to advance (R. Chan 2013). Mr Shanmugaratnam reiterated this at the Institute of Technical Education's (ITE)[14] twenty-fifth anniversary celebrations, where he emphasized that lifelong learning would depend on the skills desired, not on the formal academic qualifications that one already has (Shanmugaratnam 2017). Integral to the idea of continuous meritocracy is mastering skills, which necessarily entails continually developing skills and talents, as well as a broader and more collaborative view of society that considers others' strengths in addition to one's own weaknesses (R. Chan 2013). Societal respect for everyone, regardless of their jobs, should therefore be a defining characteristic of this ideal society (Toh 2013). In this new global economy, there will be a constant demand for new skills, and thus a constant need to keep acquiring new skills (Shanmugaratnam 2016b). This example, along with many others, demonstrates Singapore's ability to anticipate and plan for flux. It also shows that career disruptions are part of the norm.

This necessitates a rather radical shift in mindset towards work and meritocracy. This might be one of the biggest obstacles to creating a continuously meritocratic society in Singapore. Equating one's academic qualifications with one's ability is understandable and even economical since it is costly to gather deeper qualitative information on different learning abilities and styles, but it is also one-dimensional and does not allow for diversity in skills (Toh 2013). Cost, convenience, and a reluctance to take risks play a huge role in the inertia that prevents the employment model from being revamped to make it more inclusive. However, the ball is not entirely in the employer's court either; employees are equally, if not more responsible for the situation. Gog Soon-Joo, the former executive director of the Institute for Adult Learning, identified three types of barriers that employees may face: informational, situational, and dispositional. The informational barrier refers to a gap in knowledge about the opportunities for upskilling and advancement. The situational barrier hinders progress due to choices made after weighing the pros and cons of adult learning. The dispositional barrier refers to the resistance to adopt an alternative worldview or mindset that could mark changes in one's development and progress, because it is different from what has already been deeply ingrained in one's mind (Toh 2013). While the first two may be overcome with the right types of support, the last type is possibly the hardest of the three to overcome due to its affective nature.

A total revamping of the popular mindset will mean dismantling the traditional construct of meritocracy, the education tracking system based primarily on academic performance that mainly serves pragmatic pedagogical purposes (R. Chan 2013). Acknowledging the limitations of an otherwise successful and globally recognized education system in Singapore, then minister of education (Schools) Mr Ng Chee Meng said in the Ministry of Education Fiscal Year 2017 Committee of Supply debate speech that planning for education in Singapore should not only take a long view and focus on lifelong learning, but, more critically, should be tailored to meet future economic needs. It should move away from the traditional view of meritocracy, and the emphasis on academic achievements, and pursue a more holistic model. Implications for this are in line with the overarching aim of the government to be future-ready; not only do students have to develop skills and stay relevant through lifelong learning, they also have to develop soft skills and resilient, innovative attitudes to be ready for future challenges and uncertainties. In addition to the above, Ng also emphasized the need to nurture students' "joy of learning" and asserted the government's commitment to providing "equal access to opportunities" for all, regardless of socioeconomic backgrounds (C.M. Ng 2017).

The government has already started acting on these plans. One of the first changes it made was to completely abolish the system of secondary school in 2012 and junior college rankings in 2004 (C. Sim 2014).[15] More recently, in response to widespread criticism of the Primary School Leaving Examinations (PSLE) scoring system, which pits students against each other, Prime Minister Lee announced in 2013 that changes will go into effect in 2021 (Chia and Kotwani 2016). Instead of the existing system of scoring, Transformed-Score, a standardized score that ranks students relative to each other, will be implemented that will grade PSLE subjects according to eight Achievement Levels (AL). The ALs are similar to the broader General Certificate of Education (GCE), Ordinary (O-Level), and Advanced Level (A-Level) system used by secondary schools and junior colleges. This new scoring system aims to reduce competitiveness by evaluating students' performances individually (Ministry of Education n.d.). While this is a positive step, the views of the parents surveyed indicates that two things will first need to change before parents are fully convinced about this new system: the perception of the PSLE as the crucial exam for their children, as well as the competitiveness of the Singapore education system, a change that will not take place overnight (Chia and Kotwani 2016).

Other solutions proposed include a more egalitarian system like that in Finland, where students are not streamed, and a more holistic system like that in the United States, where a much larger pool of subjects is offered and students are allowed to pick and choose according to their strengths. Derrick Chang, CEO of PSB Academy in Singapore, concurs, and suggests having a curriculum that places less emphasis on how students perform in examinations, and more emphasis on their soft skills in projects. While soft skills such as sharing, collaborating, and negotiating will continue to be important, other types of soft skills, such as social and emotional intelligence, will also be needed to navigate a highly connected future where cross-border communication will become the norm. Chang calls for greater levels of collaboration between industry partners to provide opportunities for students that go beyond industrial attachments to companies and internships (D. Chang 2017).

Some headway, at least in higher education, has already been made; the move to transform tertiary institutions into research universities can be seen in the establishment of a number of new institutions of higher learning. The reputation of these new universities is further boosted by partnerships with renowned institutions around the world: The Singapore University of Technology and Design (SUTD) was established in association with the Massachusetts Institute of Technology (MIT) (Fisher 2020), and Zhejiang University in China, and the new medical schools at the National University of Singapore (NUS) and Nanyang Technological University (NTU) were set up with Duke and Imperial College, from the US and UK respectively (Fischer 2013a).

The National University of Singapore (NUS) Centre for Future-ready Graduates launched "Roots and Wings," a program designed to equip its students with life skills and awareness of their strengths and weaknesses to prepare them for the future. For alumni and Singaporeans, the School of Continuing and Lifelong Education (SCALE) was started in 2015 (NUS News 2016a, b). The program collaborates with other institutions, for example the Employment and Employability Institute (e2i), an NTUC initiative to provide skill upgrading programs, and aims to identify and address skill gaps in the workforce (e2i n.d.). More recently, in January 2018, it was announced that in an unprecedented move, NUS would start opening up more places for working adults, 20 per cent more per class over the next five years, and allow non-alumni to sign up for a wide range of courses as part of the university's efforts to align itself with the SkillsFuture vision (Mokhtar 2018). In 2021, NUS is launching a new interdisciplinary school in humanities and sciences to prepare students for the digital careers of the twenty-first century (J. Ong 2020). These will not be without challenges, because there need to be considerable changes in the mindsets of students, parents, and educators, who may be nervous about trying something outside their comfort zones and worry about how students might fit into conventional professions' norms of specialization (J. Ong 2020). However, interdisciplinary and multidisciplinary education that mixes and matches STEM with humanities and social sciences will clearly provide a competitive edge for young graduates. They can then fit into multiple professional roles and take on the challenges of lifelong education and career changes in the flux society, which, even beyond the current global health crisis, are full of complex problems, such as climate change and automation, which require integrated and continuous learning. NUS president Tan Eng Chye said in an opinion piece that the university should transform itself so that students can deal with "wicked problems" that change all the time (E.C. Tan 2020).

Like NUS's SCALE, NTU has set up a new College of Professional and Continuing Education (PaCE) in collaboration with NTUC, aimed at providing opportunities for skills upgrading (Nanyang Technological University 2018.). To accomplish this aim, not only is it adopting a more holistic approach by incorporating working experience into the admission criteria so that the focus is less on academic background, it is also looking into making the classroom aspects, such as how students interact and where classes are located, more flexible. In August 2016, twenty-eight part-time undergraduate-level courses catering to sectors such as digital electronics and data analytics were launched (Khamid 2016).

SUTD, Singapore's design and technology-centric university, has also set up the SUTD Academy to provide skills-based education and training courses for people with varying levels of work experience. The programs are designed to fit into "today's knowledge-intensive and technology-driven economy," and are primarily technology-based (Singapore University of Technology and Design n.d.-b). Some examples include courses in cybersecurity, digital marketing, data science, and technology and management (Singapore University of Technology and Design n.d.-b).

The universities in Singapore are also rethinking their admissions processes and criteria. Although academic competence is still one of the primary criteria for university admission, universities are broadening their scope to include non-academic qualities in their admissions processes. The cap for the Discretionary Admissions Scheme, which assesses prospective students based on criteria that are not limited to their academic performance, was increased from 10 per cent to 15 per cent of university admissions in 2017 (HR in Asia 2017a). To assist in the selection process, Professor Tan of NUS said that the aim of the university is to admit students with attributes that would enrich the academic community. A number of new strategies have been adopted to look out for such students. One is that alumni who have experience in evaluating candidates are recruited to assist in the interview process. Non-academic aptitude tests may also be administered to pare down the number of prospective students. Singapore Management University (SMU) has always adopted a holistic approach to student admissions, admitting more students who should, ideally, be adept at soft skills like time management and possess desirable characteristics like perseverance and resilience. Similarly, NTU looks for students with strong non-academic qualities, such as enthusiasm in broad areas like community service and leadership, as well as relevant work experience (HR in Asia 2017a). SUTD considers aspects such as the passion of the potential students and how well they will integrate into the university's interdisciplinary culture and curriculum (Singapore University of Technology and Design n.d.-c). All of the above is considered in addition to academic achievements to foster more innovation and create future-ready Singaporeans.

A revamp of the popular mindset includes not only what meritocracy now constitutes, but also what the former deputy prime minister Shanmugaratnam called "evolving [Singapore's] culture" (Shanmugaratnam 2016b). Employers will have to adopt a collaborative attitude, where they also train employees outside of their own organizations, even if such an approach is counterintuitive. The idea behind this is to nurture a pool of employees trained up to the same standards, so that even if an employee leaves, the same skill set levels will remain stable across the labour pool (Shanmugaratnam 2016b). Matthew's experiences with the recruitment in his software consultancy firm reflects this idea. For him, engineers should be employed based on soft and hard skills that are necessary for the workplace, not primarily on academic credentials. By focusing on these skills, he ensures that his employees are able to perform their jobs well.

It is clear then that though the upskilling challenges are many, the government's SkillsFuture initiative is one of the first steps to addressing these issues. So far, the take-up rate for SkillsFuture programs has been encouraging (Y.K. Ong 2016b).[16] In 2016, the year the SkillsFuture initiative was launched, Singaporeans aged 25 to 29 reported the highest average use of SkillsFuture credits, amounting to almost SG$400 per person. Information and communications technology courses were well-received by Singaporeans young and old. Older Singaporeans favoured learning basic skills such as the functions of a computer, and their younger counterparts opted for courses such as data analytics. The majority of the 6 per cent of Singaporeans who used their credit on Massive Open Online Courses (MOOCs), such as web design, programming, and search engine optimization were also young Singaporeans, aged 25 to 39 years old (HR in Asia 2017c). The number of courses eligible as SkillsFuture credits is also on the rise. Currently, more than 18,000 are being offered by over 700 public and private training providers (SkillsFuture 2017).[17] These numbers are steadily growing.

While these findings also reflect the substantial share of the resident workforce that participated (42 per cent) in 2016, those who benefit the most from training are young professionals, managers, executives, and technicians (PMETs) who are employed full time (Manpower Research and Statistics Department 2017a, 2017b). Chris shared his experience about using SkillsFuture to upskill himself:

> It was a bit of a rush to use my SkillsFuture subsidies. I only found out near the end of my university life that students received 100% subsidies on data science courses. I think many other students were aware of the subsidies. Most of my class was filled with students and I have some friends who told me they also took it before after we talked about it. Going into work, I knew I wanted to do more data analytics, so I took the classes. For my friends though, a lot of them just wanted to add something to their credentials and did not really think the class was useful.

The actual effectiveness of upskilling remains unknown (HR in Asia 2017c). Nevertheless, it is important to consider the various groups of people that benefit or fail to benefit from these training programs. The Labour Force in Singapore 2016 survey found that those employed full-time underwent training at a rate double those employed part-time (45 per cent and 21 per cent respectively). Compared with the unemployed, the disparity is starker: while the rate of training participation for the unemployed did not change from 2015 to 2016 (26.3 per cent and 26.7 per cent, respectively), those employed saw an 8 per cent increase in their training participation rate. This increase is largely accounted for by PMETs (10.6 per cent increase) and those working in the clerical, sales, and service sectors (6.5 per cent increase). Fewer blue-collar workers, like cleaners, labourers, and production and transport operators, on the other hand, participated in 2016 compared with 2015 (16.2 per cent and 20.7 per cent respectively) (Manpower Research and Statistics Department 2017a, 2017b). Therefore, more may need to be done to bridge this gap, especially for unemployed and blue-collar workers. One example is the Skills-Future Engage initiative launched in 2016 with a community outreach focus that aims to provide information and advice on finding the right training programs and skills to prepare for the future (Y.K. Ong 2016a).[18]

Even those serving National Service (NS), a two-year period of mandatory conscription for all male Singaporean citizens and second-generation permanent residents, are not left behind under Skills-Future.[19] Under the SkillsFuture scheme, skills acquired during National Service, such as teamwork, leadership, and technical or specialist skills, were also formally recognized by SkillsFuture Singapore in 2017. Full-time and operationally ready NSmen (those who have completed their two years of training) will be able to have their NS competencies accredited by the Workforce Skills Qualification, a national credentialling system for employees (HR in Asia 2017b).[20] For male ITE graduates who serve NS before starting work, arrangements to be updated on job-related matters will be made in the six months before their ORD (Operationally Ready Date-completion of national service). These job-related updates can be job opportunities, career-matching services, and opportunities for upgrading through both ITE's Work-Learn Technical Diplomas as well as the Earn and Learn Programme by polytechnics (Shanmugaratnam 2016b, 2017).[21] These are just some examples of how skills that are outside the conventional definitions of competency are being recognized as a response to the work of the future; work that will be diverse and "a lot more flexible, collaborative and mobile," and may require employees to take on different roles and flexible job descriptions (D. Chang 2017).

The relevance of technology to a future-ready Singapore is also one of the areas of focus in the SkillsFuture initiative. iN.LEARN 2020, a learning innovation initiative geared towards linking Continuing Education and Training (CET) partners and practitioners, was launched in October 2015 (SkillsFuture SG and Workforce Singapore n.d.). A total of SG$27 million was also committed to the initiative, whose aim is to encourage the use of technology-enabled learning (Y.K. Ong 2016a). With an increasing emphasis on ICT (information and communication technology) to make Singapore a Smart Nation, there is a corresponding demand for professionals in data analytics, information security, and software engineering, areas that have been identified as crucial to Singapore's growth and development as a more productive and competitive information-driven economy. In response, SCALE is beginning to offer courses in collaboration with the School of Computing at NUS. Three new bachelor of technology degrees in business analytics, cybersecurity, and software engineering started being offered in August 2017 (NUS News 2017). True to its goal of promoting lifelong learning and continuous meritocracy, the programs, which support the SkillsFuture initiative, will take in students regardless of their computing background, allowing both career changes from non-IT industries as well as faster graduations for those with computing experience (NUS News 2017).

Smart Nation Initiative

Singapore is moving from an investment-driven economy, to one that is going to be innovation-led.

Dr Beh Swan Gin, Chairman, EDB (Beh 2017b)

In the 2002 science fiction film *Minority Report*, the city of Washington enjoys a murder rate of zero, thanks to the work of PreCrime, a police department dedicated to preventing murders. PreCrime achieves this via its arsenal of three "precogs," mutated humans with the ability to predict crimes based on visions from the future. The Japanese anime series *Psycho-Pass* works on a similar premise, except that information on violent crimes is not obtained via clairvoyant beings but from public sensors placed everywhere that scan everyone who walks through them. After calculating the probability of a crime being committed by a citizen, the information is fed to the authorities, who then take the necessary actions to apprehend the would-be offender.

While technology today has not reached the heights seen in *Minority Report* or *Psycho-Pass*, the idea of a "smart city" empowered by technology to bring improvements to lives and increase business opportunities is not new, with cities around the world attempting to deploy policies and technologies that would realize their aim of becoming a smart city. The term may bring to mind the fantasy and grandiose high-technology structures of science fiction, but the objective is more practical, embracing current challenges to be future-ready. One way this can be seen is in how the advent of technology has dramatically changed how cities work, especially in data storage and analytics (Totty 2017). In this age of the information revolution, access to large quantities of data means that it is now possible to pre-empt potential issues. One example of this can be found in New Orleans, where, starting in 2015, data from two Census Bureau surveys has been used to identify neighbourhoods with high fire risks, to streamline its smoke-detector distribution efforts. This has resulted in an almost eightfold increase in the number of smoke detectors installed, from fewer than 800 a year to some 18,000 in a matter of three years since the inception of the program. A similar approach has been taken in Chicago to prioritize its health inspection checks. In the process, it has increased the number of violations found, which in turn would likely increase the standards of food hygiene in the city's eateries. Other technologically enabled measures include sensors that monitor traffic – vehicular and human – in cities such as Kansas City and Louisville, and enlisting the help of citizens to be data collectors in cities like Los Angeles, Mobile, and Boston (Totty 2017).[22] Shoshana Zuboff writes about how the modern workplace introduces an updated model of Bentham's panopticon (Zuboff 1988, 2015).[23] The widespread use of information technology tools has also enabled those sitting behind these, such as employers, to scrutinize the behaviours of those being observed, such as employees (Zuboff 1988, 2015). Similarly, installing these sensors everywhere to improve public services may have the additional effect of acting as a panopticon; as a result of feeling like they are always watched, citizens end up behaving more civilly and obediently.

Singapore has also hopped on the surveillance bandwagon. The Smart Nation Platform (SNP), a system of sensors that collect data from areas with high traffic, is similar to what some American cities have in place (SPRING Singapore 2015). On a much larger scale is Virtual Singapore, a project designed to build a 3D digital model of Singapore with the aim of improving government services through technology, fostering better connections between its citizens, and encouraging innovations by the private sector. This will be achieved via vast collections of data on daily living in Singapore using sensors and cameras all over the island nation (Watts and Purnell 2016). Virtual Singapore is still in progress, but upon its completion, it is expected to offer four major capabilities: virtual experimentation, virtual test-bedding, planning and decision-making, and research and development (National Research Foundation n.d.). The possibilities are varied, and the information collected can be applied in many ways, one of which is to enable the government to see how the country is functioning in real time and to make predictions on how infectious diseases are spread (Watts and Purnell 2016). Those who can expect to benefit from Virtual Singapore include not just the government, but citizens and residents, as well as businesses and the research community.

The Smart Nation Initiative, a government project launched in 2014 (by Prime Minister Lee Hsien Loong) aims to promote the harnessing of technology in a systematic and integrated manner in everyday problem-solving and living. It will enable Singapore to be better positioned to take on the challenges brought about by trends in the future that will affect the nation (H.L. Lee 2014; SPRING Singapore 2015).[24] The urgency to embrace technology in daily living is not only a matter of keeping up with global trends but, more critically, a matter of survival. The familiar rhetoric of survival and vulnerability that has brought Singapore this far has now evolved to include a technological caveat: "If we don't innovate, we will die" (Ho 2016).[25] Becoming a Smart Nation is not a luxury, but a necessity.

To that end, the Singapore government has set up the Smart Nation and Digital Government Office (SNDGO) to bring together the different ministries and integrate their ideas (H.L. Lee 2014). This office was restructured in 2017 to combine the resources and expertise across the Ministry of Finance (MOF), Ministry of Communications and Information (MCI), and the Prime Minister's Office (PMO). In Prime Minister Lee's speech at the launch of the Smart Nation Initiative, he emphasized that the push for technologically enhanced living is not only a matter of convenience, but also one of community living. One of the examples raised is how, in view of Singapore's aging population, technology can be used to care for the elderly at home, in healthcare, and even to provide IT services, making IT accessible to everyone, including seniors, who would then be able to stay connected and productive (Smart Nation Singapore n.d.).

The initiative is already making inroads into these areas: telemedicine trials are being conducted by some public hospitals in Singapore, and the Housing and Development Board's Smart Enabled Homes initiative not only aims to achieve sustainable living, but also harness technology to enhance the lives of the elderly and the care they receive (Housing and Development Board 2017). Mobile device applications are also part of the services rolled out to serve the public. Some of these help plan travel routes, make e-appointments at government agencies such as the Immigration and Checkpoint Authority, keep track of one's health, report municipal issues, and access library services. One of the apps launched in 2016, as a response to global incidents and threats of violence and terrorism, is the SGSecure app, part of the bigger SGSecure movement, which aims to prepare and protect the public for acts of terrorism (Ministry of Home Affairs n.d.-a). The application is used to raise awareness of violent incidents around the world, and for the public to report emergencies to the authorities (Ministry of Home Affairs n.d.-b). The responsibility of protecting the country from external threats is not merely the government's, it is also a collaborative effort with the people. This idea of collaboration draws its inspiration from the smart-state concept, where "state adaptability, access to information flow, facilitation of global networks, and responsiveness to market incentives" are prioritized above state-directed transformation, and it is also seen in how the smart state approaches social protection, economic development, and foreign policy (Calder 2016, 62).

The government's vision for the Smart Nation Initiative is a nationwide endeavour that began its conceptual journey in Singapore's school system (Calder 2016). Prime Minister Lee emphasized the necessity for a "first class workforce in Singapore, one which has the right skills and capabilities," and the government is committed to growing and nurturing such a labour force by equipping its people with digital skills. From basic coding skills in schools to compulsory undergraduate modules on digital literacy in universities, the intention is to take a long-term approach, from childhood to the university years (H.L. Lee 2017b). By exposing children from a young age to IT and programming, and giving them opportunities for hands-on learning, the government hopes to nurture and enable those who show an interest and an aptitude in IT to further develop their skills in tertiary institutions and thereafter contribute to the Smart Nation Initiative in their work (H.L. Lee 2014). The financial costs invested in the realization of this aim are high, with 17 per cent of its total budget, or SG$12.9 billion, devoted to education alone. However, according to Kelvin Seah, an economics lecturer at the National University of Singapore, the efforts are likely to reap benefits in the form of increased human capital and worker productivity (Cheok 2017). Lim Soon Hock, founder and managing director of boutique corporate advisory firm PLAN-B ICAG Pte Ltd, concurs. In an interview with Channel NewsAsia correspondent Bharati Jagdish, Lim suggested that entrepreneurship education should start early in schools, and that the way to cultivate an entrepreneurial mindset among the young is to implement a structured program, which takes students through the entire business process (Jagdish 2017).

The universities are also beginning to collaborate with other partners to support the Smart Nation Initiative. NUS has begun rolling out projects in "healthcare transformation" and "Smart Nation research," according to Professor Tan Chorh Chuan, NUS's then president, in 2016. One of the healthcare-related projects that NUS is working on with other partners is patient-centred health delivery models that would allow patients to access care from home, but still be supervised by a primary healthcare team. As for Smart Nation research, there are the Institute of Data Science, the National Cyber security R&D Laboratory, and a Cybersecurity Consortium and more in the works over the years as new educational collaborations are formed (see NUS News 2016c, 2017). Cybersecurity is also an area of focus for SUTD, which is partnering with ST Electronics and has established a laboratory that looks into cybersecurity and big data analytics as well as develops trusted cyber monitoring and mitigating techniques. With support from the NRF under its Corporate Laboratory@University scheme, the laboratory is also the first corporate laboratory working on cybersecurity. This is a collaborative endeavour by the respective organizations. Dr Yaacob Ibrahim, formerly the minister of communications and information as well as the minister in charge for cybersecurity in Singapore, said that this partnership would see academia and industry working together with government investment to "better align academic research with industry needs, so that research efforts will be directed towards solutions that can be readily commercialized in the marketplace" (Hio 2016). With this project underway, ST Electronics and SUTD expect the

Smart Nation Initiative to benefit from the anticipated increase in professionals trained in cybersecurity (C. Lee 2016; SUTD, 2016.).

The initiative is not meant to be solely a government effort; the public is also encouraged to propose innovative ideas for consideration (H.L. Lee 2014). Nor is it intended to be an inward-looking endeavour; in fact, the Singapore government is looking beyond its own shores. It is actively cultivating an environment favourable for technology and innovation to thrive, with the hopes of encouraging entrepreneurs and technology builders all over the world to leverage the nation's smart infrastructure to test new ideas (SPRING 2015).[26] German electronics and electrical engineering firm Siemens has done just that (Siemens n.d.). The Smart Nation Initiative received a boost when Siemens set up its Siemens Digitalization Hub in Singapore in July 2017, with the intention of collaborating with Singapore companies and universities to develop and commercialize projects, especially in areas like urbanization and digital industrialization (R. Sim 2017b). Prime Minister Lee said in his speech that having the Hub in Singapore would also "scale up innovative digital solutions for overseas markets," reflecting the nation's aim of creating an environment conducive to trying out innovative ideas before they are rolled out to the region and the world (H.L. Lee 2017b).

Singapore is also looking to groom its own innovators. The 6.5-hectare JTC LaunchPad @ One-North, supported by a number of governmental agencies, such as the Agency for Science, Technology and Research (A*STAR), Infocomm Development Authority (iDA), Media Development Authority (MDA), National Research Foundation (NRF), and Enterprise Singapore, is an initiative aimed at bolstering relations between members of the tech community in Singapore, such as entrepreneurs, investors, incubators, and accelerators (JTC Corporation n.d.).

One area in which the government is investing resources is design, which is nothing new for Singapore. Prime Minister Lee pointed out in the 2018 Ministerial Forum that design thinking was key to establishing and developing Singapore's nationhood, economic success, and multiracial harmony (H.L. Lee 2018). Dr Beh Swan Gin, chairman of EDB, says that the drive to invest in design started in 2003 with an established pool of designers in the areas of architecture, product design, and interior design as well as growing interest in other areas of fashion and furniture design (Beh 2017b). This resulted in the establishment of the DesignSingapore Council, which aims to develop the design sector for economic growth (DesignSingapore Council n.d.). Beh says that Singapore is no longer merely "a sophisticated user of technology" but also "a creator of technology." With the spotlight on Asia as a growing region, design in Singapore is poised to meet the needs of a huge pool of consumers in Southeast Asia, which has a market of some 600 million consumers (Beh 2017b). Furthermore, Singapore has also invested in setting up SUTD to drive greater research and innovation in design, with a focus on nurturing students in the art and science of design (Singapore University of Technology and Design 2010).

Considering the scale of the initiative, communication and collaboration among those involved, such as the various government bodies, planners, developers, and manufacturers, is of the utmost importance. Critical to the successful execution of the initiative is a unified understanding of definitions, technical specifications, and best practices, for which standards at both international and domestic levels have been implemented. The International Organization for Standardization (ISO) developed the ISO 37120 standard series to cater to smart cities and their sustainable development, while locally, the Information Technology Standards Committee (ITSC), formed in 1990, serves as a neutral meeting point for government bodies and industry parties to discuss and agree on technical matters (ISO 2018).[27] The Internet of Things Technical Committee also took shape within the ITSC to focus on technical references and standards vis-à-vis the Smart Nation Initiative. The necessity for standards is especially salient in an age of disruption, which calls for integrating different policies and information systems in a manner, and at a pace, that is unprecedented. By having a common framework of standards, smoother channels of communication and participation between the relevant parties can be established. In turn, these will play an important role in the successful development of the Smart Nation Initiative (SPRING Singapore 2015).

The Smart Nation efforts have been acknowledged in several global studies. Two years after it was implemented, Singapore came in first in a global ranking of smart cities and was named Global Smart City 2016, beating out 2015's winner, Barcelona, as well as London, San Francisco, and Oslo. The cities were evaluated based on a rubric of some forty metrics, such as technology, transport, energy, open data, and the economy (Juniper Research 2016). The study of the cities revealed that Singapore led in the application of smart mobility policies and technology. Its fixed and cellular broadband services, city applications, and strong open data policy were also instrumental in clinching the top spot. Another feather in Singapore's cap was grabbing the top spot in Asia, and seventh globally, in the Global Innovation Index 2017 (Bhunia 2017).[28] The Index evaluates countries based on the two Input and Output Sub-Indices scores.[29]

The accolades, however, may not accurately reflect the situation on the ground. Progress has been slower than planned, as Prime Minister Lee himself acknowledged at Camp Sequoia, Sequoia Capital India's annual technology summit (H.L. Lee 2017a). Despite the efforts of the government to achieve a Smart Nation, experts believe that the private sector's lack of initiative in exploiting the opportunities is due to a dearth of deep technology (robotics, machine learning etc.) entrepreneurs, software engineers, and data scientists (W. Tan 2017). Echoing these thoughts is Harminder Singh, a senior lecturer in business information systems at the Auckland University of Technology in New Zealand. Singh thinks that the private sector's inertia in producing real innovation is a result of too much government intervention, which means that communicating ideas may be problematic (Vaswani 2017). On the other hand, Goh Swee Chen, the former chairman of Shell Singapore, feels that the passivity may have come from what she calls a "managed economy mindset," and suggests that preparing for the challenges from disruption has to be a joint effort between the government and Singaporeans (O. Ho 2016).

The work of building up the local innovation scene should be a joint effort between the government and the start-up community, according to Serene Chan, industry manager of information and communication practice at global research and consulting firm Frost and Sullivan (W. Tan 2017). This highlights the necessity for both public and private sectors to collaborate to successfully build a smart city (Smart Cities World 2021). Lim Chee Kean, co-deputy of the IoT Technical Committee and chief executive of Ascent Solutions, feels that the reliance on grants and subsidies can be reduced by implementing tax holidays and concessionary tax rates. This would create an environment that encourages the development of "high growth market-shaking innovative companies," with financing, regulation, facilities, and culture (Yeoh 2017).

The spotlight now is on how feasible the implementation of a Smart Nation is in Singapore. There are two schools of thought. One considers Singapore's compactness and excellent infrastructure to be its strengths, whereas the other camp argues that Singapore's size is an impediment to innovation because of its small population and limited market (Calder 2016; W. Tan 2017).[30] Size aside, there are other issues to consider. Besides having to contend with emerging debates on cyber-security, data protection, and data sharing, the Smart Nation Initiative may also be dwarfed by issues such as the need for smoother coordination, as well as getting the views of citizens and meeting their needs.

Dr Lim Wee Kiat and Dr Kim Hyungkyoo, from the Lee Kuan Yew Centre for Innovative Cities, have a different perspective. They are of the opinion that smart cities should also implement technology that is sustainable. Recognizing Singapore's resources, in the form of abundant sunlight, developed transport networks, and population density, they suggest rethinking the ways Singapore generates and uses energy, and how it can creatively rechannel the energy output in sustainable ways (Lim and Kim 2015). Some of the ways they propose include using energy harvesting tiles to tap the energy from marathon runners, and human traffic to power vending machines, public lighting, transport ticketing (known in Singapore as the EZ-link card) machines, and toll gantries (known in Singapore as the Electronic Road Pricing (ERP) system). The measures they propose to reduce energy consumption include refraining from setting temperatures lower than 25 degrees Celsius in publicly accessible areas that experience high volumes of human traffic, and possibly leveraging technological advances that can either reduce the amount of heat retained in the atmosphere, or channel the energy output from certain appliances to others (Lim and Kim 2015).[31]

The potential is endless, but the ethical considerations that come with the mass collection of data cannot be ignored. Despite the best efforts to remove information that may be used to identify oneself, it is virtually impossible to completely obliterate one's digital footprint because of other data that can be pieced together to reveal information about anyone (Totty 2017). In the case of Virtual Singapore, while not all the sensors have been completely deployed yet, careful consideration will be given to their benefits for citizens before the systems are built and data is collected. However, although the issues of privacy and security do not yet have complete solutions, the government is committed to maintaining citizens' privacy. Data will be anonymized as much as possible and measures used to protect the information collected (Watts and Purnell 2016).

Another area that has received less attention in the media but is no less important in Singapore's preparation to be future-ready is neuroscience. With the advent of technology come the possibilities for therapies and cures. In view of population and public health issues, interest in neuroscience goes beyond its potential for economic growth; it may provide solutions for aging populations. This explains the spotlight on neuroscience around the world, seen in but not limited to the Human Brain Project by the European Union, the Canada Brain Research Fund, the United Kingdom's Brain Banks Network, and the United States National Institutes of Health Blueprint for Neuroscience Research. Singapore is no exception. Interest in neuroscience in Singapore is not new; it was listed as one of the top research priorities for Singapore in 2007, and extensive funding by the NRF as well as by NUS, A*STAR, and the Ministry of Defense was pumped into both the Singapore Translational and Clinical Research in Psychosis program and the Singapore Institute for Neurotechnology (Fischer 2013b).

PLANNING FOR THE FUTURE

It seems, therefore, that a proactive state is not just one that predicts future trends, but one that also implements measures and initiatives to help its citizens comfortably ride the waves of future trends. The measures may not even be limited to skills and technology. Especially in a nation with an aging population like Singapore, urban infrastructures that are more socially driven are needed. This is not limited to hard infrastructure, such as healthcare and housing. Soft infrastructure that allows people to participate socially is also necessary to aid citizens as they age and to create a livable environment, not just for the elderly, but for all ages (Chong, To, and Fischer 2017).

The Singapore government began looking into elder care as far back as thirty years ago, and in the process brought in various government agencies to revamp urban infrastructure and social programs. One of the areas is in public spaces, where a variety of initiatives have been implemented, including giving residents access to small plots of land for gardening, and using the ground floor of public housing flats, or void decks (open spaces for community activities in public housing flats), for activities catering to senior citizens, which they use to socialize informally (Chong, To, and Fischer 2017).[32] As a result, many of these decks were formally converted into

"Senior Citizens' Corners." These, among others, are initiatives by the Committee on Ageing Issues (CAI), a committee established to coordinate efforts by governmental agencies to anticipate and prepare for future needs (Chong et al. 2015).

Thinking about public spaces can go beyond the idea of physical, tangible spatial entities, and involve more of the social aspects of these spaces. One example of how this is done is one of Singapore's community programs, which trains shopkeepers, among others, to appropriately identify and manage individuals with dementia who walk into their shops. Even the Senior Citizens' Corner is not used equally everywhere. It is only when senior citizens are able to access and use it that it becomes truly useful to the senior community. For the elderly to use such public spaces successfully, more is required than merely providing them with infrastructure (Chong, To, and Fischer 2017). The Senior Citizens' Corner is one example of the government having its ear to the ground, thus enabling it to respond to what it perceives as the needs of its citizens (Calder 2016).

To cope with an aging population, Singapore has, for a long time, been attempting to increase the fertility rate. This is one of the goals of the Ministry of Social and Family Development, which provides aid to couples and encourages early marriages and childbirths through policies such as the Baby Bonus Scheme (Ministry of Social and Family Development n.d.). However, that alone is not sufficient. A proactive state needs to collaborate with various stakeholders in its approach to addressing a problem. In line with this idea, Minister Josephine Teo remarked that there is a need to consider "the career aspirations of workers and the needs of employers as well as giving couples and families a helping hand" (Sin 2018). The sense of collaboration can be seen from the unconventional groups that are involved in the policy enactment process, such as dating agencies (Sin 2016). Furthermore, Singapore is consulting with the younger generation through surveys to find out their needs and attitudes towards marriage and parenthood. For example, the Marriage and Parenthood Surveys were conducted in 2004, 2007, 2012, and most recently 2016. The 2016 survey suggests that everyone has a role to play in promoting positive mindsets and social norms towards marriage and parenthood in Singapore (Strategy Group Singapore 2017).

Singapore is always on a quest for ways to remain competitive in the face of new economic, political, technological, and social challenges, while maintaining a commitment to social integration and harmony

(B.H. Chua 2005; Y.L. Lim 2015). Two qualities are socially venerated in Singaporean society: scholastic achievements and civic and social responsibilities. While this has created a culture of working hard to attain success, some recent concerns have emerged about the need to rethink the education system and imagine how it can be more inclusive in a Smart Nation. Including the initiatives discussed in this chapter, concerted efforts have been made to introduce new thinking into the system and foster openness, without compromising Singapore's core values of meritocracy and self-reliance (Beh 2017a; Calder 2016; Cheok 2017; Sinnakaruppan 2017; Yeoh 2017). For instance, there are policy initiatives that strengthen early childhood education to better prepare children from diverse family backgrounds, alongside initiatives that focus on retraining older citizens to help them remain employable (Seow 2017). Students who have completed higher education can also obtain scholarships to attend universities locally or overseas if they show academic success along with a strong spirit of volunteerism. This building of intelligentsia across all generations of citizens is facilitated by a set of pragmatic policy responses, including infrastructural investments, allocation of social goods, and strict adherence to the rule of law.

The proactive governance model suggested in the previous chapter is an example of how the state, citizens, and institutions can collaborate to counter flux in the fourth industrial revolution to create a knowledge economy based on technological innovation and entrepreneurship. This model, as well as the discussion of Singapore as a proactive state, is one suggestion of how states might respond to flux and create better opportunities for millennials who are experiencing flux.

When I asked Thomas, the professor, who has an expertise in education policies, what he perceived to be the most significant difference between millennials and older workers, he said:

[The millennial is] living with the changes in the technology. And I think in the workplace, I suspect that he is intuitively tuned for changes in the workplace, in the greater introduction of technology. That he is not going to be a Luddite wanting to basically trash all the technology, he will embrace it … the pace of change may be greater, but they're younger, and younger people can adjust to change much, much better than older people.

In addition, I sought the opinion of a few millennials on whether emerging trends, including disruptive technologies and external com-

petition, posed a threat to their job stability. While their responses varied, most of them had a similar degree of confidence in their ability
to remain employed. Rather than feeling insecure because of new
technologies that may disrupt their current jobs, these millennials
sounded quite optimistic and willing to work alongside technology:

> Xavier, a worker in a start-up: I was actually laughing about it, my
> friends and me. Like we hear about robot teachers and all that.
> And my friend actually cracked a joke saying, "You know what,
> don't worry, it's fine. You're the one making the robot, so you will
> still have a job."

> Nelson, a biomedical engineering student: I guess, not necessarily
> [affected by economic instability]. Competition is not necessarily
> a threat; it is an opportunity. At least that's the way I view it. I'm
> not too concerned that some guy is doing some good stuff. I guess
> I'm confident enough of my own abilities ... if that guy is doing
> that, then why can't I do that as well?

> Wayne, an entrepreneur: Not really. A lot of tech trends we see as
> huge opportunities, like AI and blockchain, we are thinking of how
> they can be applied to our business as well. For example, using AI
> for the recommendation engine and stuff. For us, as a tech compa-
> ny, we can move much faster in adopting these technologies.

In fact, five of the millennials I interviewed lamented the fact that
automation has not become more ubiquitous in their fields. To them,
automation is helpful in assisting them to complete tasks, including
eliminating repetitive tasks and providing a safeguard in judgment calls.

> Verena, a recent biological sciences graduate: In science, definitely
> better. Because in science you have to work with a lot of data.
> Experiments have to be repeated, several times. Data has to be
> logged in. It is difficult to keep track of what is what. So, if there is
> an automation that can do it, it would be so much better.

Verena further shared with me her experience in the laboratory,
where she had to repeatedly count worms as part of a project. She felt
that this process could have been automated instead. She begrudged

the fact that she "had to count worms every day" and that the required machines to automate this task were only installed after she left the laboratory. She firmly believed that "automation is good." Interestingly, Verena highlighted to me that the university had altered the curriculum for the next few batches of students, making the learning of programming skills compulsory. Thus, the understanding that students and workers need to be capable of handling technology has extended beyond millennials to influence institutions such as universities. Moreover, the sentiment that "automation is good" is not unique to students working in the sciences. Big data has become ubiquitous and even careers that rely more on soft skills can be improved through automation (Agar 2019).

Perry, a psychology graduate who just started his career as a counsellor, concurs. He said the following.

> What automation can serve to help is, it may be able to access all these data, all these large amount of information with a more objective, objective. So, this may help us to not be blinded by our own emotions. So, it serves as a warning or a guideline. But it will definitely not be able to replace us in whatever we do. I am quite familiar with coding, especially on the macro side of things. Because I feel that it simplifies your job a lot. And you don't have to do tedious things over and over again. Coding is important because when you are doing jobs that involve a lot of data, a lot of information. If you don't use automation or you don't use coding, some data or information get lost in the process when you are trying to make sense out of it. But coding can really make your data a lot cleaner. So, you can see trends, you can see patterns that you would normally miss out if you do not have coding.

Furthermore, Perry highlighted to me that it is important to be "subjective" in his role as a counsellor. He remarked that if a counsellor had experiences similar to a patient's, the counsellor might be able to offer suggestions. This action cannot be replaced by automation. Thus, he was looking forward to incorporating automation in his work.

Nevertheless, while the millennials interviewed did not express any particular anxiety about automation, they echoed similar sentiments about keeping up and staying ahead in an increasingly competitive society. About 80 per cent of the interviewees did not hesitate to change jobs for small pay raises. Wayne, a young entrepreneur, said to me, "We want to have a shot at doing something which we want to embark on instead of looking back 10 years later and regret not doing it." Lifetime commitment is clearly a thing of the past in most organizations. Millennial employees are likely to be more committed to their network than the current organizations they work for. Eli, a millennial early career technology firm employee, echoed this sentiment in the interview, "Be committed to the job not the organization."

The Smart Nation Initiative is Singapore's response to such anxieties and outlines how it envisions progress in the digital age. It is too early to tell how Singapore's vision of the Smart Nation will pan out, but the significance of this case study lies in helping us understand both the microcosm and macrocosm of multiple actors coming into play in what Manuel Castells terms the "network society" (Castells 1996/2010). With the entry of information and communication technologies in society, the social relationships within the network society also evolve, at both economic and cultural levels (Castells 1996/2010). The story of Singapore's policies, along with an in-depth analysis of its millennials' anxieties and responses, provides examples of what such a network society of institutions and actors might look like.

In light of the numerous state-driven initiatives to equip and prepare its people for a work future characterized by disruptive technologies and uncertainty, the question now is: how do all these apply to the upcoming group of Singaporean workers, the millennials and Gen Z? Are they just like all the other millennials around the world, or are they unique? And more important, how do they view and conceptualize the work ethic and their future of work? The following section focuses on the research findings on Singaporean millennials' attitudes to work.

5

Millennials in Singapore

Nearing the end of my master's program, the job anxiety kicked in as I was running out of time and could no longer hide ... when relatives or friends ask: "So what are you doing now?"

Jane

This book began with a discussion and analysis of millennials as the newest entrants to the workplace (the next generation, Gen Z, born after 2000, has yet to enter the workplace in substantial numbers). In this chapter, I provide a primary account of millennial interviews.[1] Compared with their counterparts globally, Singaporean millennials generally view their future prospects with cautious pragmatism and are seriously engaged with meritocratic norms of self-reliance and hard work as the route to economic success, and ethnic integration and family support as the route to social stability. This is because self-reliance and citizen cooperation are strong narratives in social and economic future-making in Singapore, as discussed in the previous chapter. Yet, millennials here have anxieties about the future, which shows their vulnerability to disruption and flux. While they welcome automation, they also have concerns about their job prospects in an increasingly competitive Singapore, where the economy is facing job losses caused by the COVID-19 pandemic and global trade challenges or just automation in general (L. Tan 2020; Agar 2019). They wonder about the durability of their skills, fear failure, and are more critical about the future, but at the same time trust the state the fix economy (ManpowerGroup 2016). Although the state is trying to create more jobs and encouraging young graduates and older workers to retrain, it needs to better understand the changing values of the younger generations and communicate to their diverse voices with more feedback in a conversational style discussed in chapter 2 (see Turco 2016; L. Tan 2020).

The millennials and (and those on the cusp in Gen Z) I interviewed and observed were smart, technologically empowered, entrepreneurial, and with a drive to excel. However, I felt that some still needed better opportunities to hone their analytical skills, get global exposure, and find better ways to navigate volumes of real information for a better future of work, with good human to human communication skills (see Agar 2019; Kochan 2015; Kochhar 2020). They also needed to adapt quickly to mitigate risk and failure and learn from experienced mentors. Some were very keen about cryptocurrency investments despite the risks involved. Others wanted to move to China to enter entrepreneurial ventures despite having good jobs in Singapore, sometimes just on a whim.

All the millennial interviewees had college degrees and were either part of a start-up venture, employed, or soon to be employed. They had their hands and heads in many ideas to avert job insecurity and maintain their options. They liked collaborating, but were sometimes forced to work in teams they did not choose and disliked working in teams they did not choose. Sometimes their verbal communication styles could improve, because they were better at online communication. A deep look at their curricula vitae showed lots of changes in different industries till they settled down to what they really liked. The ambitious ones seemed more stressed by the competition and their ability to find their dream jobs.

Faith, a manager in charge of university collaborations with industry, explained that her students have no way of avoiding the career pressure:

> When you talk to industry, they only want to hire the best, everybody just wants the top student from every university. If you are not at the top, just mediocre or scraping through, I think that anxiety does build up. When everybody is getting internship acceptances and interviews and you're not getting yours, then you start to panic and worry, thinking "What's wrong with me?" As a society, we are very competitive. If you go talk to all employers out

there, they just wanna hire the best. So how do you, as a student, ensure that you are the best?

The fear of not being able to make it seemed common in the multiple conversations I had with millennials. Their fears could be summarized as follows: 1) not knowing what was expected of them, 2) fear of making the wrong choice of employer or career, and 3) not knowing how to make money fast enough. These anxieties might be unique to these interviewees, but they reflect similar anxieties among some groups of young people in the United States, according to studies done by the Pew Research Center (2010). Elizabeth, a career coach at a local university, discussed career anxieties during my interview with her:

> In this university, I see the anxiety to be an entrepreneur. Because being an entrepreneur is very different … it makes staying in this educational process, sometimes a little redundant. They can do a lot for themselves; they can really make a market as well that can change the world. So, I see the anxiety to really dream big and do big. I feel like they tell me that they don't read that much anymore, but they get a lot of feeds, so they go on Instagram. They go on Twitter. They go on Facebook. They follow, for instance, these high-profile people. Celebrities, Obama or whoever, and then there's almost always guaranteed some wise saying that is then viral and that is then imbued into them, and then comes out in our conversations.

Henry Doss (2014) also discusses how opportunities for innovation depend heavily on perceptions of risk and cultural values in organizations.

> A foundational element of innovation is always risk and failure such as how they are perceived, how they are contextualized in systems, how they are viewed culturally. As an innovation leader, you will want to make the same demand for risk on yourself as you do on others. You will be making evaluations and judgments constantly about your organization's risk culture and how it is, or is not, supportive of innovation; it will be equally as important, and perhaps more important, that you evaluate your own internal

ecosystem of risk. You cannot ask others to take risks, if you are not willing to take risks yourself.

The millennials who were interviewed were highly anxious to have the next big idea that might eventually make money for them or their ventures. Wayne, a millennial start-up founder, even shared with me how it was important to market himself as being a risk-taker, so that he could differentiate himself from his peers who had all had similar educational experiences. Even though he started the business venture as a way of writing a stellar college application, he ended up finding his passion and interest in the process of building his business. After a semester at his dream college, he ended up dropping out to dedicate his time to the start-up.

> I got a scholarship, I got into a school I wanted to, and the ironic thing was that I started the business to fulfill that path so that I had something to write about in my college application. I was trying to just study well and get the best grades possible. I was also very deliberate about building my portfolio, doing Student Council etc. But I think what I did differently was that I had a lot of side projects that I was interested in, like the business competitions. Even though part of the intention back then was to build my portfolio, I was genuinely interested in that, and the biggest takeaway from that was the exposure.

From this account, it is clear that he saw the importance of marketing and signalling to others by starting up his own company, and that he was a risk-taking and creative person despite his anxieties about the future.

In my interview with Connor, another millennial, he said he had similar anxiety in his career planning:

> I have heard managers and lawyers tell me that one should never work for the same company for too long for the fear of being outdated and redundant, and that growing old with a company was not possible, because employers do not risk their resources on older workers.

Furthermore, an older millennial had this to say about hedging risk. Jasper, a senior manager in his forties, said, "As you get older, it is important to be a revenue generator rather than an expense to the firm. They are more likely to fire you if you are the latter."

Millennials, like the generations before them, are anxious about career success and are doing their best to build know-how around the practical aspects of earning a living. The main difference now is that millennials and the companies they work for have much more information and choices but also much greater insecurities (Kochan 2015). Just having tech savviness clearly does not help them avoid insecurities.

All the millennials I interviewed were adept at collaborating through social media, crowdsourcing, crowdfunding, the sharing economy, start-up firms, and entrepreneurial competitions because of the pressure to keep up and their personal interest. These experiences highlight how collaboration has been reorganized to focus on producing and servicing cultures of innovation, and the willingness of millennials to take on jobs in less conventional sectors, such as those emerging in the sharing economy. This has also led to the promotion of stereotypes about this generation, i.e., that they don't seem to comprehend the meaning of work, or care about the work or the firm (Weeks 2017).

A significant number of interviewees relied on Facebook and LinkedIn for connections while relying on news feeds for information. They barely read physical newspapers or an entire book. They have little face-to-face interaction and what they do have is brief. As the connected generation, they are considered, in the corporate studies discussed in chapter 2, to be job-hoppers and multi-taskers with little focus, but, paradoxically, are required to be innovative multitasking employees. Both employers and employees had perceptions of one another that were often founded on stereotypes.

Visits to four multinational technology firms revealed that managers often hard-sell ICT-enabled collaborative workspaces and flexible organizational structures as the antecedents and catalysts of flexible work arrangements, and, thereby, innovation. Now, due to the pandemic, remote work has become the white-collar norm (Lavelle 2020). This is often mentioned to potential millennial recruits, as well as to students who visit these firms on field trips. Furthermore, flexible work arrangements, particularly in roles where employees deal with clients, are a big selling point for millennials. However, when I asked prospective millennial employees at recruitment events what they thought about open-plan offices and flexible work arrangements, not all viewed them favourably. About a third of those I spoke to felt that having flexible work arrangements was convenient, but they also felt that open offices meant that they might not have the privacy they desired from their colleagues and bosses. Also, five millennials felt that they preferred to be working fixed hours in a more traditional company, which had a clear management hierarchy, because they wanted to separate home and work. All of them felt that they were more unlikely to get promotions if they were not seen at the office every day or were physically unavailable when their bosses needed them. This may seem ironic in the information age, but it is perhaps the result of not being able to sift through the heaps of information about employers. About three-quarters of the interviewees did not bother to research the companies they were planning to join but were clearly aware of well-known firms. Some of millennials' inadequacies include:

1 Lack of information: Company rhetoric showed great infographics but were obviously meant to entice millennials based on stereotypes. Companies are not answering big questions about the effects of innovation and the future of their workforces, such as what jobs should look like in the future, with input from their current employees. Because most of these recruitment drives focus on studies of either their own employees or others employed predominantly in developed economies, the demographics captured are hardly representative of all millennials.

2 Unwilling to make structural changes: Company surveys show that employee turnover rates are particularly high in technology-related industries due to millennial attitudes of entitlement, rather than organizational structures and values. The ADP Workforce Vitality Report Q1 2017 found that in spite of a 9.1 per cent increase in wages, almost twice the national average of 4.6 per cent, more than half of millennials 24 years old and under still left for other jobs (Fisher 2016). This is a disincentive to make structural changes in companies for long-term employment opportunities. Those I interviewed clearly felt this lack even after they had been working for a few years. There was a conscious concern about their jobs being insecure.

3 Lack of real, constructive feedback: Innovative firms place too much emphasis on feedback, with little perception about the effect it might have on individual employees. In TechCo, a com-

pany studied by Catherine Turco that aims to achieve openness in all its operations, Turco (2016) observes that real, constructive feedback is not given to employees, which may be an ironic result of the company's constant push to share ideas. In my own observations at recruitment talks, potential recruits were often tempted by an open culture of feedback but had little knowledge about how organizations work. Typical temptations for openness are free food, open-plan offices, remote-work opportunities, and playful work cultures.

4 Disruption talk: IoT, AI, and social algorithms seem to drive innovation in technology organizations, but its users do not give significant thought to the changes those will have on job restructuring. None of the employees I interviewed had a clear idea of how automation would change their jobs, but they knew they would change, and that they had to learn and keep learning.

5 Lack of clear alignment: It is unclear from the existing studies in chapter 2 whether employees and companies are aligned in their vision and goals for the organization. All the millennial interviewees felt that they were never really sure if their goals fully aligned with the organization's goals. They felt that they hardly knew what the real picture of the organization was about or where it was heading in terms of future employment prospects.

The stories below reflect these and more concerns expressed by millennials. Therefore, it is very important for the state to come up with clear policies to manage the expectations of the workforce, corporations especially, with growing geopolitical and supply chain tensions, which will affect all millennials with mounting job insecurities.

SINGAPOREAN MILLENNIAL STORIES

How do the perceptions of millennials in Singapore compare with the perceptions of millennials entering the workforce discussed in chapter 2? I observed that they have different levels of preparedness for the future of work. Some of them are based and educated in Singapore, and some are abroad, but what they all share is their exposure to the Singapore education system. I aim to showcase the very richness of millennials' histories, anxieties, and trajectories, and provide readers with a perspective on how these individuals have experienced the proactive state: its ideologies, institutions, and policies. The stories show that even the most tech-savvy generation is only partially prepared for the age of flux.

It does not serve as a comprehensive typology, but I have attempted to draw some similarities between the ways the interviewed Singapore millennials have responded to flux and their attitudes towards work. These categories may not capture many other nuances to each of their stories, but they do show most of the recurring themes: *a spirit of opportunism, a moral duty to work, a constant need to update oneself,* and *trust in the way the system works.* These themes also reflect various themes I discussed in chapter 2. First, while global literature suggests the possibility that millennials feel self-entitled, interviews with Singaporean millennials only partially suggest that. They embody *a spirit of opportunism* and approach work life instrumentally to achieve their goals. Second, the interviews support my assertion that millennials are not merely job-hoppers. Instead, they mainly seek jobs that provide moral meaning to their lives. I suggested in chapter 2 that millennials globally are willing to work longer hours in exchange for greater flexibility in their work arrangements. I see a similar trend in Singapore. However, some millennials focus on other factors in their job search, such as traditional work arrangements. Third, though anxiety about automation varies among global millennials, they understand that they need to constantly update themselves, because of their strong sense of meritocracy. Fear about automation is much less prominent, but they do have career anxieties despite that. Last, with a system based heavily on meritocracy, Singaporean millennials tend to be optimistic that as long as they embody the key ideals of meritocracy and can perform, they will have a safe and stable future. However, they also know that underperformers or non-conformists have had few opportunities in this system, hence they feel much anxiety and put a lot of pressure on themselves to get ahead.

A Spirit of Opportunism

The instrumentally rational individual (someone who pursues any means to arrive at an end) focuses on pursuing a well-calculated end in mind, in contrast to the value-rational individual, who acts on a set of underlying values and beliefs, whether or not these actions lead to success (Weber 1922/1978). The millennials I interviewed seemed to be more opportunistic when it came to making decisions about their own ambitions. This sense of opportunism encompasses a kind of measured idealism that is guided by pragmatic concerns. This is an important qualification, because the opportunism that I have observed is not a blind opportunism, taking on just *any* kind of job. The millennials I interviewed are open to taking on different and additional opportunities that come their way, even if the job renders them underemployed, but these roles must be relevant in some way to what they care about. One should be gainfully employed and earning money, rather than sitting idle to find out what one is truly passionate about. These millennials are not worried about taking stopgap jobs, but they are deliberate about which opportunities are going to move them closer to their future goals. About 30 per cent wanted to do several things, such as work full time and have a small side business. The idea was to earn money in as many ways as possible. This can be seen from the interviewees who spoke with me.

Wayne: When my co-founders and I started out … we didn't have an idea, we just wanted to do something. It could be anything. I mean the first company was a silly idea, a shirt company and imagine this, three guys wanting to start a fashion company! We didn't have any customers and two, three months in, I finally spoke to my cousin who was a fashion designer. He just told me all about these manufacturing processes, design processes, and then at the end of the meeting, we looked at each other and knew that this was not for us. So, then we pivoted to something else. We were interning for a co-working space, as interns to run their internship program. That was when we realized that there was an opportunity there because there was demand. We didn't do any advertising, but a lot of start-ups wanted to use the service to recruit interns, so that's where we started.

Dominic: I am trained as an engineer in a local university and started working in a big tech company a few years ago. I think that I first began thinking strategically about my career since I was a youth. I would call myself a resourceful opportunist. While I knew that knowledge was a key to opening doors of opportunities and attaining a reputable status in society, I was also aware that I needed to know how to attain specific skills and apply them in the right environments. This is why I decided to get a part-time job outside of school when I was a teenager. In addition to earning a small sum of money, I was able to gain some real-world experience ahead of my friends.

Kaleb: When I was in polytechnic [before university], I did really well. I didn't really spend too much time on curriculum, but instead placed most of my efforts working on side projects and competitions. I got into the hackathon scene at around the right time and won a few of them in my second year of polytechnic. I was quite interested in finding out about start-ups and their culture back then. Before I graduated, my friends and I even did a small venture in 2012 ...

On my decision of university, I wanted to choose the path less travelled. I wanted to be able to make an impact and leave a mark somewhere. I decided to choose a new school with no fixed culture, because it seemed like it had a lot of room to grow. The unknown was exciting, and I decided that this would be the school where I could make my mark.

I had spoken to Dominic when he was still new at his company. Despite his relative youth in the workplace, Dominic's sense of opportunism and career aspirations had already led him to start thinking of Plan B. He shared that his objective was to gain as many resources from his time at this company as possible, while simultaneously learning and exploring outside of working hours, whether to develop new skills or learn more about entrepreneurship. He opined that acquiring knowledge voraciously is the only way to open the doors of opportunities. He had a deep-seated sense that he could not afford to be complacent or satisfied with his current state, and that it was only by seeking out the best that he would be able to stay ahead. Kaleb, like Dominic, had been driven by a sense of ambition since he had been at school. While he attributed it partly to his dislike for rote learning, Kaleb was already looking for opportunities outside the classroom to gain real-world experiences. From taking part in hackathons to choosing his university, Kaleb sought the opportunities that would most allow him to make an impact. While this meant that he took slightly unconventional paths, these decisions to be unique and set himself apart were deliberate and careful. Far from being idealistic, this attitude seems to be an example of a new pragmatic way to differentiate oneself from one's peers and stay ahead.

Wayne: The other reason was because we were applying to schools, and we saw all the testimonials of people who went to big schools like Wharton, Berkeley and thought, Whoa, I need something to write about! So, the ironic thing was that while we started the company so that we could have a good story for college applications, we ended up dropping out of college for the company in the end. The real honest reason was that we needed a story to write, but we ended up getting hooked into the whole business.

Dominic: The rat race is inevitable. For myself, I seek to thrive in the rat race and climb the corporate ladder. After all, this will be my main source of income. However, it should not be the only one as the reality is that people will get axed out of the rat race when they pass their prime. Therefore, the attitude I hold towards the rat race is to gain as many resources from my career while seeking out other opportunities outside of working hours.

When I asked if any of them were anxious about venturing out or committing to responsibilities at a young age:

Wayne: No, I wasn't afraid because I had nothing to lose ... I figured that I was learning a lot from this and I was meeting with a lot of brilliant business people mentoring us, so I had nothing to lose at all.

Dominic: I have always been driven by the desire to give back and create a positive impact on society. Growing up, I always had a seize the day attitude and ensure that I do everything I can to make an extraordinary impact ... since life is short. Along the way, there will be obstacles and how you handle obstacles will shape how you respond to situations in the future. When obstacles arise, it is an opportunity to train oneself. The more obstacles you overcome, the greater your momentum to achieve success ... as you realize that things are always not as hard as you imagine.

I had earlier discussed how Singapore's founding fathers embraced a pragmatic approach to running the country. This enduring sense of pragmatism is clearly evident in the way these millennials seemed to feel under pressure to make sensible and safe choices. Former dean of the Lee Kuan Yew School of Public Policy Kishore Mahbubani posits that one possible reason for such pragmatic mindsets is the extensive pressure that parents are placing on their children these days (Mahbubani 2016). After all, most parents of millennials in Singapore grew up in a newly independent Singapore, where pragmatism was seen as a tool, for both the government and citizens, to cope with widespread poverty. Based on the conversations that I had, parents continue to play a big role in millennials' decision-making processes, but they do not always have the last word.

Zachary: Regarding my parents, they are very typical old school Asian parents. From young, they just push me to go to tuitions [after school classes] and just study all day all night, that kind. So, they aren't really appreciative of me doing entrepreneurship or doing my own things that deviate from the norm, which is study hard, get good results, get a good job, that workflow. So how I managed to go around it is actually by not really telling my parents much regarding like oh I am doing my own things. Basically, in fact in the early days of doing my start-up, I think I just kept them in the dark. I just said, oh I'm doing a school project … So, I just basically masked it in a way. Then I guess when there's some recognition or the profits start coming in and get recognized in the media, in competitions or something like that. Then I just let them know. I happened to be featured in the news and stuff. Then just let them know a bit. And then, them being practical will say "oh okay, he is doing a good job." Part of it is knowing how to manage your parents. What's their attitude?

Kaleb: Thus far, I've mostly followed a very standard path in terms of education, and I suppose I went to a pretty decent primary and secondary school. The path really diverged for me when I scored a pretty decent [secondary school aggregate] score to go to junior college but decided to go down the polytechnic route. Initially, my parents still wanted me to go to a junior college … but I really hated rote memorization and sitting still for an entire day. I never really did enjoy much of secondary school, which was why I was adamant on going elsewhere.

Veronica: I was born in the 1980s and I consider myself an early millennial. I grew up in a lower-middle-class family and was brought up with the understanding that an education in the hard sciences would guarantee a path to better job prospects, and anything else would be valued less in society. Even though I developed an early interest in arts and humanities subjects in school, my parents did not hesitate to nip my interests in the bud, pushing me towards the science stream in secondary school. This persisted even as I grew of age to enter university. Despite my stellar results in the General Paper and my teacher's recommendations, I still chose to pursue chemistry instead of law or English literature to please my parents. I eventually got my first job as a research chemist with a local firm, feeling the pressure to justify the tuition money spent on studying chemistry.

Though Zachary's parents did not support his decision to become an entrepreneur until he had found success, his story exemplifies that the final decision still lies with the individual. For Zachary, pursuing his dream involves managing his parents' expectations as well. Similarly, while Kaleb's parents did encourage him to pursue the junior college path, he eventually had the last say in what he wanted to do. Veronica, on the other hand, experienced outright rejection of her interests from her parents at an early age. Even when she came of age to decide for herself, she chose the path that would please her parents. That is not to say that parents are the ones holding Singaporean millennials back from pursuing less conventional aspirations. Instead, these millennials appear to have an innate desire to prioritize stability, to self-regulate, and to limit their choices.

Veronica: A tiny part of me also wants to do it for my parents, who have been nothing but unfailingly supportive since they realized I am not going to be the scientist of their dreams, but to whom I have always felt sorry for my failure to fulfill their aspirations for me. To make matters worse, jobs in academia are scarce and a PhD is no guarantee that I will get the job I want. I also sometimes feel the pressure from my JC [Junior College] classmates who are all doing very well and are all well-established in their careers, but I understand that everyone is different.

Furthermore, the background of the parents also affects their acceptance of their children pursuing non-traditional paths, such as entrepreneurship. In an interview with a team of three millennial members of a start-up, they echoed this sentiment.

Anderson: So, I think I speak for the whole team. We all came from families that have an entrepreneurial background. So, my father is a master mariner. Used to sail professionally, but then he's a ship captain turned businessman. So, I mean, I grew up in that environment where my parents just did business. So, my dad's business ventures are as old as I am ... I mean, yeah, I grew up in that environment ... I wouldn't say that it had a particular impact in ... my entrepreneurial pursuit. But it definitely had an impact on ... getting an understanding and an approval from ... your family to do something that is risky.

Titus: My parents didn't have office jobs. They also started their own businesses. They started from [a] minimart and [got] involved in other businesses like a noodle factory and stuff like that with their friends. Yeah, I guess because they have gone through it, so they don't want their kids starting their own venture.

Judy: My grandfather is an owner of a factory that makes sesame oil. Yeah, so that's for my grandfather on my dad's side. So, all the siblings work in the factory. So, there's this family business. Yeah, that's like my background, I guess. So, I used to always go to the factory to play around or help out and see what they are doing.

The interviewees are trained and work in a wide range of disciplines. I was surprised to find that to some extent pragmatism and hard work are still a modus operandi among the younger generation in Singapore. Even with encouraging parents, millennials still feel a need to be pragmatic. For Anderson and his team, while their parents are largely supportive of their endeavours, there is still a sense that they need to be pragmatic and find a job that pays well. As Anderson puts it:

No one was outrightly [sic] against it. The responsibilities are on us. Like, you know, not a disservice [to us] by doing this. How long can you go not earning as much as your peers? And you know, so you eventually have to start thinking about the future and find something that … you can sustain.

Serene, who studied business in a local private university, has a similar viewpoint. She expressed to me that "I just don't want to lose to my dad you know. So, I must do better than him." I noted earlier that I had not observed a single emergent millennial work ethic, both from my experiences as an educator and from the primary data. However, these millennials' choices are still guided by a common emphasis on practicality. I started out with the hypothesis that the flux society might have ingrained a different set of values among the younger generation. I was particularly interested in the millennials in Singapore since they had grown up in relative comfort, compared with the poverty and uncertainty that their parents and grandparents had witnessed in Singapore's earlier years. The underlying nuance was always a sense of anxiety to succeed.

John: I'd be lying if I said that the monetary value [of a job] doesn't count. It definitely does, especially in Singapore where the standard of living is so high. Actually, I thought to myself a few years ago, saying, you know, I can earn S$3k a month and I'll be fine. But when you grow older, you realize that once you have a wife, and there are kids … and to raise a kid costs nearly a million dollars now? It's crazy, you can't do S$3k a month to raise a kid. That'll be quite unfortunate.

Eric: Purpose is different from Passion. In short, Purpose is rational, like doctoring saves lives, working 9–5 provides an income to feed a family … while Passion is irrational. For example, a musician believing he/she would be lucky enough to create a hit song …

Serene: I do it purely for the money. To be honest, what I wanted to do as a kid, cannot be done in Singapore. I wanted to either study volcanoes or go and dig up bones. So … it cannot be done in Singapore … A job is a means to an end. I want to make money and I can do a second degree [for passion] in the future.

Moreover, in Serene's case, her pragmatic thoughts extended beyond her career choice and influenced her choice of university and degree, with a sense of anxiety about what the right choice was.

> Serene: One thing about local university is that you had to … study three or four years minimum because that is … the whole curriculum. Then I was thinking … I don't want to waste so much time studying because there's no better payoff you get out of a public school versus a private school … My school was only … two years.

Singapore's forefathers could be considered idealistic, because they had sought to achieve what had never been done before: transform a small fishing village into a bustling global economic hub with one of the highest GDPs per capita in the world, all in the span of just over fifty years. Many praise this "Third World to First World" transformation. Along with this economic development has come the opinion that Singapore's initial priority of economic growth could take a backseat to developing other aspects of its economy. One of these alternative priorities is growth in developing the arts and other cultural sectors. More specifically, proponents have argued that the literary arts, for one, can nourish "not just of the body and mind, but of the soul" and offer its citizens a "more rounded, richer understanding" of their identities (M.H. Chua 2016). Likewise, Kishore Mahbubani also argued that Singapore needs more idealists and dreamers who are daring enough "to strive to make the world a better place" (Mahbubani 2016). In his plea, Mahbubani continues to share how his own "unwise, impractical and idealistic decision to study philosophy" proved to be the right decision as an adult, when he found that the skills he had learned from studying philosophy, being able to reason, write, and argue, enabled him to be a more effective diplomat.

What this suggests is that Singapore's comfortable position and global standing ought to give its citizens some room to channel their energies towards personal, motivational ambitions, like developing their sense of self and nourishing their soul, as opposed to only pursuing practical goals like financial stability, which, according to all the interviewees, is becoming harder.

In my interviews, millennials said that they did not see the two goals of financial stability and pursuing an ambition of interest as being mutually exclusive. I spoke to Glenn, who is an executive in an organization that provides underserved students with mentorship opportunities. He thought that the distinction between passion and financial stability was not a rigid dichotomy.

> Glenn: The most important factor people will look at is how good they are at it. Like I said, normally it relates quite well to passion. The more passionate you are at something, the more willing you are to work at it. Spend time on it and plug your gaps. Work on your mistakes. And then develop deeper skills in it. But you know, there is still a question of which one you look at first. I would say it's how good you are at it first. Because how good you are will determine your productivity, which then determines your wage or how far you can go, how easily you can get promoted. That is the main driving force.

Thus, although his organization aims to allow students to discover their interests and careers through various mentorship or internship opportunities, which of the various programs these students are placed in is also determined by their capabilities. Passion and financial stability become conflated, perhaps with a clear anxiety about staying economically relevant and viable.

Clement, a millennial who founded his own music media company, shared with me his story of tying passion together with financial stability.

> Clement: I knew I wanted to do music ... because I was really passionate about music. And then I went overseas, and I wanted to be a professional performer. So, I went to Berkeley College of Music, global performance program. But it was there that I realized, actually, I'm not as good as I thought I was. Secondly, I wasn't really ready for the kind of a musician's life which is very ad hoc ... there are dry days and wet days, you know, it's very unpredictable ... You hear stories of graduates from top music universities who end up being like waiters in restaurants, you know that kind of thing ... I started asking myself what was my comparative advantage? And I realized, ok, maybe it is more for the music business. Because firstly, I have passion for the subject. Secondly, I feel I'm a bit more risk taking. I used to solve problems. I like to you know, group people together to work at a common goal. So, I figured that's where I could play a role in this music scene is in the business side of things.

In my interview with Beatrice, a human resources manager, she shared her observations about the work ethic of the millennial generation in Singapore. In the twenty-five years she has spent in the field, she found this generation to be the most ambitious, creative, and enthusiastic. However, the affluence they grew up with leads them to seek job satisfaction and fulfillment, placing more emphasis on making a difference than on their financial returns. In the workplace, this translates into the desire to feel empowered and have their opinions heard, rather than blindly abiding by instructions or bowing down to authority. Because this generation grew up with technology and information at their fingertips, older managers in the workplace no longer hold a monopoly on knowledge. Knowledge is power, and older managers will find themselves having to relinquish power to millennials, giving them more collaborative opportunities to gain their own buy-in. There is some agreement that they are seeking a level of fulfillment in their careers that money alone will not satisfy, somewhat echoing Turco's findings (2016) in the United States.

John: So of course, the initial monetary value may count but we have to draw a line between whether you're working too hard, too much and not enjoying it. Sometimes when I go out and see something that costs $15, then I'll be like, Oh my goodness, this costs 3 hours of my pay! Or if I go for a buffet, I'll be like Oh my goodness, I've to work one more day!

I know some of my friends who work in the construction sector, and sometimes they just walk the entire construction site, then write a report every day and pass it up. It's just an 8-to-5 job, and they think, "I'm only paid until 5 o'clock so I'm not going to work any longer than that. It's not worth my time." So, in the end these things also shape your mindset as well. If you're not willing to put in the extra mile for your work, then your boss won't see the effort you're putting in. And you can't actually rise up the ranks.

Angie: Finance isn't a huge motivator for me right now. I think money will definitely get more important once I settle down, have a family and my priorities change. But for right now, I think what matters to me the most when it comes to finding a job is whether there are good mentors around me and whether I can learn something from my job. It is more of that than … money. Which I feel … is the case for most millennials nowadays … they would rather take on a lower paying job where they can learn more and be more engaged in.

This also means that these millennials are open-minded and, to some extent, humble about the options with which they are presented. Sometimes, they are even willing to fill their time with other opportunities while waiting for the right one. In Veronica's case, she was willing to do a short stint in editing, and even going abroad to do volunteer teaching, if it could buy her more time to consider whether or not to pursue a postgraduate degree in English. Rather than jumping impulsively at opportunities, millennials often factor in a whole host of considerations before taking a leap.

> Veronica: Working as a chemist in my first job did not work out in the end; I decided then that I would leave the field of chemistry and attempt to find my way back to language. But before that, I had to pay off my student loan, and so I entered the workforce immediately. I first worked as an editor in an educational publishing firm, and then moved on to an administrative position in the public service. Life was easy then, but hardly fulfilling. I left after two and a half years in the middle of a recession, and without a new job. I was in my mid-twenties then.
>
> It was then that I heard of an opportunity to do volunteer teaching in a Southeast Asian country, and I went for it. I fell in love with teaching English, and with interacting with people of different cultures. So, when I returned to Singapore, I dived into teaching ESL. After working as an ESL teacher teaching for about six years, and ten years after obtaining my bachelor's degree, I finally made the decision to return to school to pursue my love of language. This meant giving up financial security and a very comfortable lifestyle, but I took the plunge anyway because I figured, being in my early thirties then, I would probably never get another chance to do it.

It might be premature to claim that all millennials are not dreamers or risk-takers, because they grew up in a relatively comfortable and safe environment. I suggest that there is a tension between the need to innovate and wanting to conform. This was apparent from some of the interviews, where millennials expressed the idea that they felt compelled to take on jobs to earn money for survival due to the lack of job they desired. Nevertheless, they still held on to some desire to move towards the jobs they wanted.

> Hana: I am looking towards establishing a career that is policy analysis oriented. So, as a first job, in order to get towards that eventual goal, I am currently looking for jobs within the government sector as well as within think tanks and journalism ... I am definitely open to any other opportunities that come my way ... You just need a job. Like whatever is offered to me, I am more willing to just take it up, because ... the sheer fact that an employer wants you is a huge factor. When you don't have a choice ... Of course, you are going to take it right? You don't really have a choice in that matter. Factors like just an income. The fact that you have to [be] responsible now ... The sheer fact that you just need something to do.

> Jessica: Now that I have graduated and am an adult right. I should be more responsible financially. Even though my parents can still take care of me financially, I still feel like it is only right for me as a person and as their daughter to at least be able to take care of myself. So, I started my job search and things like that from both private and public sectors. And I don't really get replies from them. I get a lot of calls from like RecruitExpress and what not, for insurance, which irritated me because I didn't want to do insurance.

In both cases, Hana and Jessica viewed their non-STEM degrees as less desirable in the working environment (this is just their opinion and not based on researched facts). Thus, they felt that they just needed to secure any job to start their careers. However, they still expressed some optimism about the possibility of moving towards their desired jobs in the future. Jessica in particular regarded her first job as an opportunity to learn more about what she might want to do eventually as her life-long career. Hana also remarked that even during the search for her first job, she would like to consider company culture:

> Company culture is quite important though. I think that helps in determining ... how long you will stay in your first job. Because ... I feel that the first job isn't the job I am going to stay for long.

It is just my stepping-stone. [How long I stay there depends on] how the office politics is [and] the sort of benefits they give me, am I satisfied with the work I am doing, am I getting personal growth out of it? ... Am I learning new things? ... Is it repetitive? Is it boring? That leads to job satisfaction and the significance of the work.

I heard similar thoughts from other millennial interviewees, especially from those early in their careers. Many of them value personal growth in their careers. For some millennials like Victor, the opportunity to have strong personal growth factors into their decisions to build a start-up instead of taking on a job at a multinational corporation. According to Victor:

All my internships and all of my past jobs have always been at smaller companies where there are a lot more responsibilities on you to make things happen, and you have more autonomy in terms of ... the decisions you make, which I think helps me to grow a lot as a person.

I noted with interest that the need to be practical changes depending on circumstances. For example, perceptions about risk-taking for potential entrepreneurs tend to change according to their phase of life, as echoed by Colin, a Singaporean millennial software engineer working in a start-up in Silicon Valley:

I am generally more risk-taking than most people. I figured that while I am still young, I have the ability to take risks because it's not like I have a family and have finances to take care of. Even if eventually the company fails, I only have to support myself. But that may change as I get older in life and have family responsibilities.

Many other interviewees also reflect the need to be more practical when financial stability is a problem. Jessica expressed some sense of that anxiety when she heard that all her peers had already found a job, and when she asked a university senior how early graduating students usually get a job offer. Thus, while idealism still exists, the idea of self-reliance has been inculcated into the lifestyle of Singaporean millennials and has made practicality a part of their life-course decisions. In these ways, Singaporean millennials constantly navigate the path between practicality and idealism as they transition to the working life and beyond.

A Moral Duty to Work

One very common idea central to millennials' work attitudes is the desire to derive meaning from work. An IBM study reported that millennials ranked having a positive impact and tackling social and environmental challenges as their top goals (Baird 2015). Elizabeth, the career coach, also observed this in the millennials she coached, sharing that millennials tend to feel distracted and pulled in multiple directions because they are always on the lookout for where they could be making the most impact.[2] The combined effects of technological advancements and the loose use of the word innovation have pressured many of these millennials to feel like they have to make something of themselves, because all the success stories they read about in social media and their immediate social circles continuously paint the picture that it is possible.

When it comes to motivations for work, most of the primary findings corroborated business literature in showing how millennials aspired to make a positive impact on the larger community around them through their work. The idea that one must do a job that has a strong moral meaning to it heavily influences millennials' career decisions. In my interviews with Singaporean millennials, most of them wanted to leave a mark somewhere, and were simultaneously hoping to pursue personal ambitions. One engineer, Kaleb, even mentioned that he had chosen to enroll in a new and unestablished school because starting somewhere new seemed to offer the most opportunities for him to be distinctive and make his mark. Another millennial, Dominic, who works in a multinational software company, talked about how he continues to take classes and acquire new skills outside of work to prepare himself for any opportunities that might come by. Even though he occasionally loses motivation to do so, he pushes himself by reminding himself that this is the only way he can make a positive impact on society. As the literature suggests, I have found that millennials tend to set big ambitions, which they tirelessly pursue. Moreover, they have a common fear that they will stray from their ambitions. They were mostly hopeful about the future of technology-led work. However, they felt anxious about the competition in accessing various work options, such as banks, technology firms, the civil service, manufacturing, research, and education.

The first aspect of the moral duty that they assume is their aversion to meaninglessness, which weighs on them almost as much as their fear of being left behind. The stopgap opportunities that these millennials pursue are not just time fillers, but often stints from which they felt they could derive some meaning. In one conversation with a millennial who took a gap year, he seemed to deeply regret his decision to pursue a gap year because it ended up being of little use:

Eric: I took a gap year between completing army and beginning university. I believed that I was an autodidact and resourceful. After 13 years of instructed education, I wanted to self-learn. However, I was complacent and lacked discipline. My gap year wasn't productive. I still played computer games every day. Truth is, I squandered my gap year. In retrospect, I believed taking risk, any risk, meant success. I think taking a gap year without some kind of accountability was a mistake.

Because every decision had to be evaluated for its level of usefulness, it can occasionally come across as an overly formulaic way of functioning. Eric himself acknowledges that, occasionally, his pragmatism leads him to view hypothetical scenarios as binaries:

Eric: Schooling in what I'm good at will probably give me a fulfilling life (decent grades, meet interesting people, go to faraway places), but I will lose my ideals (only a big idea guy with no ability to make a direct impact) leading to a meaningless life. Schooling with my ideals will probably gave me a very miserable life (maximum effort to attain minimum grades) but I will be able to directly make an impact.

Elizabeth, the career coach, who also used to work as a banker, told me that she observed that millennials entering the banking industry had different motivations and aspirations from her and her counterparts. Instead of valuing certain jobs for their money-making abilities, millennials are more likely to look for opportunities to make a larger impact:

Elizabeth: I spoke to someone recently and he said that he is in banking right now, but he intends to be a motivational speaker, because he thinks that that's probably going to give him more money and more impact. Because there is that level of fulfillment now.

Fiona exemplifies this observation by Elizabeth well. Fiona was three years into her first career stint as a researcher when she decided to leave work to pursue a master's degree in international relations. Even though she said that she made this decision out of interest, she still expected that her career change would allow her to have an effect on the community around her. As Allison Pugh suggests, work has always been, and still remains, an important identity marker for workers. That is much less true for millennials today (Pugh 2015b). Fiona's anxieties stemmed from a fear that she would not find a job that accurately reflected her identity or offered a comfortable space to express her true self, that it would fail in helping her to reach the goal of "improving the lives of people." For Fiona, finding meaning in her work was intrinsically tied to the moral imperative she felt to uplift and make a change in her community:

Fiona: I had anxiety about what this program would be like for me, whether I'd fit in, and find work that engages me and reflects who I am as a person ... I have not yet scored the job that becomes a career, or found my true self in the workspace yet, but I have an enormous amount of hope that day will come ... One day, I hope, I'll be able to work to achieve this goal of improving the lives of people, but rather than just research it, I hope I'll be able to be a part of writing it. I want to become a representative of my country and my community, and also be accepted as different from the norm in my hybrid identity.

I spoke to Joyce soon after her graduation from university. In similar ways, Joyce wanted to seek a career that would represent her identity. Unlike many millennials who spoke with me, Joyce was not concerned about finding her first job. Rather, she had a specific goal in mind: to enter a medical school. This was shaped by defining moments in her life:

Joyce: I want to do medicine ... I know it is what I want. Why do I want it? It is a journey. I always wanted it since I was in secondary, because I have been through the experience, I know the · pain and also ... I realize I want to be there with the doctors and the nurses. They were able to reassure me. And I know I am in good hands ... I wanted to ... help people in that way ... That actually was a very strong driving factor for me. After "A" levels, we had quite a long time right? So I worked in a gynae clinic. That was very interesting also ... It gave me two main exposures. One was ... the general setting like with the nurses and everything that medicine is team-based work. And I really enjoyed the environment. And ... how the nurses are. It really is like a family. If you really know how to follow social niceties and ... bring out your personality, actually it is very family based ... It is something I appreciate a lot. People are my thing. So ... I really enjoyed that. And ... also, another thing was ... When I observed the doctors, I realize that they have three main qualities in general: they are usually very driven, they are usually very composed, they usually have a lot of character. And I think that that is very inspiring. It is something that even without medicine, it is something I wanted to work towards. Along the way, it starts to confirm that there is something that I want to. But I think ... what really ... made me decide was ... when I was in Thailand and I got hit by a motorcycle ... At that moment, I didn't have anything on my mind. You know ... they say ... if you die you will think of your greatest regret? ... It is the afterthought that provoked my career choice ... I realize that I don't have a drive in life. And that is the scariest thing in life ... The scariest thing is not to die. It is to be on your deathbed and realize that your whole life has passed you but you have never had a drive in life ... I really question myself. What is my purpose? What is my drive? What do I want in life? I started to think and I realize that what has driven me so far in life ... is always when I am doing something related to healthcare or medicine.

Joyce's identity was shaped around this drive to being a doctor. Interestingly, she was willing to do a gap year after graduation to bolster her curriculum vitae for her medical school application. Rather than giving up on her dream, her backup plans for failing to be admitted to a local medical school were to apply for what she perceived as easier overseas medical schools. This notion of having a moral meaning to work sometimes goes beyond the millennial individuals themselves. Parents might hold the same desire for their children. For Kon, a millennial data scientist working overseas, finding a good job that is meaningful is a desire of his parents:

> Kon: They are very open to me working in any kind of role, any industry, as long as it's a good job generally. They are okay with me being ... a doctor or not a doctor, it doesn't need to be a specific job just as long as I'm doing something meaningful, they are okay with it ... They definitely wanted the best for me, and they wanted me to pursue my dreams within reasonable constraints.

The moral duty that these millennials feel towards their work is not limited to the impact or mark they expect to leave on their communities. The second aspect of their moral duty pertains to the self-imposed pressure to attain these opportunities by their own effort. The meritocratic spirit in Singapore rewards hard work and competence, implying that one should appear to be deserving of the rewards that one attains in the end. This ethos re-emerges clearly among these millennials who have been brought up in Singapore. They do not want to just have good things given to them; they want to feel like they have worked hard, have proven themselves, and are deserving of that merit. In a country that prides itself on identifying and rewarding merit, it then becomes important to prove that one did not take any shortcuts to succeed.

> Jane: I grew up in an upper-middle class family in Singapore, where education was prioritized with the mild obsession over a paper chase through reputable schools, and the values of being a respectable member of society was always upheld. I would say with certainty that the decisions I have made in my life thus far and the person that I am today are almost completely shaped by a reaction to the Singapore culture and my family upbringing. This culture being the omnipresence of meritocratic elitism throughout my childhood to adolescent years. Being put in a highly sought-after primary school, in which the quality of education carries the expectation of you advancing to an elite high

school thereafter, I felt the pressure of doing well academically from a young age. This was coupled by my father's respectable status within the grassroots and business community that brought home conversations about school rankings and scholarships to the dinner table (albeit he never directed those remarks to me, but was simply a casual conversation to him), as well as my brother's natural inclination in academics that brought out a little sibling inferiority in me. Going through school I never felt like I was good enough and the first blow to my self-esteem came when I received my PSLE (Primary School Leaving Examinations) results when I missed the cut-off mark to enter my ideal "elite" high school. This was followed by my parents' push to ... get me an interview of appeal ... in that school, which did in the end secure me a place ... While I feel grateful to have had those opportunities, it further intensified the feeling of insufficiency, because I had to rely on my family ... and had not earned my place like most people did. As such, I found myself in a dilemma of liking the comforts of being protected by my parents, while internally detesting and resisting ...

Jane's acute awareness of her family's socioeconomic situation and the relative comfort that she was afforded caused her to internalize a belief that she was inadequate; having to depend on her family's connections to get into her dream school as opposed to earning a place meant that she missed out on the chance to prove her own worth and abilities. Jane's admission of this tension becomes even more interesting given that other millennials admit that there is a formula underpinning the success of most students in Singapore:

Nelson: If you're an ambitious young upstart, from a good school and good family, then I would say it's easy. To just follow the routine, get the grades, and you'll be pushed up to these places. But I would say if I was someone who wasn't from the best family or best school, it wouldn't be easy. Let's say I was from an ordinary secondary school, you wouldn't know where to begin, you wouldn't have the friends to speak to, you wouldn't have the resources. In that aspect, Singapore isn't exactly the best place to be. If you manage to not slip through the cracks, I will say it's very easy. But you need to know the formula. I'd say [the formula is] good grades ... and I'd say your parents, they need to know. They need to know what's important and when, because lots of these opportunities, lots of these things in school ... you have to prepare for way in advance.

Wayne: Back in my school ... it felt like success was already defined for us. Definitely not just for us, but a lot of the other junior colleges as well. Success was defined as doing well in A levels, getting a government scholarship, and then going to Oxbridge or one of the Ivy Leagues. I felt like there was only one path.

Even though having well-informed parents who emphasize academic excellence and going to good schools are perceived to be significant in getting millennials ahead, Jane still felt a sense of guilt that her achievements were not purely of her own making. Even though it was her family's economic and social capital that inspired these goals of wanting to attend a prestigious high school, those factors and an internalized meritocratic ethic caused her to feel like she did not truly deserve to be in those schools.

It is important for these millennials to be conscientious, not only in their work, but also in the way they pursue their ambitions, knowing that the totality of their motives and achievements will reflect how well they have thought through their plans. As a result, they appear deliberate in pursuing endeavours that will testify to their abilities. While there is a sense that they desire recognition for their efforts, they rarely feel they are entitled to the kind of help they think they deserve along the way:

Jane: My main career interest is in arts and cultural policy because it combines my own passion in dance and my previous academic investments in studying the creative economy and arts pedagogy. It was something that had meaning to me and felt consistent with my purpose. However, being interested in an uncommon and non-prestigious field of arts administration also meant that I did not always receive the most encouraging remarks: "Oh ... what is that?" "I think it is quite hard, why don't you work for your dad first? Ask your dad for connections! I'm sure he knows many people ... in arts-related fields." To be asked to tap into those networks and privileges made me feel insufficient despite having a master's degree, and so I actively avoided asking my father for help.

Another millennial, Sarah, shared about how she had never assumed that she would have the opportunities to pursue her studies abroad, even though her parents recognized that it was a prestigious path that would set her on a promising future:

Sarah: My parents made it clear from when my sister and I were teenagers that they could not afford to send us abroad to study. I've met friends whose parents had mortgaged their flats and took out bank loans to send them abroad, but that had never been a likelihood for me. Despite knowing how prestigious an overseas education was, my parents never considered paying out-of-pocket for us to be educated abroad. This stemmed from their desire to instill fairness. I had an older sister who studied in a local university, and they had set aside the exact amount of money, nothing more, for me to do the same and from a genuine belief that our local universities were just as good. More crucially, they felt it important to ensure that I would not unconsciously allow myself to feel entitled to the privileges that some of my peers seemed to easily access. My mother often reminded us that she, after all, grew up in a poor family and had to work in a factory's assembly line while she was still in school to support my single grandmother in supporting a family of four children. This was her way of reminding us that our middle-income position was a hard-earned status that we should never take for granted or grow greedy about. It was more important that we developed a deep sense of where we came from and what we could afford, lest we mistake the lifestyles that we aspire to have for that which we can have. Growing up with the expectation that studying overseas was an unlikely prospect meant that I had to fork out extra: extra time to prepare, extra time to research, extra energy to find the support and affirmation until I was confident enough to apply for a scholarship. In my world, the combination of getting a scholarship and going abroad to study was also the exception rather than the norm.

This meritocratic work ethic does not seem to be coerced. However, these millennials also expressed that they felt a sense of duty in wanting to give back to their communities in spite of the stiff levels of competition that such a system puts them through. There is definitely a lot of stress and anxiety.

Sarah: When I first got awarded the scholarship to study overseas, I felt like the term bond created unnecessary negative perceptions.[3] Some of my bonded peers viewed the six years of service as an obligation that tied them back to Singapore, putting a lid on what could otherwise have been an illustrious career trajectory. On the contrary, the scholarship had given me opportunities that I would never have dared to imagine for myself! It relieved my family's financial burden, assuaged pragmatic concerns and allowed me to wander into unknown territory ... which was a seeming luxury to a risk averse and stability seeking family.

Jane: I don't know what lies ahead for my career path, but I know that whatever I end up doing should be meaningful to me, grant me a level of autonomy and freedom for decision making, and serve a larger purpose towards progressing social and cultural development.

Dominic: What drives me to make my choices? It boils down to my ambition to give back and create a positive impact on society.

Chris: My family was burdened with a lot of debts before my entry into university as my father, the sole breadwinner of the family, had passed away due to cancer. I felt really fortunate that I could receive financial assistance and bursaries from the university and the community that helped sustain me through my undergraduate days. And now, I am also looking at possible scholarships for PhD study. I think receiving these assistances made me want to give back to society. I want to help improve the world in whatever ways I can.

Max Weber's work helps us to understand the work values of early Calvinist Protestants (Weber 1904/1998). The Calvinists developed a work ethic of self-discipline, frugal living, and hard work, and saw spending their money as being indulgent, or sinful. While they had an obligation to obtain a secular job in society, their economic position was primarily meant to demonstrate their obedience and to glorify God. This work ethic manifested as a result of their anxiety about salvation; they did not know what God's plans were for them, only that they should not be ostentatious (ibid.). The parallel of the Protestant work ethic today in Singapore is the anxiety to stay ahead. There is a similar sense, that only merit and hard work can save one from the tides of change. As a result, this develops millennials' urge to prove that they have attained their success by relying on their own effort, not by shortcuts that would deem them undeserving (see Leong et al. 2014).

A Constant Need to Update Oneself

Irene Wu, a social innovation management fellow at the Amani Institute, argued that Asian education systems are still heavily characterized by rote memorization and rely excessively on examinations to determine students' success (Wu 2018). Singapore's education system is no exception. Rapid growth and an increasingly disruptive global economy are throwing these traditional methods of learning into question. Syed Ali Abbas, the group human resources director of Global Fashion Group (GFG) also mentioned in a public lecture that many countries in this part of the world are all very "certificate-driven, qualification-driven" (Aubrey, Abbas, and Nadu 2018). Yet, this approach may be worth questioning given that many technical skills and expert knowledge will become less relevant in many of our future jobs (Agar 2019). Are these skills still relevant? And are they sufficient for preparing our future workforce for the flux society?

Competing in a meritocratic environment like Singapore's means that there is a constant need to stay ahead and keep innovating and updating oneself by learning relevant skills for the future. I found out through my interviews that John and Kaleb had already had jobs lined up even before they graduated. This did not stop them, however, from worrying that their skills would soon be deemed irrelevant.

> Kaleb: As for anxieties, I fear that one day I won't be able to learn as fast as the younger generation can. Our education is being augmented so much by technologies that enhance cognition, and the younger generation are still getting the brunt of it. What would be one's edge if experience (the factor that sets apart juniors and seniors) can be emulated by automation (big data, interpreted experience from historical data). Why would companies hire older people? Ageism has already become a thing in Silicon Valley, so why would it get any better in the future?

For many, these come in the form of acquiring some technology skills to prepare themselves for an increasingly automated economy.

Even Veronica, the graduate student in linguistics, had considered taking on computational linguistics so that her skills would be more marketable in the future economy. In some sense, growing up in the flux society and understanding change as a constant, has imbued millennials with a disposition of never resting on their laurels and existing credentials. Moreover, as they begin to view certain skills as critical for the future, they may feel compelled to take these courses.

> Minnie: Coding is very popular nowadays right? And everyone is doing it. That's why I started doing it. I felt like this is a skill that is essential for the future digital economy ... The years [underclassmen] below me. They have to take this compulsory coding module as part of their accounting course. But for my year, it wasn't necessary ... My prof always says that eventually one day the accounting industry will shrink because there is no need for so many accountants because of automation, right? I was thinking that eventually my friends will have a hard time reskilling, upskilling, but then, just one year below them, they will have a much easier time.

Minnie's experiences are not uncommon in Singapore. With the strong emphasis on programming for the digital economy, many millennials feel a need to upgrade their skills. Interestingly, Matthew, who heads a software consultancy firm, felt that this anxiety is unnecessary as, even in the future, there will be a need for people with specialities besides programming.

One way that these millennials attempt to stay ahead and relevant is by updating themselves, in the form of learning new skills, talking to friends, and getting buy-in from the people around them to find out what's new and trending. In other words, they are constantly tapping into various sources of information to find out the state of the job market, and where they stand relative to others. Whether it is the latest version of a computer software or a piece of global news, I have observed that it is common for millennials to casually exchange practical information among themselves. By offering new and updated information to their peers, they can signal that they are updated. In addition, they also stand to gain new insights and perspectives from the comments made by their peers, which they then use to assess their own relevance in the job market. James Coleman would say that this is evidence of the social capital that these millennials can access, and then tap into resources within their social circles for their own benefit (Coleman 1988). Coleman defines social capital as a way of facilitating a desired end. It differs from other tools because it is uniquely situated between two or more interacting actors. By necessity, the efficacy of social capital as a means becomes dependent on the strength of ties within a relationship (Coleman 1988). The closer and more trustworthy these social relations are, the more likely that exchange of information can take place genuinely. This brings significant advantages to millennials within these circles, and, likewise, has implications for those who fall outside of these circles.

John: The few friends that I have in university … they are the ones who actually shaped me the way I am. I wasn't the brightest bulb, I wasn't the most adventurous, I wasn't someone who was decisive. When I first went to engineering, I happened to be paired up with this guy who knew a few people, and they were all in the same clique. And all of them were all very high achievers, highflyers. They all knew what they wanted out of life. So, the kind of people you meet in this kinda program … are people who really want something out of their lives. So, I was the only odd one out, obviously. And you know, the class wasn't big. It was around 14 people and you had to make groups and I just so happened to sit with them. Because of this, we had to do projects together. And because I had to keep up with their hype of doing the project, it just became normal to be adventurous like them. It was like a 5 versus 1 thing, and the only way to survive there was to conform to the culture of the clique.

While the process of exchanging information and measuring themselves against their peers keeps them updated, it can also get competitive. About some of the students that she mentors, Elizabeth, the career coach, observes:

Elizabeth: I think the anxiety sometimes creates this dissatisfaction for them in the space. Some people can just live for the anxiety and then they get, you know, slightly depressed about what they're doing here. But I see this, not as a function of their peers being entrepreneurs, I see this as a function of them being fed information and images and ideals of what they can do, where they should be. These types of information create a different sort of expectation that they have to live up to.

As a result of these expectations, millennials often do not feel good enough and feel anxious about whether that reflects some incompetence. This is why they also feel the competing fear of being an outlier in their community. It seems particularly important to these millennials that they are doing what their friends are doing, because this is their way of gauging whether they are picking up the right trends. Friends and social networks have become their primary source of information, signalling whether they are conforming to society's existing norms. It has become almost instinctive for them to consider how others perceive them through the choices they make, not only because it is a face-saving mechanism, but because of the ingrained understanding that being in close proximity to their peers assures them that they are still relevant.

Nelson: My closest friends ... I'd say we are similar in the way we think and process. So, I think the behaviour I mentioned just now, if I want something you can just go forge your own path. That's pretty much all of us. But we recognize there's a right way, proper way to do it. From primary school, secondary school. The primary school guys were the brightest, from the GEP. But it's inevitable. If you're with driven, motivated people when you're young, when you grow older, you also seek out driven, motivated people. All the way through, I've been looking for ambitious, bright, driven people. Yeah, I guess it's subconscious. I didn't operate like this when I was younger.

Colin: Growing up in a good secondary school and junior college ... I got to be around very smart people. A lot of them had ambitions to go overseas as well so it didn't seem too abnormal to want to go abroad. I ended up going overseas, and even though it was out of my parents' pockets, it didn't seem so out of the norm. I think I was on a relatively different track ... I knew I wanted to come to the US and going through the SATs to get admission was not something that most of my peers were doing since they were either going to United Kingdom or staying in Singapore. So, I definitely chose the less taken route, but like I said, the concept of going overseas was not foreign.

Eric: Many of my close friends and family always wondered why I did not choose to study social science. Furthermore, my grades in social science are consistently better than my technical subjects. A good friend once joked that he would vote for me if I run for office.

Sarah: I went on to pursue a course in Sociology at a public university in the United States, but most Singaporeans at my university studied engineering and economics; I was the first Singaporean studying sociology in five cohorts of students. Pursuing a different track from the typical crowd was not easy. I often felt like I lost out on the sense of camaraderie that my peers who were taking the same courses enjoyed. This was accentuated by the fact that most of the Singaporean students studying abroad tended to stick together because it accorded precious familiarity and comfort as an international student ... that offered some way of organizing ourselves on a large and cosmopolitan campus. Pursuing an unusual major on my own did not only mean that I did not have Singaporean peers to depend on for advice, but also led me to regularly question if there was a reason why so few people had chosen this path. To be honest, sometimes I felt like I was accorded less respect because studying something like sociology was deemed to be less useful or valuable ... to them, it was simply too irrational and "un-Singaporean" to spend hard-earned money on a course that offered no clear "returns."

This sensitivity to how their peers perceive them is not always the result of discussions between peers. Most of the time, these perceptions appear to be internalized, and then projected onto themselves as expectations that they must meet.

Veronica: I do some part-time work in a local university and seeing so many young PhDs (some 10 years younger than me!) makes me wonder if I could ever be as competitive, given my age and my family commitments in particular. To make matters worse, jobs in academia are scarce and a PhD is no guarantee that

I will get the job I want. I also sometimes feel the pressure from my JC [junior college] classmates who are all doing very well and are all well-established in their careers …

Jane: I think that what I struggle with the most about Singapore is that there is a fixation over determining one vocation and sticking with it for the rest of your life … Too many career shifts and inconsistencies would make you appear an unsuccessful individual.

Anderson: And also … in the last two terms of your university, most of your conversations with friends would only start with "which job did you apply for? Which interview did you go? I went for so many interviews and I got this many offers" and stuff like that. Every single conversation starts the same way. And then … after a while it just gets to you … you know, you're not doing anything wrong. But you just start questioning yourself.

Anna, a career coach, shared with me her observations of students from the arts and social sciences department in her university in response to the notion of internships, which are important for finding jobs. According to her, internships help to bring out that clarity, of knowing I have done something similar in school, like writing up a research methodology or a report, and link the knowledge to the required workplace skills. In the past, there was a lack of awareness about the importance of internships. However, Anna has observed the trend changing, with an increasing focus on career skills early in the university years by both students and firms.

Anna: There is definitely a rise in interest in people going for internships early. Or those who cannot go know the importance of internships even as a freshman. Increasingly, I see more freshmen coming for career guidance such as how to actively seek out internships and student exchange programmes that best suit their interest. In addition to recruitment events, companies are interested to reach out to Year 1s and Year 2s to start building relationships through information sessions. The aim for these companies is to create awareness and share about their culture. We see this in some internships and information sessions that specifically look for students graduating in a few years' time. For example, the Economic Development Board also has case exercises for freshmen to let the students know the company and the culture.

As universities, students, and firms continue to emphasize training for appropriate career skills from a younger age, the job search process becomes more complicated and the pressure to improve oneself plays a stronger role in the lives of individuals. Interestingly, intragenerational differences may exist among millennials about their attitudes towards work. In a group interview session with three millennials with varying levels of work experience, I found that, in response to my question on their attitude towards upskilling in programming skills, they offered different views on the issue.

Benedict, an early-career millennial: I think it is natural for me. From a young age, I have been exposed to technology ... When I go to work, I see the computer in terms of the number of hours a day more than my friends, more than my parents, more than my dog. So, I think being able to speak to the computer is a prerequisite. More recently, I think instead of brushing up my programming skills and picking up a variety of languages, I realize it is important to be able to communicate this language to other people who don't understand the language ... It will be more useful as a skill to be able to explain to someone what coding is.

Alice, a mid-career millennial: While learning different skills is good, it has to be buildable and have some linkages to what I am doing ... Currently I am doing programming. So, I will prioritize perhaps on the domain skills such as in the banking industry ... For me, it has to be something relevant so I can apply my skills.

Quinn, a late-career millennial: It is very important to stay relevant. You probably can't keep doing whatever you have been doing in the past. You must have an open mind and be willing to pick up new skills ... So, if all these things add value and help me understand how to apply better, how to improve, how to increase productivity, it actually motivates me to pick up something new ... It is difficult for me to go into the details [of the work] without first understanding the basics.

Benedict sees the skills involved in technology as a requirement for surviving in the workplace. To younger millennials, skills have become a form of prerequisite for work life. Alice and Quinn view skills upgrading as important in staying relevant for the workforce. Thus, rather than being a prerequisite, they provide additional benefits. Furthermore, Alice was more open to the idea of learning skills that might not be directly relevant to her current job. In her words, the career trajectory is a lattice-structure; one can move across various industries and need not stay within a single industry for an entire lifetime. These different views towards upskilling also reflect the idea that millennials are not a homogenous group but have different work values due to their different experiences. Nevertheless, in all three cases, there is a sense that one needs to continue to be relevant and updated, even if the underlying motivations may differ.

Millennials' innate sensitivity to remaining relevant and updated, coupled with the pragmatism that they have been socialized to maintain, creates a unique work ethic. On the one hand, their idealism keeps them constantly on the lookout for opportunities to keep up with their peers; on the other hand, their constant eye on practicality helps to balance these dreams and keeps them humble and open-minded to opportunities that come their way, even if they may not be glamorous or immediately fulfilling. There is a willingness to delay gratification if it means they will be able to reach their ambitions eventually on their own merit.

Trust in the Way the System Works

Finally, while millennials may be anxious about how to achieve their goals, they appear to have an inherent trust in the system and in the promises of institutions. In the "Reputation Age," as Nelson (an interviewee) coins it, millennials are worried about how others perceive them; not just the fear that they are not good, but that they are perceived to be undeserving. At the same time, they have been witnesses to and beneficiaries of the various opportunities awarded by the Singapore government. They know that they are likely to succeed if they also embody the beliefs within the system: meritocracy, self-reliance, and pragmatism. This is the effect of proactive governance on more than one generation. I did not get a sense of entitlement among the interviewees. They acknowledge that the system is not easy. They know that the fundamentals in the system work and that things are progressing quickly in Singapore. I asked Isaac, a Singaporean software engineer based in Silicon Valley, if he would consider returning back to Singapore to work.

> Isaac: Yeah, if opportunities arise. For example, right now I'm monitoring the cryptocurrency scene. Even MAS [Monetary Authority of Singapore] has said that they're very open to it, and they're not going to restrict it or regulate it as tightly as China, United States or India. So that's very exciting. As you know, if they see that there are developments in that space, then there's definitely going to be a burgeoning industry around it. I see the overall culture [of the technology space] also changing. When I went back, I went to visit one of the local start-ups, they already seemed to have the Silicon Valley mindset. Like if you don't come in, that's fine. So, I see it slowly changing but there's still lot more to catch up on. The scene is definitely very exciting.

> John: So, for the start-up scene, it's very supportive, especially from schools. In my university they often send out emails saying, "If you have an idea, come pitch to us for funding!" It comes about thrice a semester. So, there are many options for you to pitch your idea, and I think it's very good. It's a very good platform for us to explore what we really want and test out this start-up scene.

My interviews with several millennial entrepreneurs confirm that it is not a predestined trait that differentiates them from their peers. Instead, they often simply attribute it to being at the right place at the right time, and to their ability to take advantage of the opportunities.

> NR: Did you ever feel anxious not subscribing to a typical career path?
> Wayne: No, because I actually did subscribe to it, right? I got a scholarship, I got into a school I wanted to, and the ironic thing was that I started the business to fulfil that path, so that I had something to write about in my college application. It was only when I had time to explore my options that I went to this accelerator … and that was when I was exposed to this whole new world outside about what people are doing.
> NR: Do you know if your co-founders were motivated by similar things?

Wayne: Broadly, we were motivated by very similar things. We have very different needs as individuals and are driven by different motivations, but broadly we were all looking for the same thing. Initially, how to get into best schools and best scholarships. Later on, it was how to do well in the business.

NR: Did you see many of your friends in high school doing similar things?

Wayne: I wouldn't say what I did was unique, I was also trying to just study well and get the best grades possible. I was also very deliberate about building my portfolio, doing student council etc. But I think what I did differently was that I had a lot of side projects that I was interested in, like the business competitions. Even though part of the intention back then was to build my portfolio, I was genuinely interested in that, and luckily for me, the biggest takeaway from that was the exposure.

I took a particular interest in what engineers had to say about this anxiety of being outdated one day, since they are the ones creating the technologies and enabling automation. Arguably, they may be the ones who are most equipped with the skills and knowledge to ride the tide of automation. Here is one exchange that I had with Nelson, a biomedical engineer:

Nelson: Am I feeling more anxiety? No ... nothing has really changed. If you don't stay relevant and try to adapt you will just be out of the picture. There isn't really any shift.

NR: You mean that human beings have always had to stay relevant?

Nelson: I would say yes, at least for Singapore. The majority of my adult life, I've always thought this ... especially right now, it's all about information and information exchange. The game has changed. It's no longer the Information Age, it's the Reputation Age.

NR: Assuming that you're in a start-up and that doesn't work, will you be anxious?

Nelson: I'd say ... I would have something at the back, so I won't be destitute. But I won't put too many eggs in that basket. But I've some idea on how to hedge my bets. If I was worried about being out of a job, I think where I am now, in Singapore, as an engineer and in university, I'm fairly confident in my abilities. I think I have decent interpersonal skills. I'd say I'm already ahead of the curve. I guess, it's about how to stay ahead of the game within your own field. The fear now is becoming irrelevant. Not so much falling behind but becoming obsolete. That's the primary fear. It's not so much about winning. But the fear is that you are useless and what you have won't cut it.

What is interesting is that even though they know the system works, these millennials continue to create backup plans for themselves to hedge against possible failure. This may initially come across as a paradox. However, it is this very spirit of self-reliance that motivates their desire to depend on themselves and not what the system provides. This strategy of preparing a multiplicity of options for themselves enables them to remain competitive in the face of unprecedented change. As Nelson said, he is able to remain fairly confident of his ability to keep a job, because he would have "some idea on how to hedge [his] bets" in every situation.

John, likewise, is trained as an electrical engineer but has already toyed with the prospect of running his own business for a while. Even though entrepreneurs are often portrayed as adventurous, risk-taking individuals, John's decision to pursue entrepreneurship was made cautiously. He was only willing to make the jump when he was certain that there would be no significant financial costs.

John: My mum used tell me a lot about business. She used to say it's a combination of timing, luck and God's blessings. Because even if you're competent, if the timing is not there, then it's just too bad ... so it's very vulnerable. I still remember my mom when she first started her business in 2007, her first client came after 8 months ... it's very difficult to actually see how much your business can progress and how much you actually have to wait to see your business prosper. So, growing up, she actually told me that I must have a backup plan in case something like that happens.

My position is that this desire to prepare backup plans in anticipation of change is one possible way to cope with change, whereas others view such behaviour as a fear of failure. In a country where the system works well, it may be possible that people gradually develop a preference for taking the safe route. Rather than taking care of the fundamentals in a way that allows individuals to pursue their passions, proactive governance might conversely shelter generations to the extent that they are doing everything they can to avoid dealing with flux. It becomes a question of whether the successes of this country will also eventually impede the generation that it aims to serve. As Kishore Mahbubani puts it, "The advantage of living in Singapore is that we live in a stable, well-ordered society. Paradoxically, the disadvantage of living in Singapore is that we live in a stable, well-ordered society" (Mahbubani 2016). This is not entirely false, given that some of the millennials that I have spoken to have also expressed their aversion to failure:

> Veronica: The most prominent barrier is my lack of self-confidence in my ability to be able to complete a PhD successfully, and coming in close second is the fear of having to start all over again. I loathe to rely on my safety net (teaching ESL [English as a Second Language]), but the thought of restarting in my mid-thirties is indeed intimidating.

> Jane: Being a child in Singapore meant that you could be berated for every little mistake you made, so mistakes I avoided. I then delayed this process even further by taking up a master's program in another interdisciplinary field ("unacceptable"), but at an Ivy League institution ("acceptable") – once again, playing the balancing act.

The kind of failure they are referring to does not exactly portray the desolate conditions that come to mind. For Veronica, failure is "having to start all over again." For Jane it is the possibility of being "berated for every little mistake." Some of them develop a kind of risk aversion that is enough to stop them from pursuing certain paths that would force them to leave their comfort zone and become creative. When I interviewed Steven, a director of a university's entrepreneurship centre, to solicit the possible reasons underlying this risk aversion, he attributed it to millennials not having enough global exposure:

> Steven: Not enough exposure maybe. It's very important that they think beyond Singapore. The market size here is too small ... and things also work too well in Singapore ... They may not be prepared to handle chaos and that may be an issue. I hope they can adapt of course, but they have to be more exposed to messier parts of life. That makes you more competitive and street smart. In Sin-

gapore, the preferred route is to get an established career, whether in the government, MNCs or GLCs. There has to be encouragement and support to get younger people who are talented, who know how to make things happen, to be part of the entrepreneurship scene. We've been trying to do it since the 1990s, but it's still hard. Younger people still prefer a safety net, not just them, but their parents as well. I also try to tell my students very honestly. Statistics show that 90% of the start-ups fail. So, students have to be aware of that.

The benefit of going abroad temporarily to expose oneself to new experiences was echoed by Isaac, another millennial who had studied in the United States for his undergraduate degree. In our interview, he admitted that it was only after he had left the country for a while that he began to notice that it was very easy to get comfortable, perhaps even complacent, in a safe environment like Singapore.

Isaac: I think the main thing that stuck out to me was that Singaporeans tend to think more about the problems and harp on it instead of trying to solve it. Over here at Silicon Valley everyone shows it through their actions, like "Okay, the aircon is broken, let's try to fix it." So, as a result, it instills a sense of creativity, there's a lot more creative juice flowing around, and people are very open to discussing solutions and ideas. Naturally, there's a lot more discussion and collaboration over here. There's always a sense of a team working towards solving a problem, and that creates a sense of community. But back home I would say a lot of the problems we face are smaller, because we are a small country, and there's a habit of just talking and talking and not doing, which I really hate.

The stories of the Singaporean millennials have revealed how Singapore's proactive governance and ethos of meritocracy and self-reliance have influenced their life courses. Their stories closely resemble a policy report that interviewed millennials in polytechnics (Teo et al. 2018), which found that 76 per cent of the interviewees thought that meritocracy exists in Singapore. Furthermore, among the 76 per cent, 93 per cent believed that job prospects and economic well-being were dependent on individual efforts (ibid.). Thus, the ethos of meritocracy and self-reliance permeates other segments of the millennial population as well. The question now is whether proactive governance should still be a good thing, given that it tends to over-prescribe what people should or should not do to succeed. For example, it is not surprising that many millennials still largely seek to pursue careers in conventional fields like banking, medicine, and law. These were the jobs once perceived to be the most prestigious ones and are still perceived that way by many baby boomers and Gen Xers who aspire to have their children be successful today. While these career aspirations were uncommon among the millennials I interviewed, human resources practitioners like Syed Ali Abbas have pointed out that it is this very trend that may make Singaporeans particularly vulnerable to automation (Aubrey, Abbas, and Nadu 2018). It will become a very dangerous trend if people do not want the jobs (such as nursing) that are here to stay, and only seek the jobs that are already being affected by automation. I argue that as long as the Singapore government continues to proactively anticipate future changes and adopt policies that enable citizens to move towards those directions, millennials and post-millennial workers will be able to adapt to the flux society and assuage the anxiety that arises from their uncertainties about the future of work.

6

Conclusion

This book looked at the future of work from various angles, recognizing that a proper and thorough treatment of the subject requires an integrated view of work and the many complex problems and solutions embedded within it. Chapter 1 looked at the phenomenon of anxiety about the future of work, in the areas of innovation, networking, and performance. It is not only individuals and corporations that face anxiety; states and governments are also under pressure to ensure that their people will be ready to tackle the challenges of the future. The chapter presented an argument about the effects of anxiety on work cultures and introduced the forms of anxiety faced by different stakeholders in the flux society.

Many of the anxieties discussed thus far have arisen in tandem with the emergence of automation and new technologies. Many of the millennial stories later in the book shed light on how the new generation entering the workforce finds it imperative to incorporate some "tech" into their portfolio of skills. Even if it is not a primary skill set, they see technological competence as the new baseline, whether they are trained in engineering, STEM, social sciences, or another field. Millennials' primary anxiety is perceiving that they must incorporate technological skill sets, such as programming skills, into their work, regardless of their education and careers, for fear of being outdated. Some millennials, like Perry, feel obligated to learn such skills despite not needing programming skills to perform their jobs. Other millennials, like Veronica, who are not trained in STEM fields, feel they need more explicit skills, in Veronica's case adding a computational element to her linguistics degree. In other words, millennials are vulnerable to the increased quantification-, data-, and algorithm-driven work cultures with rather precarious job opportunities, unless states and firms work to proactively provide better re-training, job opportunities, and working conditions. Millennials do not enjoy the near-stable work environments of previous generations, despite older generations' worry that they might be facing retrenchment later in their careers due to organizational restructuring, economic downturns, and technological upgrades (Kochan 2015; Raghunath 2019).

Developed economies are driven by the imperative to innovate. That is why disciplines like engineering, sciences, social sciences, and interdisciplinary connections are perceived as the tools that will enable and prepare workers for that future. But does this make technology responsible for the changing future of work? Though I recognize evidence that society is moving towards a technologically deterministic model, I have argued against a view about the future of work that focuses solely on technological determinism, and reject a fatalistic view of anxiety. Instead, I argue that the model is being promoted by various social actors who are worried about being left out of the capitalist race for success if they do not self-disrupt with innovations. Technological disruption is thus both welcomed and feared. Alternative viewpoints, especially those that concentrate on people rather than technology in shaping policies, have to be considered as well. Rather than feeling anxious about the threat of job loss from the entry of automation, that anxiety should be redirected or channelled to collaboration and upskilling, especially in making sure that workers have the right skills for the jobs of the future. Erik Brynjolfsson and Andrew McAfee argue that the right skills and education will stand a worker in good stead in a time of rapid technological progress (Brynjolfsson and McAfee 2014). Michio Kaku, a futurist and theoretical physicist, agrees that while repetitive blue-collar jobs such as those in the automobile and textile industries will be severely threatened by automation, blue-collar jobs are not all equally at risk, nor are all white-collar jobs safe (Kaku 2016). This is a sentiment echoed by Alan Blinder, whose study on offshorable work shows that both those highly and less skilled are equally vulnerable to offshore work. A study by the Martin School also found that not all jobs are as much under the threat of unemployment as some other studies have suggested (Bakhshi et al. 2017; Blinder 2007). The wonders of automation notwithstanding, so far robots are unable to map forms to real-life meanings; for example, advanced facial analysis programs can monitor individuals' emotional responses but they lack the ability to fully comprehend human experiences and emotions (Manyika 2017).

What does this mean for the types of jobs that will be threatened? When I interviewed Crystal, a professor researching machine learning and artificial intelligence, she offered the view that jobs traditionally viewed as "very good jobs requiring high qualifications," like that of a surgeon, are more likely to be replaced today by a robot than the job of a plumber. Robots have the ability to learn from the best surgeons, and with practice over time attain an even higher level of precision than humans. While they may not be better in technique or improvisation, robots also do not have physiological needs, which means they can work more efficiently than human surgeons. A plumbing job might be more difficult for a robot to pick up since every new household will have a different problem scenario; no two households share identical plumbing systems. For the robot to know how to deal with the infinite combinations presented in every new scenario, it would have to learn from a very extensive range of possibilities. In such situations, the general skills of adaptation and improvisation that a human plumber has will be more valuable. Likewise, blue-collar jobs such as garbage disposal, sanitation, gardening, policing, and construction are expected to thrive because they are non-repetitive, whereas repetitive white-collar jobs such as accountancy, bookkeeping, travel agents, and banking will be particularly vulnerable to automation.

Who, then, would thrive in the new white-collar world? Kaku believes that it will be those who engage in intellectual capitalism, which he defines as using common sense and qualities such as creativity, imagination, and leadership.[1] Other skills that are valued in intellectual capitalism include analyzing, telling jokes, writing scripts or books, and doing science. Citing the example of England earning more revenue from rock music than coal, Kaku believes that the future of work is moving from commodity-based capital, such as coal, to intellectual capital, such as rock and roll music (Kaku 2016). In a world systemized by flux and constant upgrading, the ones who will be left out are those who are not aware of the new skills sought in the market and are unable to acquire the means to upgrade their skills to enter this space. The ability to fail and rise again is ever so important for those who want to thrive in disruption and innovation (see Fleming et al. 2017; Higginbottom 2017).

Thus, it appears that the kind of human capital required to thrive in the work scene of the future will have to encompass many forms of capital. It will have to go beyond mere social capital, which can be defined in terms of community solidarity, or access to and use of social network resources (Lin 1999). This is especially true for millennials, who have been raised in an age of digital devices. They may lack more traditional forms of social capital, like face-to-face relationships, but they are superior to other generations in the extent of their digital networking capital (Gallup 2016). One's network connections correspond to one's reputation as well; it is common for professionals to enroll in MBA programs to build up their own networks, and signal that they are engaged in continuously upgrading their skills, rather than acquiring the specific skills taught in the program. Also, despite the reality that social capital is no longer the only capital needed in the flux society, it still has a role to play in the creation of human capital, as argued by those who define social capital as access to and use of social network resources, such as James Coleman (1988). An example of the importance of social capital is the sharing economy model, considered by some to be "the new world of declining transaction costs and rising consumer interest in sharing" (Botsman 2013). On the one hand, existing literature points to the possibilities of the sharing economy for strengthening ties within a community (Andreotti et al. 2017). Specifically, new models, where users share resources from couches and cars, can foster intimacy and "act as catalysts of collaborative action" within these communities (ibid., 24).[2] In the absence of an intermediary in their transactions, users are dependent on reciprocal relationships founded on trust. Since trust becomes an important antecedent for the sharing economy to work, there is good reason to believe that the sharing economy can create and strengthen social capital (Andreotti et al. 2017).[3]

Rather than having one set of skills or educational qualifications, today's economy prizes those who have the ability to continuously change to keep being relevant. It has become more important for a candidate to list their ability to continue adapting, upskilling, and expanding their networks, than just stating the schools they graduated from or the degree they acquired. One example of this is LinkedIn, the world's largest professional employment-oriented social network (LinkedIn n.d.). In addition to the usual details that one would see in a traditional CV, the site prompts users to "add 5 skills to showcase what you are great at," claiming that "members with more than five skills are 27x more likely to be discovered in searches by recruiters" (Jangid 2017).

I stress the element of collaboration in this new work ethic because the discussion on the future of work cannot only focus on millennials in the working population but must also include existing workers such as Gen Xers and baby boomers, who are living longer and retiring later. Life and work longevity are increasing in developed societies due to advances in medical science and health. Lynda Gratton and Andrew Scott calculate that the average person with a lifespan of one hundred years would have to work into their eighties if they planned to retire on half of their final salary. Not only that, the challenges of working into one's eighties include having to constantly upgrade, re-skill, and re-train to remain productive and employable in the face of a rapidly evolving employment market. Gratton and Scott also predict a shift from the traditional three-stage life (education, employment, and retirement), which will become unsustainable with the possibility of one-hundred-year lifespans being unexceptional. Instead, they propose a multi-stage life where two or more different careers are possible. This has a few implications. First, this may mean that mapping one's age to the life stage one is currently at may no longer apply, in a way that the authors call "age-agnostic" (Gratton and Scott 2016). Because one is no longer expected to be confined to a certain life stage, and because one's lifespan is going to be longer, opportunities for change will not only increase, but may need to be kept open for a longer time. Also, cross-age friendships are more likely to occur, as it becomes more possible to find people of different ages in similar life stages. This could foster better inter-generational understanding.

On its own, living longer might seem like a plus, but it is only one side of the aging-population coin. On the other side is the issue of decreasing fertility rates, a problem plaguing many developed Asian countries, including Japan, South Korea, and Singapore. Japan, and many more globally, is facing a labour crisis; Japan's population is projected to shrink by about one-third in the next fifty years, largely due to declining birth rates, which dropped to under one million for the first time in 2016 (Reynolds 2017). Similarly, South Koreans are not only living longer, but are also opting not to have more children. They now have one of the world's lowest birth rates (Cho 2021). Singapore faces the same problem. In a bid to create a stopgap, the nation has been actively encouraging immigration (K. Ng 2015). Citing James Smith and Barry Edmonston (1997), Putnam also reports that immigration plays an integral role in offsetting the fiscal effects of the exit of baby boomer workers, especially in countries with aging populations (Putnam 2007; Smith and Edmonston 1997).

Clearly, strategies for the future working population are not going to be straightforward; these policies will have to be conceptualized in light of concurrent demographic and immigration developments. All of these, especially the reality of an aging population, point to a need to reconsider the concept of retirement and even the logic of a retirement age. Given Gratton and Scott's (2016) calculation that one would have to work well into one's eighties, our current retirement ages in the sixties would no longer make any sense. Josephine Teo, former minister of manpower, suggested that one way to ensure financial independence for older workers would be to increase the retirement age to prevent companies from retiring them because of their age. This would allow workers more time to accumulate wealth and to continue providing for themselves (J. Teo 2019). Globally, countries have been increasing their retirement age. For example, Denmark and Netherlands link their retirement age to the life expectancy of their populations (ibid.). This is all the more pertinent in non-pensionable societies like Singapore (Calder 2016).[4] Working longer seems like a viable solution, but as one ages, incomes may also decrease because companies are less willing to pay more or to maintain the same salary. To combat this, workers may then have to consider multiple sources of income. Therefore, not only will traditional models of employment and retirement have to change, flexibility at the workplace should also go hand in hand with flexibility for later retirement as new business and work models emerge in the flux society, where change is constant (A. Lee 2018).

All these issues may point to a stark reality: not only could the current, almost obsessive, fixation on millennials and Gen Z as the future stakeholders be myopic, it may also be equally simplistic to reduce the future of work to a single employment model, whether it be the traditional corporation type or the current in-vogue model of the sharing economy. What this means is that while lifelong employment might involve many disruptions, and may no longer be available to all, states have to be proactive. They must craft and shape policies in ways that allow the individual to pursue or create lifelong employment and allow them to be able to proactively find ways to provide work for themselves. One way to do this is to facilitate continuous retraining and upskilling. A possible model that could enable this is freelance work, where the individual is the epicentre of lifelong employment. Rather than large and hierarchical corporations, one-person organizations can instead act as service providers. Today's idea of employees and corporations might change so much that they might no longer be the norm in the future of work. Instead, start-ups and self-employment models might just become the mainstay of the future work scene, with smaller nuclei of business models the norm. This is not to say that there is no place for corporations. Empowering whole communities should still be a priority, but there is also a need now to cater to individualistic expectations, especially when individuals can be equipped to work on their own as entrepreneurs. The role of the state is, hence, one that is more like a facilitator or an enabler in addition to its numerous roles. The core concepts of inclusion and continuous meritocracy are key factors in this new perspective of a collaborative approach to the future of work. Governments and corporations can no longer be the only drivers in the flux society; instead of a single driver of the future of work, multiple stakeholders have a part to play.

We cannot afford to have a myopic view of progress and leave groups out by focusing only on key players. Many more conversations are needed across industries about the parties involved; not just about millennials, but about everyone who has a stake in the system. An example of this type of conversation can be seen in an online exchange between Prime Minister Lee and Tan Min-Liang, the Singaporean CEO of US-based consumer technology company Razer. Tan replied to Prime Minister Lee's tweet on plans for implementing a unified e-payment system in Singapore and seamless e-payment system. To the surprise of many, Prime Minister Lee responded favourably to the suggestion: "Thanks @minliangtan! Make me a proposal, and I will study it seriously" (Koh 2017). In the words of Tan Min-Liang, "When Singapore's PM responds on ideas through Twitter you can be sure they're serious on the Smart Nation Initiative. Kudos" (M.L. Tan 2017).

In chapter 4, I discussed some initiatives undertaken by the Singaporean government as one illustration of a model of proactive governance. In this model, the state does not merely feed financial resources to achieve certain outcomes, but seeks to achieve a dynamic, reciprocal relationship with the populace. The Singapore government has developed a comprehensive package of policies targeted at actively providing opportunities for Singaporeans to engage in innovation and collaboration, ranging from setting up funds and programs in local universities, to encouraging entrepreneurship, to providing the Smart Nation Scholarship to develop talent in the field of technology. Anticipating changes and dealing with them before they take place serves as the basis for these initiatives, in order to equip people with the latest skills and opportunities to remain competitive in the job market. Coupled with these platforms is an overall attitude that the country cannot rest on its previous successes. It should constantly question existing structures and processes. In more recent conversations about social mobility, ministers and community-led groups alike have even attempted to rethink the relevance and meaning of meritocracy, a long-standing value that Singapore's founding fathers swore by. While meritocracy used to be synonymous with academic excellence, today it is understood more in terms of one's perseverance and willingness to adapt. The SkillsFuture and Smart Nation Initiative are just two of the multiple efforts that the Singapore government has carried out to equip its population to embrace lifelong learning as a way of adapting to the future of work (SkillsFuture 2017 n.d.-a; Smart Nation Singapore n.d.).

So, are the millennials at the receiving end of these systems ready for the future of work? The millennials in Singapore that I spoke to in chapter 5 reflect some of the protracted effects of having such a model of proactive governance. They come from a myriad of backgrounds: some are engineers, and others are social scientists and humanities graduates; some are from upper-middle-class families; others had to base their career decisions on attaining financial stability. Yet, what commonly defines their experience is the way they have interacted with and navigated the education system: being subjected to the competitive environment of standardized testing, while also being exposed to the various opportunities offered along the way to equip themselves to be more competitive. An important normative mechanism appears to have emerged from such a system of proactive governance; it socializes an already highly educated population to constantly think of how they can prepare themselves to be relevant and to keep up with economic and social changes. The first-hand accounts in chapter 5 also offer a human touch to challenge the millennial typologies that are featured in the literature (chapter 2). I chose to look specifically at millennials in Singapore to let the reader understand how the nation's development efforts through implicit norms like meritocracy, and more explicit education policies, manifest in the generation of millennials that retain a deep sense of idealism and pragmatism amid the anxieties of the flux society.

That said, the picture that I paint of these millennials as products of a national system and psyche is not flawless. While the rigorous education system in Singapore has trained a generation of hard workers, it may not have adequately prepared them for the failure and rapid change that comes with the flux society. Although they are good at future-proofing and devising alternative plans, they might not be at the right level of future-readiness because they remain largely risk averse. They still rely heavily on tried-and-tested methods and predictable systems, and don't have enough of an appetite for forging new and unconventional tracks. Ironically, it is this very attitude of being forward-thinking and cushioning their future against failure that holds them back from actions that would lead to them becoming more adaptable, innovative, and having breakthroughs. However, while the national system provides lots of opportunities for millennials to succeed in the system, inevitably some in the race are left behind. Although the millennials I interviewed were largely successful in navigating the national system, the anxieties and difficulties they expressed over the need to constantly compete with others for opportunities are highly relevant. Failure to obtain these opportunities may result in a lifelong struggle to fight the changing work climate. Kelly, a millennial working towards her PhD, acknowledges the merits of meritocracy in Singapore, but she highlights problems with it as well.

Kelly: I think that the country generally does strongly believe that if you work hard, you will succeed. And that's the cornerstone of meritocracy, right? But of course, I personally don't agree, because I think meritocracy is a bit of a sham, right? I mean, I am a product of it. It works for me because I'm academically inclined. And so, I shot up in school I did well and everything I'm supposed to do, right. And it's easy for me. I never worried about my grades ... But then I know that that's a very specific system that rewards a very specific kind of intelligence. Yes. And it's crushing. It's limited. I know that for example, I could never do what my sister does. She's in no way not as smart as me. I am smart in a very limited academic way ... But meritocracy only rewards one kind of intelligence and that is academic intelligence.

In a country where income inequality is becoming a hotly debated topic (Y. Teo 2018), there is a need to consider millennials who might be left behind because they cannot obtain the required resources to survive the flux society. This book draws heavily from the stories of educated millennials because this population is most at risk at falling behind in the race for innovation. An analysis of Federal Reserve data by an advocacy group, Young Invincibles, showed that American millennials are already falling behind their baby boomer parents in income levels and overall net worth (including assets such as home-ownership and student debt), even if their education levels are higher (Boak and Antlfinger 2017). The predominant narrative places the blame on poorer economic conditions today, with parents claiming that opportunities appear to be fading away (ibid.). From the data I have gathered, I go a step further. I argue that it is their reliance on these formal structures of education and recruitment that expose them to the most risk in the flux society. A college degree today is no longer just a ticket to success; it is more important for millennials to enter the workforce with a mindset of being ready for flux. A Pew Research Center study showed that Americans of all ages feel that their jobs are more precarious and recognize that they will need to constantly upgrade their skills to stay employable (Pew Research Center 2016). I analyzed the anxieties of the millennials entering the workforce in Singapore. These millennials may not be finding it hard to get jobs after graduation due to enormous efforts by their universities and themselves, but that does not stop them from worrying about staying relevant in the future. In the same vein, their degrees seem to do little in assuaging their concerns that the changes in the economy will soon outpace them. For governments, corporations, and citizens alike, the challenge is in having to constantly reinvent themselves with no idea where the finish line is. Nevertheless, the sense of optimism that Singaporean millennials embody suggests that it is possible to adapt to the flux society through a system of proactive governance, and with collaboration between stakeholders.

WHAT'S NEXT?

In my study thus far, I have focused my analysis on millennials' anxiety in light of the changing nature of work. However, the spotlight is not on them as manifestations of stereotypes, but more on equipping them to increase their productivity, creativity, and readiness to take on future work challenges. However, adopting a view of the future of work that largely focuses on a single group, millennials, is not sufficient. A more holistic discussion of this topic will also be needed to incorporate the perspectives of other stakeholders affected by the economy in flux, including older workers whose skills may no longer be relevant, as well as corporations and businesses that have been replaced by automation.

I propose that cities and countries consider an approach of proactive governance to prepare their citizens for a flux society, as illustrated through my case study of Singapore. It is necessary to qualify that a model of proactive governance can only work when citizens are receptive and seek to take advantage of the opportunities provided by the government. This entails sufficient public trust in the state. The Singapore government benefits from its citizens' high level of trust. The foundations of this trust have taken time to build and maintaining it in the future will take many more conversations and inclusiveness on all sides: from maintaining a clean record in public service and having zero tolerance for corruption, to remarkable economic growth over fifty+ years, to the kind of transparent communication and reassurance that the government has provided to citizens during unprecedented crises, like the SARS outbreak in 2003 and now during the Covid-19 crisis. However, even Singapore's former head of the civil service, Peter Ho, warns of the need to understand how technology can erode public trust and decentralize the government's power in Singapore (P. Ho 2018). In a world of crowdsourcing, mobile applications, and social media, people are turning to each other for positive and negative feedback, encouragement, and technical advice, and putting more trust in the opinions of their peers. These technological changes highlight the need for a proactive state like Singapore to continue adapting its methods to reflect more consultative avenues and opportunities to rebuild livelihoods for those who are unable to succeed economically in the current system, despite the enormous support provided. Also, too much mollycoddling by the state might dampen the local entrepreneurial and innovative cultures, which involve more risk taking. Likewise, this model of proactive governance cannot be applied wholesale. Instead, it should be adaptive and strengthen economic cooperation and community ties.

Another example of a country proactively trying to deal with flux is Finland, which spent two years testing a universal basic income (UBI) pilot. The UBI trial was first proposed as a potential alternative to the current welfare system in 2015 and appealed to Finns because of the changes to the digital economy (Oltermann 2016). On the one hand, a UBI would guarantee a "necessary injection of cash" that allows people to afford technological devices and keep up with changes made to the workforce (Oltermann 2016). On the other hand, the UBI would remain an important source of social security and is favoured as a more prudent alternative to existing welfare payments (Henley 2018). In April 2018, the government decided not to extend the two-year pilot. While this response to flux may not be directly applicable to other countries, the Finnish government has provided another example of proactive governance: an ability to anticipate how changes to the workforce will affect social security, a recognition that its existing systems needed updating, and a willingness to learn from other countries and systems.

A final aspect of this book that requires further discussion is how societies have sought to understand innovation. The concept of innovation is probably one that requires a redefinition. It has been popularly understood as a good idea for changes to an existing product. But innovation goes beyond merely adding elements to an existing concept. Samantha, a design professor, suggested to me that "real innovation is when something is completely different." She added that innovation is something that has not only been designed, but also sold on the market. Not only does it have the potential to change the way things are done, it also has an effect that can be positive as well as negative.[5] A single definition of innovation is impossible, and there may also be different standards of innovation in different countries. Innovation has been conceptualized to encapsulate more than just mere technological affordances. Rather than studying only technological determinism as the driving force behind innovation, the reverse relationship, of humans driving technological change, should also be studied. The implications of this phenomenon are that the actors of innovation are humans, and that technology is not inherently right or wrong. Instead, how technology is being used, and whether it is used ethically or not, is dependent on the human actors who harness it.[6] The question then is, what does it take to make a society more innovative? Is it possible to balance regulation and innovation? If so, how does one retain the rule of law and yet encourage innovation in the face of changing business models?

What this book does not discuss is the complex nature of how technology has changed the way people communicate, live, and work with each other. Who will create new forms of communication with the younger generation affected by flux? Who will dictate the norms of communication? What will the new expectations be? Who will be left behind? All these questions throw up a vision of a future of work, which could involve a number of scenarios driven by different forces. The need to expand our scope of vision to include perspectives on connections and interdependencies of various factors means that we also need to point all the stakeholders, namely individuals, businesses, employers, and social and governmental institutions, in the same direction. Collaboration between different stakeholders has never been as crucial as it is now. The uncertainty of the future of work means that all parties need to work together instead of venturing out on their own to face the issues (Hagel and Schwartz 2017). This has immense implications for the individual, for businesses, and for public institutions. The challenge, then, is to put everything that has been discussed into action.

Appendix

1–10: Managers and employees (some are non-millennial)
11–50: Millennials

Index	Pseudonym	Description
1	Matthew	Director of a software consultancy firm
2	Thomas	Senior policy expert on education policies and a professor at a local university
3	Elizabeth	Career coach
4	Crystal	Professor researching machine learning and artificial intelligence
5	Samantha	Design professor
6	Anna	Career coach for arts and social science students
7	Gavin	Senior manager of a multinational bank
8	Faith	Manager in charge of university collaborations with industry
9	Steven	Director of an entrepreneurship centre
10	Jasper	Senior manager of a bank
11	Lucas	Manager in a software firm
12	Beatrice	Human resources manager
13	Victor	Computer scientist
14	Clement	Founder of a media music company
15	Anderson	Co-founder of a creative education agency
16	Titus	Co-founder of a creative education agency
17	Judy	Co-founder of a creative education agency
18	Isaac	Employee in a technology firm in Silicon Valley
19	Luke	Employee in a technology firm in Singapore
20	Hana	Graduating university student with a social science major
21	Ronald	Founder of a virtual reality company

Table (*continued*)

Index	Pseudonym	Description
22	Zachary	Entrepreneur
23	Eli	Employee in a technology firm
24	Kelly	Student completing her PhD
25	Serene	Recently graduated from a private local university
26	Xavier	Employee in a start-up
27	Verena	Graduate with a biological sciences degree
28	Perry	Graduate with a psychology degree and just started his career as a counsellor
29	Benedict	Early-career employee
30	Alice	Mid-career employee
31	Quinn	Late-career employee
32	Wayne	Start-up founder
33	Dominic	Employee in a technology firm
34	Kaleb	Engineering graduate
35	Veronica	Linguist
36	John	Engineering graduate
37	Eric	Engineering graduate
38	Nelson	Engineering graduate
39	Colin	Employee of a technology firm based in Silicon Valley
40	Sarah	Sociology graduate
41	Jane	Sociology graduate
42	Fiona	International Relations graduate
43	Kon	Data scientist working overseas
44	Zoey	Graduate with a degree in engineering
45	Jessica	Graduate with a social science degree
46	Joyce	Graduate with a biological sciences degree. Taking a gap year to apply for medical school
47	Minnie	Student learning coding
48	Chris	PhD student
49	Angie	Financial broker
50	Glenn	Executive working in a mentoring organization

Notes

1 The term *algorithm economy* is largely attributed to Gartner, a global technology research company, who defines it as a phenomenon with "entirely new markets to buy and sell algorithms, generating significant incremental revenue for existing companies and spawning a new generation of specialist technology start-ups" (Sondergaard 2015a). In the algorithm economy, businesses are founded and run on "a piece of software code that solves a problem or creates a new opportunity" (Sondergaard 2015b). The more sophisticated and effective this code is, the more valuable the product that is created.

2 Zygmunt Bauman (2000; 2007) discusses the ideas of constant change and risk associated with late and liquid modernity. While I do not discuss the debates around modernity, the idea of constant changes in risk societies is relevant.

3 Thierer (2012) cites T.S. Eliot (1948, 19) on his assertion, "[O]ur own period is one of decline; that the standards of culture are lower than they were fifty years ago."

1 See the blogs at COMPASS, University of Oxford, by Nilanjan Raghunath and Tony Tan (2020a, b).

2 What can governments learn from the ways in which technology firms handle millennials? Young people need to be heard and given avenues for the diversity of their voices. Clearly, on the one hand, institutions

have stereotypes of generations, and on the other hand, organizations promote openness that is also subject to constant technological presence and surveillance. However, innovative organizations need to be on top of things when it comes to creating new cultures of consultations and safe feedback to shape flux and disruptive innovation (see Christensen 1997; Turco 2016). Disruptive innovation has thus become a clichéd term used in forums and talks about the future of work and IoT, but it simply means getting software and machines into a self-sufficient system with less human intervention. Disruptive innovation is defined as small companies taking on product and service lines for customers that are overlooked by larger firms, because they are less profitable (Christensen, Raynor, & McDonald 2015). Uber, Lyft, and Airbnb are often cited as examples of disruptive innovation. Moreover, it is also said to have, arguably, shaped millennials' approach to work (Gregory 2016). It differs from sustaining technologies in that, instead of fostering better product performance like the latter do, it tends to bring about worse product performance by underperforming products already established in mainstream markets (Christensen 1997). Though disruptive technologies also contradict the conventional wisdom of hard work, customer-driven strategies, long-term perspectives, and better planning, in the long run they are likely to enter the mainstream market as full-performance players capable of competing with established products (ibid.). One way they do so is when companies, in a bid to develop products superior to their competitors', overlook the risk of over-satisfying the demands of their customers. This creates a gap in the market for lower-priced products, which is then filled by disruptive technologies (ibid.). Clayton Christensen notes that the Internet plays a role in facilitating the entry into and subsequent commercializing of disruptive technologies in the mainstream market (ibid.).

While it might be true that the inability to keep abreast of customers' technological demands can precede the downfall of a company, Christensen (1997) argues that many companies have proven capable of developing the needed technology effectively. Poor management is also not an adequate reason as these managers generally understand and develop the necessary strategies to meet the demands of their customers. However, even with technology and good management on their side, these companies may fail to make good decisions when faced with disruptive technological change. Christensen (1997) points out that factors contributing to the success of established companies, such as listening to customers, tracking competitors' actions, and investing resources to develop and build better quality products, are also the very ones that cause failures when confronting disruptive technologies.

3 A list of interviewees with their pseudonyms is included in the appendix.

CHAPTER ONE

1 Ulrich Beck, in his book *Risk Society: Towards a New Modernity* (1992), conceptualized the *risk society*, arguing that Western societies have failed to deliver the promises of modernity, and instead have generated global risks by making the entire world a testing ground for the risks that are generated. The idea of the *flux society* is influenced by Beck's work and seeks to further the point that we are never meant to be too comfortable in the world of work, because the status quo does not produce innovation. In the *flux society*, constant apathy towards the environment and social relations and boredom require signs and signals of progress. However, we need to go further and understand the effect that automation has on individuals. How are individuals coping with fast-paced change, particularly the educated class armed with university degrees? What changes are they facing in the workplace and how will they cope? My observations of workplaces have shown me that many automation changes are occurring. Some of the changes involve the reorganization of the physical workspace: creating open spaces and technology for remote work, as well as hot desking, where employees are not assigned a permanent workspace. Other changes include combining some aspects of work with recreation and play time to foster an open culture. While some of these changes suggest that companies are reacting to what they think workers want or suggest how workers should network and interact without barriers, they also reflect the trend of "Googlizing" the workplace. Google is known in the technology industry for its dynamic workplaces that mix work and play and provide free food and board games for its employees. Many believe that such collaborative environments will encourage productivity and creativity. But not everyone wants to mix work and play or is suited to work in an environment like this. Contrary to popular belief, millennials place less importance on recreation in the workplace than baby boomers and Gen X workers (Rigoni and Adkins 2016). In an interview I had with Matthew, a director of a software consultancy firm, he suggested that the trend towards Googlizing the workplace can have some negative effects. For example, one aspect of this trend is to remove work cubicles, which is supposed

to increase collaboration between employees. However, Matthew noted that this can be highly distracting for individuals who are performing jobs that do not require many collaborations with others. Thus, there is a need to consider how to best manage different groups of workers in the workplace. Connected to the ideas of new capitalist structures, such as late capitalism (Mandel 1975), there is pressure to rework the career tracks and benefits in organizations to make employees more competitive. Rapid changes in technology and other forms of disruptions involve creating new business models and workplaces that are highly adaptable and resilient. This means that companies must look at new ways of creating, managing, and sustaining the employees' work ethic. This has serious effects on how they perceive employees and the overall work culture, as the younger generation are seen as champions who can herald innovation and a sense of entrepreneurialism in the workplace. Thus, the next chapter provides detailed analysis of how firms view the millennial generation and the associated vulnerabilities that arise from these perceptions.

2 The concept of symbolic capital was developed by Pierre Bourdieu (1984, 1986, 1989). Bourdieu identified symbolic capital as a form of capital that afforded honour and prestige to an individual, contributing to the strength of one's reputation in society.

3 The McKinsey (2016) survey of 2,135 global executives identified functional and departmental silos, risk aversion, and a difficulty in forming and acting on a single view of the customer as three deficiencies of the digital age.

4 See Burt (2004), Granovetter (1973), Rainie and Wellman (2012), and many other network theorists who discuss the importance of connections in finding jobs, information, status attainment, and influence. Many firms that I visited also emphasized the importance of networks to their employees to enable better teamwork, cross-fertilization of ideas, and innovation.

5 A visit to an innovation workshop organized for employees of a multinational technology design firm showed that managers needed many activities and long debriefings to get them to communicate face to face. The organizational wiki was more popular as a tool for conversations about innovation.

6 This is from Deloitte's global Human Capital Trends Survey (2017) cited by Bersin et al. (2017).

CHAPTER TWO

1 This information came from visits to hiring and networking events in technology firms.

2 Myers and Sadaghiani (2010, 225) cite Cam Marston (2009) that millennials lack loyalty and a work ethic and contest the stereotypes about millennials in their research paper.

3 In this study, 172 business and management undergraduates from two UK universities were placed in focus groups and their responses were studied.

4 Harvey Krahn and Nancy Galambos did not define the years that fall within the Generation Y category but used the graduating class of 1996 as a proxy for observing Generation Y characteristics and attitudes.

5 Thomas is a professor who teaches education policy at the postgraduate level in Singapore. I interviewed him to better understand how the needs of the economy have shaped education policy as well as the types of skills that schools try to develop in students. He also shared some of his experiences as a baby boomer working closely with millennials in his industry.

6 This survey by Morar Consulting polled 2,000 people in Singapore, half of them millennials. The survey was commissioned by videoconferencing tech firm Polycom.

7 The respondents were 9,699 adults aged eighteen to sixty-seven in full-time employment from a variety of firms in the US, the UK, India, Japan, China, Germany, Mexico, and Brazil. About 1,200 were surveyed in each country. The weighing of the data reflects roughly the composition of the adult populations in each country, with 400 participants from each of the generations of millennials (defined in the study to be between eighteen and thirty-three years old), Gen X (between thirty-four and forty-nine years old), and baby boomers (between fifty and sixty-eight years old). Out of the 400, 100 were parents/non-managers, 100 were parents/managers, 100 were non-parents/non-managers, and 100 were non-parents/managers (Ernst & Young 2015). The limitations of an online survey have been noted by marketing research firm The Nielsen Corporation, which also administered a global online survey of more than 30,000 respondents from different generations in sixty countries in Asia-Pacific, Latin America, Europe, North America, and the Middle East/Africa from 23 February to 13 March 2015 (Nielsen 2015). The survey was administered online so it was limited to respondents

with access to the Internet. Also, respondents in developing countries with online access are likely to be younger and wealthier. Hence, the findings from both EY and AC Nielsen may not be representative of the entire population (Nielsen 2015).

8　This is one of the biggest and most comprehensive studies done on millennials by Deloitte Touche Tohmatsu Limited (Deloitte) done annually. The 2017 Deloitte Millennial Survey examined the work-related concerns, expectations, and beliefs of close to 8,000 millennials from thirty countries around the world (Deloitte 2017). Sixteen of these countries are emerging markets and the rest are developed economies. The participants, all born after 1982, are college- or university-degree-holders employed full-time in predominantly large private-sector firms of more than 100 employees.

9　The term G.I. is an American abbreviation for "general or government issue," which refers to veterans of the United States armed forces.

10　Sennett (2007). See chapter 1, "Bureaucracy," for further discussion on delayering, casualization of labour, and risk-taking.

11　Sennett (2007). This idea is expounded upon in chapter 2, "Talent and the Specter of Uselessness."

12　Sennett (2007). In chapter 2, "Talent and the Specter of Uselessness," Sennett asserts that skill alone cannot counter the "specter of uselessness" in people's lives today.

13　Sennett (2007). In the introduction, Sennett opines that it takes a particular breed of human being to be able to thrive in such unfavourable conditions and lists the three challenges that they have to tackle.

14　Turco (2016). The company studied by Turco is named TechCo, a pseudonym. See the book's preface for an introduction to the company.

15　Turco (2016), introduction, cites from Max Weber, *Economy and Society* (Vol. 2), edited by Guenther Roth and Claus Wittich (Berkeley, CA: University of California Press, 1978).

16　Turco (2016), introduction. She cites from Robert Merton (1940), "Bureaucratic Structure and Personality," *Social Forces* 18(4).

17　Turco (2016), introduction, cites from Braverman (1974), Burawoy (1979), and Edwards (1979).

18　Turco (2016), introduction, cites Meyer and Rowan (1977, 340).

19　Turco (2016). See chapter 2, "Open Communication," for more on how confidential information is made available to the company's employees.

20　Turco (2016), chapter 4, "Openness Controls," citing Ezra Zuckerman (2010, 300).

21 Turco (2016), chapter 5, "Open Culture," citing James Baron (2004).

22 Turco (2016), chapter 5, "Open Culture," citing Orlando Patterson (2014).

23 Turco (2016), chapter 5, "Open Culture," citing Gideon Kunda (1992).

24 Turco (2016), chapter 7, "Conversational Spaces."

25 Turco (2016), chapter 7, "Conversational Spaces"; see Howe and Strauss (2000). See also Alsop (2008) and PWC (2011).

CHAPTER THREE

1 The analogy of a human body to the social body in this aspect is attributed to Herbert Spencer (Urry 2000).

2 The Singapore pledge highlights the need to disregard differences between citizens and emphasizes the need to have a cohesive society to achieve the common good of Singapore. The following is an excerpt from the Singapore pledge:

>   We, the citizens of Singapore,
>   pledge ourselves as one united people,
>   regardless of race, language or religion,
>   to build a democratic society
>   based on justice and equality
>   so as to achieve happiness, prosperity
>   and progress for our nation.

3 A study by Bakhshi et al. suggests the same, that "occupation redesign coupled with workforce retraining could promote growth in [occupations that face uncertainty]" (Bakhshi et al. 2017, 13).

CHAPTER FOUR

1 Young (1992, 28). Young cites Mirza (1986, 37).

2 The Maria Hertogh riots took place from 11 December to 13 December 1950. The conflict, between the Malay community and people of European descent in Singapore, centred around a Dutch-Eurasian girl, Maria Hertogh, who was adopted by a Malay Muslim family during the Second World War. The outcome of a legal battle for her custody after the war was perceived to be biased against the Muslim community, and set the stage for the riots, which took 18 lives and injured another 173 (L. Tan 1997).

   The racial riots of 1964 between the Malays and the Chinese took place in July and September 1964, amid political tensions between the

PAP and the Alliance government in Malaysia led by the United Malays National Organisation (UMNO), Malaysia's largest political party. Feelings of dissent among the Malay community against the PAP for their alleged oppression of the Malays in Singapore were stoked by Malay activists within UMNO and reached breaking point on 21 July 1964. The first series of riots occurred over a span of almost three weeks, from 21 July to 7 August 1964, and claimed 23 lives while injuring another 454. The second took place barely a month later, from 2 September to 14 September 1964, after the mysterious murder of a Malay trishaw rider, causing the Malays to retaliate against the Chinese. Thirteen lives were lost and another 106 were injured (Han 2014). http://eresources.nlb .gov.sg/infopedia/articles/SIP_45_2005-01-06.html?s=1964 racial riots.

3 The Central Provident Fund (CPF) is a compulsory savings scheme, where Singaporean citizens and permanent residents along with their employers make monthly contributions to a fund that is set aside for the employee's retirement. This is Singapore's equivalent of a social security system. Even self-employed citizens and permanent residents can make contributions (Central Provident Fund 2020). MediSave is a national medical savings scheme that automatically sets aside part of an employee's income to help them save for future medical expenses.

4 See Huff (1995), 1424–5, 1426, 1428–9.

5 This quote is from PM Lee's letter reply to the Committee on Ageing Issues in 2006. https://www.msf.gov.sg/publications/Pages/Report-of-the-Committee-on-Ageing-Issues-2006.aspx.tens.

6 Calder (2016). Calder's model of Singapore as a "smart state" involves a minimalist and enabling approach to governance in social welfare, economic development, and management of foreign policy.

7 The Edusave account is an education-centred scheme, and comes in the forms of grants, awards, bursaries, and scholarships, to name a few. The baby bonus and child development accounts are meant to encourage and support couples financially to have more children. For more information, see: Ministry of Education, 8 April 2019, available from https://www.moe.gov.sg/education/edusave, and Ministry of Social and Family Development, 8 March 2017, Baby Bonus Scheme, available from https://www.msf.gov.sg/policies/Strong-and-Stable-Families /Supporting-Families/Pages/Baby-Bonus-Scheme.aspx; Goodman (2015). Calder (2016, 65) considers Singapore's efforts to ensure personal self-reliance and social stability through such policies as fulfilling one of the "quintessential functions of government."

8   B.H. Chua (2011, 43) says more than 80 per cent of Singapore's popula-
    tion lives in public housing.

9   Workforce Singapore, formerly the Workforce Development Agency, is a
    statutory board under the Ministry of Manpower. The agency adminis-
    ters specific programs to develop the local workforce to keep them rele-
    vant, and also works with business owners and companies to help them
    remain competitive.

10 This quote is from PM Lee's letter reply to the Committee on the Future
    Economy (2017). https://www.straitstimes.com/singapore/cfe-report-7-
    strategies-to-take-economy-forward.

11 The Future Economy Council was formerly named the Council for
    Skills, Innovation and Productivity and formed in 2017 (Ministry of
    Trade and Industry 2017a, 2017b.). https://www.mti.gov.sg/Future
    Economy/TheFutureEconomyCouncil#:~:text=The%20FEC%20will
    %20oversee%20the,initiatives%20and%20Industry%20Transformation
    %20Maps.

12 Chua Mui Hoong is currently an associate editor at the *Straits Times*.

13 NTUC (n.d.-c).

14 The Institute of Technical Education is a vocational education institu-
    tion established by the Ministry of Education to provide pre-employ-
    ment training to students from the secondary school level onwards
    (Shanmugaratnam 2017).

15 The rankings of junior colleges had been discontinued earlier, in 2004.
    For more information on the school ranking system in Singapore, see
    C. Sim (2014).

16 The SkillsFuture Credit Scheme has been so successful that the other
    initiatives under SkillsFuture have at times been overlooked. (Y.K. Ong
    2016a).

17 The top 10 training providers include local tertiary education providers,
    such as universities and polytechnics, as well as course providers, such as
    the NTUC Learninghub Pte. Ltd and online course provider Coursera
    (SkillsFuture 2017). More courses are being added each year.

18 The SkillsFuture Engage initiative has since been renamed SkillsFuture
    Advice, beginning in 2017.

19 National Service is the period of mandatory service in Singapore's uni-
    formed forces. It is for male Singaporean citizens and second-generation
    permanent residents, and lasts two years (Ministry of Defence 2021).

20 The Operationally Ready Date is the date that an NSman finishes his
    two-year term of service (HR in Asia 2017).

21 The Earn and Learn Programme allows an individual to learn and obtain a qualification while working (Shanmugaratnam 2016b, 2017).

22 Kansas City uses sensors to collect traffic data that is then used for a variety of purposes, such as parking, public lighting, responding to crowd disturbances, and even entrepreneurship. Louisville identifies areas with air pollution and distributes sensor-equipped asthma inhalers to asthma sufferers there. In Los Angeles, an application for reporting trash problems has helped the city's efforts to clean up the streets gain traction. Similarly, in Mobile, Alabama, blighted properties are identified via Instagram, a popular photo-sharing application. In Boston, a navigation application from Google named Waze makes it possible for users to share traffic and road conditions in real time, and also assists in low-cost experiments on possible traffic changes (Totty 2017).

23 The Panopticon is an architectural feature proposed by Jeremy Bentham in the mid-nineteenth century for prisons, insane asylums, schools, hospitals, and factories. As an alternative to violence, the Panopticon separated prisoners from each other in cells that were arranged in a ring around the observer, or prison guard, allowing him a panoramic view of all the prisoners (Bentham 1995).

24 Five areas identified as key to society and in which technology has the potential to make a positive impact are: transport, home and environment, business productivity, health and enabled ageing, and, finally, the public sector services (Prime Minister H.L. Lee 2014); see also (SPRING Singapore 2015).

25 Quote from Sim S. Lim., DBS Singapore's then country head. From O. Ho (2016).

26 Some 9,000 government data sets have been made available to the world's tech community to explore and test novel ideas (SPRING Singapore 2015). This number has been increasing over the years.

27 See International Organization for Standardization ISO 37120:2014, available from https://www.iso.org/standard/62436.html for more about the ISO37120 series (ISO 2018).

28 Bhunia (2017). http://www.opengovasia.com/articles/7710-singapore-ranked-1st-in-asia-and-7th-worldwide-in-global-innovation-index-2017.

29 The Innovation Input Sub-Index looks at five innovation-enabling elements: institutions, human capital and research, infrastructure, market sophistication, and business sophistication. The Innovation Output index looks at outputs as a result of innovation, in the areas of knowledge and technology, and creativity (Bhunia 2017).

30 The first camp consists of examples like Prime Minister Lee and Singa-
pore-based start-up nuTonomy CEO Karl Iagnemma; examples from the
second camp include San Francisco-based Singaporean company Razer
CEO Tan Min-Liang, venture capital firm Venturecraft CEO Isaac Ho, and
the Singapore University of Social Sciences' Dr Calvin Chan (W. Tan
2017). See also Calder (2016), who, like those from the first camp, considers Singapore's size and structure an advantage that larger states, with
more complex bureaucratic and political structures lack.

31 In an informal survey conducted by the authors, it was found that all of
the air-conditioned, publicly accessible locations, e.g., airport terminals
and shopping malls they visited, had temperatures lower than 25 degrees
Celsius. Twenty-five degrees Celsius is the recommended ambient temper-
ature in Singapore's commercial buildings (Lim and Kim 2015).
Researchers from Stanford University have come up with building materials capable of reflecting sunlight back into outer space (A. Myers 2013).
This technology can potentially reduce the amount of air-conditioning
needed in Singapore (Lim and Kim 2015). Ngee Ann Polytechnic has
developed a heat-recovering prototype that is capable of channelling waste
heat from air-conditioning compressors to appliances like shower heaters.
If implemented, that could lower electricity bills (Lim and Kim 2015).

32 The authors note that void decks are often purposely left empty, but can
be used for permanent and temporary uses, for example kindergartens
and weddings. They are meant to foster a sense of belonging or be used
as spaces for events (Chong, To, and Fischer 2017).

CHAPTER FIVE

1 For confidentiality purposes, I have withheld the identities of all the
millennials that I have spoken to. All interviewees' names in this book
are pseudonyms.

2 I interviewed a career coach who runs her own business consultancy in
leadership and coaching. She works closely with millennials in universities to give them career advice and guidance. In our conversation, she
said this about millennials: "I feel like everyone's kind of rushing,
almost pulled by something that they need to keep going towards. I feel
like that's what's causing them to rush and move even faster. In their
natural tendency they are motivated to create output. But then, now it's
almost like they also put that pressure on themselves to just speed up
and get it down and show. Because they need to show something."

3 The scholarship that Sarah is referring to is a full scholarship that covers the entire length of her undergraduate and graduate studies. In return, she will have to complete a "bond," referring to the length of time she is bound by contract to work for her scholarship sponsor.

CHAPTER SIX

1 Michio Kaku (2016) is a futurist and theoretical physicist at the City College of New York and City University of New York (CUNY) Graduate Center.

2 See Andreotti et al. (2017). The writers cite Molz's (2013) example of couch surfing use, and Ozanne and Ozanne's (2011) acclaim of such initiatives.

3 See Andreotti et al. (2017). The writers also cite existing literature on trust in the sharing economy, from Botsman and Rogers (2010) and *The Economist* (2013).

4 In Singapore, the Tripartite Workgroup, which comprises various government agencies, actively engages self-employed persons and businesses to decide on the retirement age, which is set to increase. See Ministry of Manpower (n.d.-a, b) for a history on the changes in the retirement age in Singapore.

5 Interview communication, August 2017.

6 The term technological determinism was apparently coined by the American sociologist and economist Thorstein Veblen (1921). In his final chapter, Veblen (1921, 102) outlines the idea of how a "soviet of technicians," who are technological experts, should come together to determine the "economic affairs of the country and to allow and disallow what they may agree on." Technological determinism can be seen as letting technology, or those who are experts at the forefront of technology, to determine the economical and societal structures. See also Chandler (1995), Finnegan (1989).

References

ADP Research Institute. 2017. *ADP Workforce Vitality Index: 1st Quarter 2017*. United States: ADP Research Institute.

Agar, Nicholas. 2019. *How to be Human in the Digital Economy*. Cambridge, MA: MIT Press.

Agency for Science, Technology and Research. 2015. *STEP 2015: Science, Technology & Enterprise Plan 2015*. Singapore: Agency for Science, Technology and Research.

Agrawal, Ajay, Joshua Gans, and Avi Goldfarb. 2018. *Prediction Machines: The Economics of Artificial Intelligence*. Boston, MA: Harvard Business Review Press.

Alberta Government. 2016. *Preparing Industry Professionals for the Classroom*. Last modified 21 October 2016. https://education.alberta.ca/recent-news /preparing-industry-professionals-for-the-classroom/?searchMode=3.

Alcorn, Chauncey L. 2016. "How Millennials in the Workplace Are Turning Peer Mentoring on Its Head." *Fortune*, 26 July 2016. https://fortune.com /2016/07/26/reverse-mentoring-target-unitedhealth/.

Alsop, Ron. 2008. *The Trophy Kids Grow Up: How the Millennial Generation is Shaking up the Workplace*. San Francisco, CA: Jossey-Bass.

Altringer, Beth. 2013. "A New Model for Innovation in Big Companies." *Harvard Business Review*, 19 November 2013. https://hbr.org/2013/11/a-new-model-for-innovation-in-big-companies.

Andreotti, Alberta, Guido Anselmi, Thomas Eichhorn, Christian Pieter Hoffmann, and Marina Micheli. 2017. *Participation in the Sharing Economy*. SSRN. https://ssrn.com/abstract=2961745.

Arntz, Melanie, Terry Gregory, and Ulrich Zierahn. 2016. *The Risk of Automation for Jobs in OECD Countries: A Comparative Analysis*. OECD

Social, Employment and Migration Working Paper No. 189. Organisation for Economic Co-operation and Development (OECD). https://doi.org/10.1787/5jlz9h56dvq7-en.

Aubrey, Bob, Syed Ali Abbas, and Sriven Nadu. 1 June 2018. "The New Asian Workplace: Who Will Take Charge?" The Head Foundation. 13:54. https://headfoundation.org/2018/06/05/the-new-asian-workforce-who-will-take-charge/.

Autor, David H., Lawrence F. Katz, and Melissa S. Kearney. 2006. "The Polarization of the U.S. Labour Market." *American Economic Review* 96, no. 2: 189–94. doi: 10.1257/000282806777212620.

Autor, David, David A. Mindell, and Elisabeth B. Reynolds. 2019. *The Work of the Future: Shaping Technology and Institutions.* Massachusetts: Massachusetts Institute of Technology Work of the Future Taskforce. https://workofthefuture.mit.edu/wp-content/uploads/2020/08/WorkoftheFuture_Report_Shaping_Technology_and_Institutions.pdf.

Averill, James, R., Kyum Koo Chon, and Doug Woong Hahn. 2001. "Emotions and Creativity, East and West." *Asian Journal of Social Psychology* 4: 165–83. doi: 10.1111/1467-839X.00084.

Baer, Markus. 2012. "Putting Creativity to Work: The Implementation of Creative Ideas in Organizations." *Academy of Management Journal* 55, no. 5: 1102–19. doi: 10.5465/amj.2009.0470.

Baird, Carolyn Heller. 2015. *Myths, Exaggerations and Uncomfortable Truths: The Real Story Behind Millennials in the Workplace.* United States: IBM Institute for Business Value. https://www.ibm.com/downloads/cas/Q3ZVGRLP.

Bakhshi, Hasan, Jonathan M. Downing, Michael A. Osborne, and Philippe Schneider. 2017. *The Future of Skills: Employment in 2030.* London: Pearson and Nesta. https://futureskills.pearson.com/research/assets/pdfs/technical-report.pdf.

Baron, James. N. 2004. "Employing Identities in Organizational Ecology." *Industrial and Corporate Change* 13, no. 1: 3–32. doi: 10.1093/icc/13.1.3.

Bartley, Tim, and Curtis Child. 2011. "Movements, Markets and Fields: The Effects of Anti-Sweatshop Campaigns on U.S. Firms, 1993–2000." *Social Forces* 90, no. 2: 425–51. doi: 10.1093/sf/sor010.

Barton, Christine, Jeff Fromm, and Chris Egan. 2012. *The Millennial Consumer: Debunking Stereotypes.* Boston, MA: Boston Consulting Group. https://mkt-bcg-com-public-images.s3.amazonaws.com/public-pdfs/legacy-documents/file103894.pdf.

Bates, Cindy. 2017. "Survey Reveals Four Secrets to Success for Attracting and Retaining Millennial Talent." *Comcast Business.* Last modified 27 January 2017. https://cbcommunity.comcast.com/community/browse-all

/details/survey-reveals-four-secrets-to-success-for-attracting-and-retaining-millennial-talent.

Bauman, Zygmunt. 2000. *Liquid Modernity*. Cambridge, UK: Polity Press.

– 2007. *Liquid Times: Living in an Age of Uncertainty*. Cambridge: Polity Press.

Beck, Ulrich. 1992. *Risk Society: Towards a New Modernity*. London: SAGE Publications.

– 2000. "Risk Society Revisited: Theory, Politics and Research Programmes." In *The Risk Society and Beyond: Critical Issues for Social Theory*, edited by Barbara Adam, Ulrich Beck, and Joost van Loon, 211–40. London: SAGE Publications.

– 2006. "Living in the World Risk Society." *Economy and Society* 35, no. 3: 329–45. doi: 10.1080/03085140600844902.

Beck, Ulrich, Anthony Giddens, and Scott Lash. 1994. *Reflexive Modernization: Politics, Tradition and Aesthetics in the Modern Social Order*. Stanford, CA: Stanford University Press.

Beck, Ulrich, and Martin Chalmers. 1996. "Risk Society and the Provident State." In *Theory, Culture & Society: Risk, Environment and Modernity: Towards a New Ecology*, edited by Scott Lash, Bronislaw Szerszynski, and Brian Wynne, 28–43. London: SAGE Publications.

Beck, Ulrich, and Christoph Lau. 2000. "Second Modernity as a Research Agenda: Theoretical and Empirical Explorations in the 'Meta-change' of Modern Society." *British Journal of Sociology* 56, no. 4: 525–57. doi: 10.1111/j.1468-4446.2005.00082.x.

Beh, Swan Gin. 2017a. "Singapore's Long Game in Innovation." *Singapore Economic Development Board*. Last modified 31 March 2020. https://www.edb.gov.sg/en/news-and-events/insights/innovation/singapores-long-game-in-innovation.html.

– 2017b. "Why Singapore is Betting Big on Designer." Yahoo! Finance. Last modified 1 April 2017. https://finance.yahoo.com/video/why-singapore-betting-big-designer-211432244.html.

Bell, Daniel. 1973. *The Coming of Post-Industrial Society: A Venture in Social Forecasting*. New York, NY: Basic Books.

Bentham, Jeremy. 1787. *The Panopticon Writings*. London: Verso, 1995.

Bersin, Josh, Bill Plester, Jeff Schwartz, and Bernard van der Vyver. 2017. *Rewriting the Rules for the Digital Age: 2017 Deloitte Global Human Capital Trends*. Deloitte University Press. https://www2.deloitte.com/content/dam/Deloitte/us/Documents/human-capital/hc-2017-global-human-capital-trends-us.pdf.

Bhatti, Zubair K., Jody Zall Kusek, and Tony Verheijen. 2015. *Logged On:*

Smart Government Solutions from South Asia. Washington, DC: World Bank Group.

Bhunia, Priyankar. 2017. "Singapore Ranked 1st in Asia and 7th Worldwide in Global Innovation Index 2017." Open Gov. Last modified 27 October 2017. https://opengovasia.com/singapore-ranked-1st-in-asia-and-7th-worldwide-in-global-innovation-index-2017/.

Blinder, Alan S. 2007. *How Many U.S. Jobs Might Be Offshorable?* CEPS Working Paper No. 142. Center for Economic Policy Studies, Princeton University. https://www.princeton.edu/~ceps/workingpapers/142blinder.pdf.

Boak, Josh, and Carrie Antlfinger. 2017. "Study: Millennials are Falling Behind Their Boomer Parents." *Chicago Tribune*, 13 January 2017. https://apnews.com/article/8b688578bf764d3998cca899a448aa33.

Bochel, Catherine, and Hugh Bochel. 2017. "'Reaching In'? The Potential for E-petitions in Local Government in the United Kingdom." *Information, Communication and Society* 20, no. 5: 683–99. doi: 10.1080/1369118X.2016.1203455.

Botsman, Rachel. 2013. "The Sharing Economy Lacks a Shared Definition." Last modified 12 November 2013. https://www.fastcompany.com/3022028/the-sharing-economy-lacks-a-shared-definition.

Botsman, Rachel, and Roo Rogers. 2010. *What's Mine is Yours: How Collaborative Consumption is Changing the Way We Live*. London: Collins.

Bourdieu, Pierre. 1984. *Distinction: A Social Critique of the Judgement of Taste*. Translated by Richard Nice. Cambridge, MA: Harvard University Press.

– 1986. "The Forms of Capital." In *Cultural Theory: An Anthology*, edited by Imre Szeman and Timothy Kaposy, 81–93. New Jersey: Wiley-Blackwell.

– 1989. "Social Space and Symbolic Power." *Sociological Theory* 7 (1): 14–25. doi: 10.2307/202060.

Brack, Jessica, and Kip Kelly. 2012. *Maximizing Millennials in the Workplace*. Chapel, NC: UNC Kenan-Flagler Business School.

Brandon, John. 2015. "Microsoft Survey Says Millennials Want These 3 Things: Vision 2020." Last modified 13 November 2015. https://www.inc.com/john-brandon/microsoft-survey-results-millennial-means-modern-worker.html.

Braverman, Harry. 1974. *Labour and Monopoly Capital: The Degradation of Work in the Twentieth Century*. New York, NY: Monthly Review Press.

Bryan, Lowell L., Eric Matson, and Leigh M. Weiss. 2007. "Harnessing the Power of Informal Employee Networks." *McKinsey Quarterly*. Last modified 1 November 2007. https://www.mckinsey.com/business-functions/organization/our-insights/harnessing-the-power-of-informal-employee-networks.

Brynjolfsson, Eric, and Andrew McAfee. 2014. *The Second Machine Age: Work, Progress, and Prosperity in a Time of Brilliant Technologies*. New York, NY: W.W. Norton & Company, Inc.

Bughin, Jacques, and James Manyika. 2013. "Measuring the Full Impact of Digital Capital." *McKinsey Quarterly*. Last modified 1 July 2013. https://www.mckinsey.com/industries/technology-media-and-telecommunications/our-insights/measuring-the-full-impact-of-digital-capital.

Buonocore, Filomena, Marcello Russo, and Maria Ferrara. 2015. "Work–Family Conflict and Job Insecurity: Are Workers from Different Generations Experiencing True Differences?" *Community, Work and Family* 18, no. 3: 299–316. doi: 10.1080/13668803.2014.981504.

Burawoy, Michael. 1979. *Manufacturing Consent: Changes in the Labor Process under Monopoly Capitalism*. Chicago, IL: University of Chicago Press. https://doi.org/10.2307/3089314.

Burt, Robert S. 2004. "Structural Holes and Good Ideas." *American Journal of Sociology* 110, no. 2: 349-99. doi: 10.1086/421787.

Business Wire. 2016. "Dell Ranks 50 Global Cities Enabling Innovation and Change Through Technology." Last modified 4 April 2016. https://www.businesswire.com/news/home/20160404005133/en/Dell-Ranks-50-Global-Cities-Enabling-Innovation-and-Change-Through-Technology.

Calder, Kent E. 2016. *Singapore: Smart City, Smart State*. Washington, DC: Brookings Institution Press.

Callahan, S. 2008. "Customer-Centric Differentiation: The Key to Market Success." *The New Era of Service Differentiation*, LOMA Resource: 22–5.

Camden Carl, Stephane Kasriel, Katherine Fleming, Diana Farrell, Michael Chui, and Susan Lund. 2017. "The Digital Future of Work: Is the 9-to-5 Job Going the Way of the Dinosaur?" McKinsey Global Institute. Last modified 21 July 2017. https://www.mckinsey.com/featured-insights/future-of-work/the-digital-future-of-work-is-the-9-to-5-job-going-the-way-of-the-dinosaur.

Castells, Manuel. 1996. *The Rise of the Network Society*. Oxford: Wiley-Blackwell. 2010.

Central Provident Fund. 2020. Last updated 3 December 2020. https://www.cpf.gov.sg/members.

CBC News. 2016. "Alberta Government Wants Kids to Be 'Future Ready.'" *CBC News*, 18 October 2016. https://www.cbc.ca/news/canada/edmonton/alberta-government-wants-kids-to-be-future-ready-1.3810112.

Chan, Heng Chee. 2020. "IPS-Nathan Lecture 3: Singapore in a Time of Flux: Optimism from the Jaws of Gloom." *Institute of Policy Studies Singapore*. https://www.youtube.com/watch?v=ikC-xoyMmik.

Chan, Heng Chee, Sharon Siddique, Irna Nurlina Masron, and Domin Cooray. 2019. *Singapore's Multiculturalism: Evolving Diversity*. London: Routledge.

Chan, Robin. 2013. "Meritocracy: Vision of S'pore as Society of Equals." *The Straits Times*, 19 April 2013. https://www.straitstimes.com/singapore /meritocracy-vision-of-spore-as-society-of-equals.

Chandler, Alfred D. 1993. *The Visible Hand: The Managerial Revolution in American Business*. Cambridge, MA: Harvard University Press.

Chandler, Daniel. 1995. *Technological or Media Determinism*. Aberystwyth University. https://www.wolearn.org/pluginfile.php/45/mod_page /content/23/chandler2002_PDF_full.pdf.

Chang, Derrick. 2017. "What Skills Do We Need for the Future Economy?" *Today Online*, 16 April 2017. https://www.todayonline.com/daily-focus /education/what-skills-does-singapore-need-future-economy.

Chang, Rachel. 2015. "Tripartism is Right for Singapore but Must be Adapted to New Challenges: PM Lee." *The Straits Times*, 26 October 2015. https://www.straitstimes.com/singapore/tripartism-is-right-for-singapore- but-must-be-adapted-to-new-challenges-pm-lee.

Channel News Asia. 2019. "Heng Swee Keat to be Promoted to DPM in Cabinet Reshuffle." *Channel NewsAsia*. 23 April 2019. https://www.channel newsasia.com/news/singapore/heng-swee-keat-promoted-deputy-prime- minister-cabinet-2019-11470768.

Chatrakul Na Ayudhya, Uracha, and Janet Smithson. 2016. "Entitled or Misunderstood? Towards the Repositioning of the Sense of Entitlement Concept in the Generational Difference Debate." *Community, Work and Family* 19, no. 2: 213–26. doi: 10.1080/13668803.2016.1134116.

Chen, Brian X., and Cade Metz. 2019. "Google's Duplex Uses A.I. to Mimic Humans (Sometimes)." *The New York Times*, 22 May 2019. https://www .nytimes.com/2019/05/22/technology/personaltech/ai-google-duplex.html.

Cheng, Chi-Yeng, and Ying-yi Hong. 2017. "Kiasu and Creativity in Singapore: An Empirical Test of the Situated Dynamics Framework." *Management and Organization Review* 13, no. 4: 871–94. doi: 10.1017/mor.2017.41.

Cheok, Melissa. 2017. "Building a 'Smart Nation' in Singapore Doesn't Come Cheap." *Bloomberg*, 12 July 2017. https://www.bloomberg.com/news/articles/2017-07-11/building-a-smart- nation-in-singapore-doesn-t-come-cheap.

Chernyshenko, Olexanser S., Marilyn A. Uy, Weiting Jiang, Moon-ho R. Ho, Seong Per Lee, Kim Yin Chan, and Trevor K.Y. Yu. 2015. *Global Entrepreneurship Monitor 2014 Singapore Report*. Singapore: Nanyang Technological University.

Cheung, Chau-kiu, Ngan-pun Ngai, and Steven Sek-yum Ngai. 2012. "Work Commitment among Unemployed Youth in Hong Kong, Shanghai and Tianjin." *International Journal of Adolescence and Youth* 17 (2–3): 66–76.

Chia, Lianne, and Monica Kotwani. 2016. "Students to be Graded on 'Achievement Levels' in PSLE from 2021." *Channel NewsAsia*, 13 July 2016. https://www.channelnewsasia.com/news/singapore/students-to-be-graded-on-achievement-levels-in-psle-from-2021-7912318.

Chiam, Ching Leen, Helen Hong, Flora Ning hoi Kwan, and Tay Wan Ying. 2014. "Creative and Critical Thinking in Singapore Schools." NIE *Working Paper Series No. 2*. Singapore: National Institute of Education.

Chin, Jit Kee, Mikael Hagstroem, Ari Libarikian, and Khaled Rifai. 2017. "Advanced Analytics: Nine Insights from the C-Suite." McKinsey Analytics. Last modified 5 July 2017. https://www.mckinsey.com/business-functions/mckinsey-analytics/our-insights/advanced-analytics-nine-insights-from-the-c-suite.

Cho, Joohee. 2021. "South Korea Sees More Deaths than Births for 1st Time." ABC News. Last modified 5 January 2021. https://abcnews.go.com/International/south-korea-sees-deaths-births-1st-time/story?id=75051328.

Chong, Keng Hua, Zheng Jia, Debbie Loo, and Mihye Cho. 2015. "Successful Aging in High-Density City State: A Review of Singapore's Aging Policies and Urban Initiatives." In *International Perspectives on Age-Friendly Cities*, edited by Francis G. Caro & Kelly G. Fitzgerald, 81–102. United Kingdom: Taylor & Francis.

Chong, Keng Hua, Kien To, and Michael M.J. Fischer. 2017. "Dense and Aging: Social Sustainability of Public Places Amidst High-Density Development." In *Growing Compact: Urban Form, Density & Sustainability*, edited by Joo Hwa P. Bay and Steffen Lehmann, chapter 10. United Kingdom: Routledge.

Christensen, Clayton M. 1997. *The Innovator's Dilemma: When New Technologies Cause Great Firms to Fail*. Brighton, MA: Harvard Business School Press.

Christensen, Clayton M., Michael E. Raynor, and Rory McDonald. 2015. "What is Disruptive Innovation?" *Harvard Business Review*, December 2015, https://hbr.org/2015/12/what-is-disruptive-innovation.

Chua, Beng Huat. 1999. "Global Economy/Immature Polity: Current Crisis in Southeast Asia." *International Journal of Urban and Regional Research* 23, no. 4: 782–95. doi: 10.1111/1468-2427.00228.

– 2005. *Taking Group Rights Seriously: Multiracialism in Singapore*. Murdoch University, Asia Research Centre.

– 2011. "Singapore as Model: Planning Innovations, Knowledge Experts." In *Worlding Cities: Asian Experiments and the Art of Being Global*, edited by

Ananya Roy and Aihwa Ong, 29–54. Chichester, UK: Blackwell Publishing Ltd.

Chua, Mui Hoong. 2016. "A Luxury We Can No Longer Afford to Miss." *The Straits Times*, 23 April 2016. https://www.straitstimes.com/opinion/a-luxury-we-can-no-longer-afford-to-miss.

– 2018. *Singapore, Disrupted: Essays on a Nation at the Crossroads of Change.* Singapore: Straits Times Press.

Chua, Vincent, Eik Leong Swee, and Brian Wellman. 2019. "Getting Ahead in Singapore: How Neighborhoods, Gender, and Ethnicity Affect Enrollment into Elite Schools." *Sociology of Education* 92, no. 2: 176-98. doi: 10.1177/0038040719835489.

Cohen, Patricia. 2017. "Steady Jobs, With Pay and Hours That Are Anything But." *The New York Times*, 31 May 2017. https://www.nytimes.com/2017/05/31/business/economy/volatile-income-economy-jobs.html.

Coleman, James S. 1988. "Social Capital in the Creation of Human Capital." *American Journal of Sociology* 94: S95–S120. https://www.jstor.org/stable/2780243.

Committee on Ageing Issues: Report on the Ageing Population. 2006. *Report on the Ageing Population, Five-Year Masterplan.* Singapore: Ministry of Social and Family Development.

Committee on the Future Economy. 2017. *Report of the Committee on the Future Economy.* Singapore: Committee on the Future Economy, 4 February 2017. https://www.mti.gov.sg/Resources/publications/Report-of-the-Committee on-the-Future-Economy.

Cooperman, Alan, and Michael Lipka. 2014."U.S. Doesn't Rank High in Religious Diversity." Pew Research Center. Last modified 4 April 2014. https://www.pewresearch.org/fact-tank/2014/04/04/u-s-doesnt-rank-high-in-religious-diversity/.

Coulmas, Florian. 2007. *Population Decline and Ageing in Japan: The Social Consequences.* London: Routledge.

"Council for Skills, Innovation and Productivity Set Up." *Local News Singapore*, 20 May 2016. https://localnewsingapore.com/council-for-skills-innovation-and-productivity-set-up/.

Crouch, Mira, and Heather McKenzie. 2006. "The Logic of Small Samples in Interview-Based Qualitative Research." *Social Science Information* 45, no. 4: 483–99. https://doi.org/10.1177%2F0539018406069584.

De Hauw, Sara, and Ans De Vos. 2010. "Millennials' Career Perspective and Psychological Contract Expectations: Does the Recession Lead to Lowered Expectations?" *Journal of Business and Psychology* 25, no. 2: 293–302. https://www.jstor.org/stable/40605787.

Deal, Jennifer J., David G. Altman, and Steven G. Rogelberg. 2010. "Millennials at Work: What We Know and What We Need to Do (If Anything)." *Journal of Business and Psychology* 25, no. 2: 191–9. doi: 10.1007/s10869-010-9177-2.

Deloitte. 2017. *The 2017 Deloitte Millennial Survey – Apprehensive Millennials: Seeking Stability and Opportunities in an Uncertain World*. United Kingdom: Deloitte. https://www2.deloitte.com/content/dam/Deloitte/global/Documents/About-Deloitte/gx-deloitte-millennial-survey-2017-executive-summary.pdf.

– 2018. *2018 Deloitte Millennial Survey – Millennials Disappointed in Business, Unprepared for Industry 4.0*. United Kingdom: Deloitte. https://www2.deloitte.com/content/dam/Deloitte/global/Documents/About-Deloitte/gx-2018-millennial-survey-report.pdf.

– 2019. Deloitte Human Capital Trends survey, 2019. https://www2.deloitte.com/content/dam/Deloitte/cz/Documents/human-capital/cz-hc-trends-reinvent-with-human-focus.pdf.

– 2020. *The Deloitte Global Millennial Survey 2020 – Resilient Generations Hold the Key to Creating a "Better Normal."* Deloitte. https://www2.deloitte.com/global/en/pages/about-deloitte/articles/millennialsurvey.html.

Deng, Zongyi, and Saravanan Gopinathan. 2016. "PISA and High-Performing Education Systems: Explaining Singapore's Education Success." *Comparative Education* 52, no. 4: 449–72. doi: 10.1080/03050068.2016.1219535.

DesignSingapore Council. n.d. "About Us." Accessed 27 July 2017. https://www.designsingapore.org/about-us.html.

Doss, Henry. 2014. "How to Lead a Culture of Innovation." *Forbes*, 29 April 2014. https://www.forbes.com/sites/henrydoss/2014/04/29/being-innovation-leadership/#ccba681180ea.

Dowdy, Landon. 2016. "How to Make a Side Job Work." CNBC. Last modified 8 March 2016. https://www.cnbc.com/2016/03/08/the-millennial-hustle-working-side-jobs.html.

Duke, Brendan. 2016. "When I Was Your Age." *Center for American Progress*. Last modified 3 March 2016. https://www.americanprogress.org/issues/economy/reports/2016/03/03/131627/when-i-was-your-age/.

Durkheim, Emile. 1893. Translated by W.D. Hall. *The Division of Labour in Society*. Rev. ed. New York: Simon and Schuster, 2014.

Economic Development Board. 2018. "Singapore Flexes Its Standing as Asia's Technology Capital." Last modified 2 March 2018. https://www.edb.gov.sg/en/business-insights/insights/singapore-flexes-its-standing-as-asias-technology-capital.html.

Economist. 2013. "Peer-to-Peer Rental: The Rise of the Sharing Economy." *The Economist,* 9 March 2013. https://www.economist.com/leaders/2013/03/09/the-rise-of-the-sharing-economy.

Edwards, Richard. 1979. *Contested Terrain: The Transformation of the Workplace in the Twentieth Century.* New York, NY: Basic Books.

Eliot, Thomas Stearns. 1948. *Notes Towards the Definition of Culture.* London: Faber and Faber.

El-Taliawi, Olga G., and van der Wal, Zeger. 2020. "Three Lessons in Crisis Governance for the Age of Coronavirus." World Economic Forum. Last modified 9 April 2020. https://www.weforum.org/agenda/2020/04/a-guide-to-crisis-governance-in-the-age-of-coronavirus/.

Employment and Employability Institute (e2i). n.d. "Corporate Information." Employment and Employability Institute (e2i). Accessed 10 September 2020. https://e2i.com.sg/about-e2i/corporate-information/.

Erickson, Tammy. 2016. "Preparing Businesses for the Next Generation of Workers." *London Business School.* Last modified 10 June 2016. https://www.london.edu/news/preparing-businesses-for-the-next-generation-of-workers.

Ernst & Young. 2015. *Global Generations: A Global Study on Work-life Challenges Across Generations.* United Kingdom: Ernst & Young. https://www.workingmother.com/sites/workingmother.com/files/attachments/2015/10/barri_benson_slides_for_app.pdf.

Ewald, Francois. 2002. "The Return of Descartes' Malicious Demon: An Outline of a Philosophy of Precaution." Translated by Stephen Utz. In *Embracing Risk: The Changing Culture of Insurance and Responsibility*, edited by Tom Baker and Jonathan Simon, 273–301. Chicago, IL: University of Chicago Press.

Finn, Dennis, and Anne Donovan. 2013. *PwC's NextGen: A Global Generational Study.* New York: PricewaterhouseCoopers. https://www.pwc.com/gx/en/hr-management-services/pdf/pwc-nextgen-study-2013.pdf.

Finnegan, Ruth. 1989. "Communication and Technology." *Language & Communication* 9, nos. 2–3: 107–27. doi: 10.1016/0271-5309(89)90013-X.

Fischer, Michael M. J. 2013a "Biopolis: Asian Science in the Global Circuitry." *Science, Technology and Society* 18, no. 3: 379–404. doi: 10.1177/0971721813498500.

– 2013b. "The BAC Consultation on Neuroscience and Ethics: An Anthropologist's Perspective." *Innovation* 11, no. 2: 2–5. http://anthropology.mit.edu/sites/default/files/documents/fischer_BAC-Consultation.pdf.

Fisher, Anne. 2016. "As Wages Keep Rising, So Does Employee Turnover."
    Fortune. Last modified 27 April 2016. https://fortune.com/2016/04/26/as-
    wages-keep-rising-so-does-employee-turnover/.
Fisher, Dara R. 2020. *Education Crossing Borders: How Singapore and MIT Cre-
    ated a New University.* Boston, MA: MIT Press.
Fishkin, James S. 1997. *The Voice of the People: Public Opinions and Democ-
    racy.* Connecticut, MA: Yale University Press.
Fleming, Katherine., Arun Sundararajan, Vasant Dhar, Tom Siebel, Anne-
    Marie Slaughter, Jeff Wald, et al. 2017. "The Digital Future of Work: What
    Skills Will Be Needed?" Last modified 21 July 2017. https://www
    .mckinsey.com/featured-insights/future-of-work/the-digital-future-of-
    work-what-skills-will-be-needed.
Foster, Karen R. 2013. *Generation, Discourse, and Social Change.* New York,
    NY: Routledge.
Frey, Carl Benedikt. 2019. *The Technology Trap: Capital, Labor, and Power in
    the Age of Automation.* Princeton, NJ: Princeton University Press.
Frey, Carl Benedikt, and Michael A. Osborne. 2017. "The Future of Employ-
    ment: How Susceptible are Jobs to Computerisation?" *Technological Fore-
    casting and Social Change* 114: 254–80. doi: 10.1016/j.techfore.2016.08.019.
Fry, Richard. 2018. "Millennials Are the Largest Generation in the U.S.
    Labor Force." Pew Research Center, 11 April 2018. https://www.pew
    research.org/fact-tank/2018/04/11/millennials-largest-generation-us-labor-
    force/.
Gallup. 2016. "How Millennials Want to Work and Live." *Gallup Workplace.*
    Washington DC. http://gallup.com/workplace/238073/millennials-work-
    live.aspx.
Gans, Joshua. 2020. "To Disrupt or Not to Disrupt?" *Sloan Management
    Review,* 19 February 2020. https://sloanreview.mit.edu/article/to-disrupt-
    or-not-to-disrupt/.
Gershon, Ilana. 2017. *Down and Out in the New Economy: How People Find or
    Don't Find Work Today.* Chicago, IL: University of Chicago Press.
Giddens, Anthony. 1991. *Modernity and Self-Identity: Self and Society in the
    Late Modern Age.* Stanford, CA: Stanford University Press.
Giddens, Anthony, Christopher Pierson. 1998. *Conversations with Anthony
    Giddens: Making Sense of Modernity.* Stanford, CA: Stanford University
    Press.
Gilchrist, Karen. 2019. "How Millennials and Gen Z are Reshaping the
    Future of the Workforce." CNBC Make It. Last modified 5 March 2019.

https://www.cnbc.com/2019/03/05/how-millennials-and-gen-z-are-reshaping-the-future-of-the-workforce.html.

Goh, Chor Boon., and Saravanan Gopinathan. 2008. "Education in Singapore: Development since 1965." In *An African Exploration of the East Asian Education*, edited by Fredriksen Birger and Jee-Peng Tan J., 80–108. Washington, DC: The World Bank.

Goodman, John C. 2015. "Singapore: A Fascinating Alternative to the Welfare State." *Forbes*, 31 March 2015. https://www.forbes.com/sites/johngoodman/2015/03/31/singapore-a-fascinating-alternative-to-the-welfare-state/#77b8fcbb76c0.

Goos, Marteen, Alan Manning, and Anna Salomons. 2014. "Explaining Job Polarization: Routine-Biased Technological Change and Offshoring." *American Economic Review* 104 (8): 2509–26. doi: 10.1257/aer.104.8.2509.

Goos, Marteen, Melanie Arntz, Ulrich Zierahn, Terry Gregory, Stephanie Carretero Gomez, Ignacio. Gonzalez Vazquez, Koen Jonkers. 2019. *The Impact of Technological Innovation on the Future of Work*. JRC Working Papers Series on Labour, Education and Technology. https://ec.europa.eu/jrc/sites/jrcsh/files/jrc117212.pdf.

Goran, Julie, Laura LaBerge, and Ramesh Srinivasan. 2017. "Culture for a Digital Age." *McKinsey Quarterly*, 20 July 2017. https://www.mckinsey.com/business-functions/mckinsey-digital/our-insights/culture-for-a-digital-age.

Goy, Priscilla. 2017. "People with Disabilities Given SkillsFuture Award to Upgrade Skills." *The Straits Times*, 30 May 2017. https://www.straitstimes.com/singapore/people-with-disabilities-given-skillsfuture-award-to-upgrade-skills.

Graf, Nikki. 2017. "Today's Young Workers Are More Likely than Ever to Have a Bachelor's Degree." *Pew Research Center*. Last modified 16 May 2017. https://www.pewresearch.org/fact-tank/2017/05/16/todays-young-workers-are-more-likely-than-ever-to-have-a-bachelors-degree/.

Granovetter, Mark. 1973. "The Strength of Weak Ties." *American Journal of Sociology* 78, no. 6: 1360–80. doi: 10.1086/225469.

Gratton, Lynda., and Andrew Scott. 2016. *The 100-Year Life: Living and Working in an Age of Longevity*. London: Bloomsbury Publishing.

Gregory, Adelia. 2016. "Millennials in the Workplace: Disruptive Tech, Open Innovation, and Investment Strategy." *California Review Management*, 15 April. https://cmr.berkeley.edu/2016/04/millennial-open-innovation/.

Gunnion, Lester. 2017. "Singapore: Plans for a Future Economy Face Challenges." In *Asia Pacific Economic Outlook, Q1 2017*, 13–19. Deloitte Univer-

sity Press. https://www2.deloitte.com/content/dam/insights/us/articles
/APAC/2017-Q1/DUP_APAC_Q1-2017.pdf.

Hacker, Jacob. 2008. *The Great Risk Shift: The New Economic Insecurity and the Decline of the American Dream.* New York: Oxford University Press.

Haftor, Darek M. 2009. "Reflections Upon Ethical Challenges of IT-Professionals." In ICT, *Society and Human Beings 2009 and Web Based Communities 2009*, edited by Gunilla Bradley and Piet Kommers, 35–42. Algarve, Portugal: International Association for Development of the Information Society.

Hagel, John, and Jeff Schwartz. 2017. "Navigating the Future of Work: Can We Point Business, Workers, and Social Institutions in the Same Direction?" *Deloitte Review* 21, no. 31 July 2017. https://www2.deloitte.com/us /en/insights/deloitte-review/issue-21/navigating-new-forms-of-work.html.

Hamel, Gary. 2006. "The Why, What, and How of Management Innovation." *Harvard Business Review*, February 2006. https://hbr.org/2006/02/the-why-what-and-how-of-management-innovation.

Han, Jamie. 2014. "Communal Riots of 1964." *Singapore Infopedia*. Accessed 18 September 2020. https://eresources.nlb.gov.sg/infopedia/articles/SIP _45_2005-01-06.html.

Hanlon, Gerard. 2004. "Institutional Forms and Organizational Structures: Homology, Trust and Reputational Capital in Professional Service Firms." *Organization* 11, no. 2: 186–210. doi: 10.1177/1350508404041613.

Heng, Swee Keat. 2019. "Speech by Deputy Prime Minister and Minister for Finance Heng Swee Keat at the Singapore Fintech Festival X Singapore Week of Innovation and Technology 2019." Prime Minister's Office, 13 November 2019. https://www.pmo.gov.sg/Newsroom/DPM-Heng-Swee-Keat-at-SFF-X-SWITCH-2019.

Heller, Nathan. 2015. "Amos Yee: YouTube Star, Teen-Ager, Dissident." *The New Yorker*, 10 April 2015. https://www.newyorker.com/culture/cultural-comment/the-arrest-of-a-teen-aged-youtube-star.

Henley, Jon. 2018. "Finland to End Basic Income Trial after Two Years." *The Guardian*, 23 April 2018. https://www.theguardian.com/world/2018/apr /23/finland-to-end-basic-income-trial-after-two-years.

Hershatter, Andrea, and Molly Epstein. 2010. "Millennials and The World of Work: An Organization and Management Perspective." *Journal of Business and Psychology* 25, no. 2: 211–23. doi: 10.1007/s10869-010-9160-y.

Higginbottom, Karen. 2017. "Why the Ability to Fail Leads to Innovation." *Forbes*, 3 August 2017.

Hio, Lester. 2016. "ST Electronics and SUTD Launch First Joint Cybersecurity Laboratory." *The Straits Times*, 13 May 2016. https://www.straitstimes.com

/singapore/education/st-electronics-and-sutd-launch-first-joint-cybersecurity-laboratory.

Hirschman, Albert O. 1970. *Exit, Voice, and Loyalty: Responses to Decline in Firms, Organizations, and States*. Cambridge, MA: Harvard University Press: Cambridge, MA.

Hirst, David. 2015. "Mind the Gap: The Digital Divide and Digital Inclusion." Last modified 1 September 2015. https://commonslibrary.parliament.uk/mind-the-gap-the-digital-divide-and-digital-inclusion/.

Ho, Olivia. 2016. "The Straits Times Future Economy Forum: Job Loss Due to Disruptive Technology 'Can Create Divisions." *The Straits Times*, 21 October 2016. https://www.straitstimes.com/singapore/job-loss-due-to-disruptive-technology-can-create-divisions.

Ho, Peter. 2018. "When Public Trust Is No Longer Centred on the Government." *Today Online*, 8 February 2018. https://www.todayonline.com/commentary/when-public-trust-no-longer-centred-government.

Hollands, Robert G. 2015. "Critical Interventions into the Corporate Smart City." *Cambridge Journal of Regions, Economy and Society* 8, no. 1: 61–77. doi: 10.1093/cjres/rsu011.

Housing & Development Board. 2017. "My Smart HDB Home @ Yuhua." Accessed 3 June 2017. https://www.youtube.com/watch?v=KnM3bL3O5TY.

– 2020. "Public Housing – A Singapore Icon." Last modified 24 July 2020. https://www.hdb.gov.sg/cs/infoweb/about-us/our-role/public-housing-a-singapore-icon.

Howe, Neil, and William Strauss. 2000. *Millennials Rising: The Next Great Generation*. New York, NY: Vintage Books.

Huff, Gregg. 1995. "The Developmental State, Government, and Singapore's Economic Development Since 1960." *World Development* 23, no. 8: 1421–38. doi: 10.1016/0305-750X(95)00043-C.

HR in Asia. 2017a. "NUS, NTU, SMU to Offer up to 2,240 Spots via Discretionary Admission Scheme for Students in 2017." Last modified 21 February 2017. https://www.hrinasia.com/news/nus-ntu-smu-to-offer-up-to-2240-spots-via-discretionary-admission-scheme-for-students-in-2017/.

– 2017b. "Skills Learnt During National Service Receive Formal WSQ Accreditation." Last modified 6 March 2017. https://www.hrinasia.com/news/skills-learnt-during-national-service-receive-formal-wsq-accreditation/.

– 2017c. "More than 126,000 Singaporeans Have Used SkillsFuture Credit in 2016." Last modified 10 January 2017. https://www.hrinasia.com/news/more-than-126000-singaporeans-have-used-the-skillsfuture-credit-in-2016/.

Institute of Innovation and Entrepreneurship. n.d. "About IIE." Accessed 13 April 2018. https://iie.smu.edu.sg/about-us.

International Labour Organization (ILO). 2017. *World Employment Social Outlook: Trends 2017*. Geneva: International Labour Organization. http://www.ilo.org/wcmsp5/groups/public/—dgreports/—dcomm/—publ/documents/publication/wcms_541211.pdf.

– 2018. *New Business Models for Inclusive Growth*. Issue Brief for Second Meeting of the Global Commission on the Future of Work. Geneva: International Labour Organization. https://www.ilo.org/wcmsp5/groups /public/—dgreports/—cabinet/documents/publication/wcms _618172.pdf.

Intellasia. 2016. "Singapore Must Take Advantage of Technologies to Create Better Jobs: DPM Tharman." Last modified 1 June 2016. https://www .intellasia.net/singapore-must-take-advantage-of-technologies-to-create-better-jobs-dpm-tharman-518925.

Institute for Management Development (IMD). June 2020. "IMD World Competitiveness Ranking 2020." https://www.imd.org/news/updates/IMD-2020-World-Competitiveness-Ranking-revealed/.

International Monetary Fund (IMF). 2019. *World Economic Outlook Data: October 2019 Edition*. Washington, DC: International Monetary Fund. https://www.imf.org/external/pubs/ft/weo/2019/02/weodata/index .aspx.

International Organization for Standardization (ISO). 2018. "ISO 37120:2018." Last modified May 2018. https://www.iso.org/standard /62436.html.

Iswaran, S. 2015. "Singapore Economy: Strategies for the Next 50 Years." *Singapore 2065: Leading Insights on Economy and Environment from 50 Singapore Icons and Beyond*, edited by Euston Quah, 102–07. Singapore: World Scientific.

Jagdish, Bharati. 2017. "Businesses Should Work on the Basis of Zero Govt. Grants: Entrepreneur Lim Soon Hock." *Local News Singapore,* 9 December 2017. https://web.archive.org/web/20170304171742/http://localnew singapore.com/businesses-should-work-on-the-basis-of-zero-govt-grants-entrepreneur-lim-soon-hock/.

Jangid, Charu. 2017. "Looking for Your Next Job Opportunity? Get Found via LinkedIn Search." *LinkedIn Official Blog,* 21 June 2017. https://blog.linked in.com/2017/june/21/looking-for-your-next-job-opportunity-get-found-via-linkedin-search.

Jasanoff, Sheila. 2003. "Technologies of Humility: Citizen Participation in

Governing Science." *Minerva: A Review of Science, Learning and Policy* 41, no. 3: 223–44. doi: 10.1023/A:1025557512320.

– 2007. "Technologies of Humility." *Nature: International Journal of Science* 450, no. 33 (November). doi: 10.1038/450033a.

JTC Corporation. n.d. "JTC LaunchPad @ One-north." Last modified 18 March 2021. https://www.jtc.gov.sg/industrial-land-and-space/Pages/jtc-launchpad-one-north.aspx.

Juniper Research. 2016. "Singapore Named Global Smart City – 2016." Last modified 17 May 2016. https://www.juniperresearch.com/press/press-releases/singapore-named-global-smart-city-2016.

Kaku, Michio. 2016. "Jobs of The Future Will Be What Robots Can't Do." YouTube. 23 November 2016. Video, 2:01, https://www.youtube.com/watch?v=8eP7nuZgNqU.

Kalleberg, Arne L. 2011. *Good Jobs, Bad Jobs: The Rise of Polarized and Precarious Employment Systems in the United States, 1970s–2000s.* New York: Russell Sage Foundation, American Sociological Association Rose Series in Sociology.

Kasriel, Stephane. 2017. "Skill, Re-Skill and Re-Skill Again. How to Keep Up with the Future of Work." *World Economic Forum*, 31 July 2017. https://www.weforum.org/agenda/2017/07/skill-reskill-prepare-for-future-of-work/.

Katz, Harry C, Wonduck Lee, and Joohee Lee. 2004. *The New Structure of Labor Relations: Tripartism and Decentralization.* Ithaca, NY: Cornell University Press.

Kearney. n.d. "Where are the Global Millennials?" Accessed 13 September 2020. https://www.kearney.ro/web/global-business-policy-council/business-policy/article?/a/where-are-the-global-millennials.

Keeley, Larry, Helen Walters, Ryan Pikkel, and Brian Quinn. 2013. *Ten Types of Innovation: The Discipline of Building Breakthroughs.* Hoboken, NJ: Wiley.

Keynes John Maynard. 1930. "Economic Possibilities for Our Grandchildren." In: *Essays in Persuasion*, 358–73. New York: W.W. Norton, 1963.

Khamid, Hetty Musfirah Abdul. 2016. "NTU to 'Open Door Wider' for PMETs to Upgrade Skills." *Today Online.* Last modified 3 May 2016. https://www.todayonline.com/singapore/ntu-open-door-wider-pmets-upgrade-skills.

Khan, Habibullah. 2001. *Social Policy in Singapore: A Confucian Model?* Washington, D.C: World Bank Institute. http://documents1.worldbank.org/curated/en/193101468758956946/016824232_2002113371001150/additional/multiopage.pdf.

King, Eden, Lisa Finkelstein, Courtney Thomas, and Abby Corrington,

2019. "Generation Differences at Work are Small. Thinking they are Big Affects our Behavior." *Harvard Business Review*, 1 August 2019. https://hbr.org/2019/08/generational-differences-at-work-are-small-thinking-theyre-big-affects-our-behavior/.

Knowledge@Wharton. 2015. "How Companies Are Managing the Millennial Generation." Last modified 5 March 2015. https://knowledge .wharton.upenn.edu/article/how-companies-should-manage-millennials/.

– 2016. "The Future of Work: How You Can Ride the Wave of Change." Last modified 29 July 2016. https://knowledge.wharton.upenn.edu /article/the-forces-shaping-the-future-of-work/.

Kochan, Thomas Anton. 2015. *Shaping the Future of Work: What Future Worker, Business, Government, and Education Leaders Need to Do for All to Prosper*. New York, NY: Business Expert Press.

Kochhar, Rakesh. 2020. "New, Emerging Jobs and The Green Economy Are Boosting Demand for Analytical Skills." Pew Research Center, 23 March 2020. https://www.pewresearch.org/fact-tank/2020/03/23/new-emerging-jobs-and-the-green-economy-are-boosting-demand-for-analytical-skills/.

Koh, Fabian. 2017. "'Make Me a Proposal': PM Lee to Razer CEO's Offer on E-payments System." *The Straits Times*, 23 August 2017. https://www.straits times.com/singapore/make-me-a-proposal-pm-lee-responds-to-razer-ceos-tweets-on-e-payment-system.

Koh, Vincent, T.H. 2006. Singapore's Transition to Innovation-based Economic Growth: Infrastructure, Institutions and Government's Role. *R&D Management*. 36, no. 2, 143–60. Research Collection School of Economics.

Kowske, Brenda J., Rena Rasch, and Jack Wiley. 2010. "Millennials' (Lack Of) Attitude Problem: An Empirical Examination of Generational Effects on Work Attitudes." *Journal of Business and Psychology* 25, no. 2: 265–79. doi: 10.1007/s10869-010-9171-8.

KPMG. 2020. "Singapore Government and Institution Measures in Response to COVID-19." Last modified 17 June 2020. KPMG International. https://home .kpmg/xx/en/home/insights/2020/04/singapore-government-and-institution-measures-in-response-to-covid.html.

Krahn, Harvey J., and Nancy L. Galambos. 2014. "Work Values and Beliefs of 'Generation X' and 'Generation Y.'" *Journal of Youth Studies* 17, no. 1: 92–112. doi: 10.1080/13676261.2013.815701.

Kuah, Adrian W.J. 2020. "Can We Really Make Singapore Students Imaginative and Inquisitive?" *Today Online*, 19 July2020. https://www.todayonline .com/daily-focus/education/can-we-really-make-singapore students-imaginative-and-inquisitive.

Kunda, Gideon. 1992. *Engineering Culture: Control and Commitment in a*

High-Tech Corporation. Organization Science. Philadelphia, PA: Temple University Press.

Kwoh, Leslie. 2011. "Reverse Mentoring Cracks Workplace." *The Wall Street Journal*, 28 November 2011. https://www.wsj.com/articles/SB10001424052970203764804577060051461094004.

– 2012. "You Call That Innovation?" *The Wall Street Journal*, 23 May 2012. https://www.wsj.com/articles/SB10001424052702304791704577418250902309914.

Lane, Sabra. 2017. "'From Awe to Anxiety': How Prepared Are We for the Coming Disruption to Job Markets?" *Australian Broadcasting Corporation*, 5 July 2017. https://www.abc.net.au/radio/programs/am/from-awe-to-anxiety:-how-prepared-are-we-for-the/8679508. Interview with Ed Husic.

Laskawy, Michael Steven. 2004. *Uncommitted: Contemporary Work and the Search for Self, a Qualitative Study of 28–34-Year-old College-educated Americans.* New York: New York University, Graduate School of Arts and Science.

Lauria, Vinnie. 2014. "What Makes an Asian Tiger? Singapore's Unlikely Economic Success Lies in Its History." *Forbes*, 10 July 2014. https://www.forbes.com/sites/forbesasia/2014/07/10/what-makes-an-asian-tiger-singapores-unlikely-economic-success-lies-in-its-history/#570fdaff6697.

Lavelle, Justin. 2020. "Gartner CFO Survey Reveals 74% Intend to Shift Some Employees to Remote Work Permanently." *Gartner Newsroom*, 3 April 2020. https://www.gartner.com/en/newsroom/press-releases/2020-04-03-gartner-cfo-surey-reveals-74-percent-of-organizations-to-shift-some-employees-to-remote-work-permanently2.

Lee, Augustin. 2018. "Trends and Shifts in Employment: Singapore's Workforce." *Civil Service College* no. 18, 30 January 2018. https://www.csc.gov.sg/articles/trends-and-shifts-in-employment-singapore-s-workforce.

Lee, Clifford. 2016. "SUTD, ST Electronics to Launch S$44.3m Joint Cybersecurity Lab." *Today Online*, May 13, 2016. https://www.todayonline.com/singapore/s443m-cyber-security-lab-be-set.

Lee, Hsien Loong. 2003. *New Challenges, Fresh Goals: Towards a Dynamic Global City.* Singapore: Ministry of Trade and Industry.

– 2006. Letter. Response to Report on the Ageing Population, Five-Year Masterplan. *Ministry of Social and Family Development*, 7 February 2006. https://www.msf.gov.sg/publications/Documents/CAI%20PM%20reply.pdf.

– 2014. "Transcript of Prime Minister Lee Hsien Loong's Speech at Smart Nation Launch on 24 November 2014." Prime Minister's Office Singa-

pore. Last modified 24 November. https://www.pmo.gov.sg/Newsroom
/transcript-prime-minister-lee-hsien-loongs-speech-smart-nation-launch-
24-november.

– 2017a. "Dialogue with PM Lee Hsien Loong at Camp Sequoia." Last modified 24 February 2017. Prime Minister's Office, Singapore. https://www
.pmo.gov.sg/Newsroom/dialogue-pm-lee-hsien-loong-camp-sequoia.

– 2017b. "Speech by Prime Minister Lee Hsien Loong at the Launch of the
Siemens Digitalisation Hub in Munich, Germany on 11 July 2017." Last
modified 11 July 2017. Prime Minister's Office Singapore. https://www
.pmo.gov.sg/Newsroom/pm-lee-hsien-loong-launch-siemens-digitalisation-
hub-munich-germany.

– 2018. "PM Lee Hsien Loong at the SUTD Ministerial Forum." Prime Minister's Office Singapore. Last modified 5 April 2018. https://www.pmo.gov
.sg/Newsroom/pm-lee-hsien-loong-sutd-ministerial-forum.

Lee, Justina. 2019. "Singapore Eases up on School Testing to Foster Creativity." *Nikkei Asia*. Last modified 13 March 2019. https://asia.nikkei.com
/Politics/Singapore-eases-up-on-school-testing-to-foster-creativity.

Lee, Kuan Yew. 1962. "Transcript of the Broadcast on August 13 at 10.30
p.m. Over Radio Singapore – Being a Speech Made by the Finance Minister, Dr. Goh Keng Swee, on July 26, before the United Nations Special
Committee on Colonialism." *National Archives Singapore*. https://www.nas
.gov.sg/archivesonline/data/pdfdoc/lky19620726c.pdf.

Lee, Marissa. 2017. "A New Singaporean Hero Must Be the Entrepreneur:
Ong Ye Kung." *The Straits Times,* 26 April 2017. https://www.straitstimes
.com/business/a-new-singaporean-hero-must-be-the-entrepreneur-ong-ye-
kung.

Lee, Soo Ann, and Jiwel Qian. 2017. "The Evolving Singaporean Welfare
State." *Social Policy & Administration* 51, no. 6: 916–39. doi: 10.1111
/spol.12339.

Leong, Frederick T.L., Jason. L. Huang, and Stanton Mak. 2014. "Protestant
Work Ethic, Confucian Values, and Work-Related Attitudes in Singapore."
Journal of Career Assessment 22, no. 2: 304–16. doi: 10.1177/10690727
13493985.

Lim, W.K., & H. Kim. 2015. *Smart and Sustainable*. Singapore: Lee Kuan Yew
Centre for Innovative Cities. https://lkycic.sutd.edu.sg/lkycic-article
/smart-and-sustainable-bt-08-09-2015/.

Lim, Y.L. 2015. "PM: Religious Harmony Can't Be Taken for Granted."
AsiaOne, 13 May 2015. https://www.asiaone.com/singapore/pm-religious-
harmony-cant-be-taken-granted.

Lin, Nan. 1999. "Building a Network Theory of Social Capital." *Connections* 22, no. 1: 28–51. http://www.analytictech.com/mb874/Papers/lin-social-capital.htm.

Linders, Dennis. 2012. "From E-government to We-Government: Defining a Typology for Citizen Coproduction in the Age of Social Media. *Government Information Quarterly* 29. no. 4: 446–54. doi: 10.1016/j.giq .2012.06.003.

LinkedIn. n.d. "About LinkedIn." Last accessed 5 June 2020. https://about .linkedin.com/.

Low, Sui Pheng, and Benjamin K.Q. Chua. 2019. *Work-Life Balance in Construction: Millennials in Singapore and South Korea*. Singapore: Springer Singapore.

Mahbubani, Kishore. 2016. "Youth Here Lack Idealism." *The Straits Times,* 20 February 2016. https://www.straitstimes.com/opinion/youth-here-lack-idealism.

Mahmud, Aqil Haziq, and Matthew Mohan. 2020. "GE2020: Opposition Vote Swing Shows People are Looking Beyond Bread and Butter Issues, Analysts Say." *Channel NewsAsia*, 12 July 2020. https://www.channelnews asia.com/news/singapore/ge2020-opposition-vote-swing-bread-butter-issues-pap-wp-12924252.

Mandel, Ernest. 1975. *Late Capitalism*. Translated by Jors De Bres. London: Humanities Press.

Mannheim, Karl. 1952. "The Problem of Generations." In *Essays on the Sociology of Knowledge*. Collected Works of Karl Mannheim: volume V, 2013 edition. Edited by Paul Kecskemeti. 276–322. London: Routledge, 276-322.

ManpowerGroup. 2016. *Millennial Careers: 2020 Vision*. ManpowerGroup. https://www.manpowergroup.com/wps/wcm/connect/660ebf65-144c-489e-975c-9f838294c237/millennialsPaper1_2020Vision_lo.pdf ?MOD=AJPERES.

Manpower Research and Statistics Department. 2017a. *Report: Labour Market First Quarter 2017*. Singapore: Ministry of Manpower. https://stats.mom .gov.sg/Pages/Labour-Market-Report-1Q-2017.aspx.

– 2017b. *Labour Market Advance Release Second Quarter 2017*. Singapore: Ministry of Manpower. https://stats.mom.gov.sg/Pages/Labour-Market-Report-2Q-2017.aspx.

Manyika, James. 2017. "Technology, Jobs, and the Future of Work." McKinsey Global Institute. Last modified 24 May 2017. https://www.mckinsey.com

/featured-insights/employment-and-growth/technology-jobs-and-the-
future-of-work.

Manyika, James, Michael Chui, Mehdi Miremadi, Jacques Bughin, Katy
George, Paul Willmott, and Martin Dewhurst. 2017a. "Harnessing
Automation for a Future That Works." McKinsey Global Institute. Last
modified 12 January 2017. https://www.mckinsey.com/featured-insights
/digital-disruption/harnessing-automation-for-a-future-that-works.

Manyika, James, Susan Lund, Michael Chui, Jacques Bughin, Jonathan
Woetzel, Parul Batra, Ryan Ko, and Saurabh Sanghvi. 2017b. "Jobs Lost,
Jobs Gained: Workforce Transitions in a Time of Automation." *McKinsey
Global Institute*. https://www.mckinsey.com/~/media/McKinsey/Industries
/Public%20and%20Social%20Sector/Our%20Insights/What%20the
%20future%20of%20work%20will%20mean%20for%20jobs%20skills
%20and%20wages/MGI-Jobs-Lost-Jobs-Gained-Executive-summary-
December-6-2017.pdf.

Marston, Cam. 2019. "Tips for Keeping Millennial Employees." *The Balance
Careers*. Last modified 14 September 2019. https://www.thebalancecareers
.com/tips-for-retaining-millennial-employees-1918679.

Marx, Karl. 1859. *A Contribution to the Critique of Political Economy*. London:
International Library Publishing Company, 1904.

Mauzy, Diane K., and Robert Stephen Milne. 2002. *Singapore Politics Under
the People's Action Party*. Politics in Asia Series. London: Routledge.

Maxwell, Gillian A., and Adelina M. Broadbridge. 2016. "Generation Y's
Employment Expectations: United Kingdom Undergraduates' Opinions
on Enjoyment, Opportunity and Progression." *Studies in Higher Education*
42, no. 12: 2267–83. doi: 10.1080/03075079.2016.1141403.

Mazzucato, Mariana. 2013. *The Entrepreneurial State – Debunking Public vs.
Private Sector Myths*. London: Anthem Press.

McGowan, Muge Adalet, and Dan Andrews. 2015. *Skill Mismatch and Public
Policy in OECD Countries*. OECD Economics Department. Working Paper
No. 1210. Paris: OECD Publishing.

McKinsey & Company. 2017. "The Digital Future of Work: Policy Implications of Automation." Last modified July 2017. https://www.mckinsey
.com/~/media/McKinsey/Featured%20Insights/Future%20of
%20Organizations/The%20digital%20future%20of%20work/Policy
%20implications%20of%20automation/The-digital-future-of-work-Policy-
implications-of-automation.pdf.

Menon, Ravi. 2015. "Keynote Address by Mr. Ravi Menon, Managing Director, Monetary Authority of Singapore, at the Singapore Economic Review Conference 2015 on 5 August 2015." Monetary Authority of Singapore. Last modified 3 October 2019. https://www.mas.gov.sg/news/speeches /2015/an-economic-history-of-singapore.

Merton, Robert K. 1940. "Bureaucratic Structure and Personality." *Social Forces* 18, (4): 560–8. doi: 10.2307/2570634.

Meyer, John W., and Brian Rowan. 1977. "Institutionalized Organizations: Formal Structure as Myth and Ceremony." *American Journal of Sociology* 83, no. 2: 340–63. doi: 10.1086/226550.

Milkman, Ruth. 2017. "A New Political Generation: Millennials and the Post-2008 Wave of Protest." *American Sociological Review* 82, no. 1: 1–31. doi: 10.1177/0003122416681031.

Miller, Jill. 2015. "Sherraden Marks Singapore's 50th Anniversary with Lecture on Social Innovation." 12 March 2015. *Center for Social Development, George Warren Brown School of Social Work.* https://global.wustl.edu /sherraden-marks-singapores-50th-anniversary-with-lecture-on-social-innovation/.

Miller, Michael J., David J. Woehr, and Natasha Hudspeth. 2002. "The Meaning and Measurement of Work Ethic: Construction and Initial Validation of a Multidimensional Inventory." *Journal of Vocational Behaviour* 60, no. 3: 451–89. doi: 10.1006/jvbe.2001.1838.

Mills, C. Wright. 1959. *The Sociological Imagination.* New York, NY: Oxford University Press.

Ministry of Education. n.d. "Changes to PSLE Scoring and Secondary One Posting from 2021." Accessed 13 July 2019. https://www.moe.gov.sg /microsites/psle/.

– 2019. "Edusave Account." Last modified 14 August 2020. https://beta.moe .gov.sg/fees-assistance-awards-scholarships/edusave-contributions/.

Ministry of Defence. 2021. Last modified 8 November 2017. https://www .mindef.gov.sg/web/portal/mindef/national-service/discover-ns.

Ministry of Home Affairs. n.d.-a. "SGSecure." Last modified 2 March 2021. https://www.sgsecure.gov.sg/.

– n.d.-b. "SGSecure: Resources." Last modified 22 January 2021. https://www .sgsecure.gov.sg/resources.

– 2021. "Safeguarding Race and Religious Harmony." Last modified 1 March 2021. https://www.mha.gov.sg/about-us/key-topics/law-and-order /safeguarding-race-and-religious-harmony.

Ministry of Manpower. n.d.-a. "What is Tripartism." Last modified 27 October 2016. https://www.mom.gov.sg/employment-practices/tripartism-in-singapore/what-is-tripartism.

– n.d.-b. "SkillsFuture." Last modified 11 May 2018. https://www.mom.gov.sg /employment-practices/skills-training-and-development/skillsfuture.

Ministry of Social and Family Development. n.d. "Baby Bonus Scheme." Last modified 26 February 2021. https://www.msf.gov.sg/policies/Strong-and-Stable-Families/Supporting-Families/Pages/Baby-Bonus-Scheme.aspx.

Ministry of Trade and Industry. 2017a. "Future Economy Council (FEC)." Last modified 9 March 2021. https://www.mti.gov.sg/FutureEconomy /TheFutureEconomyCouncil.

– 2017b. "Industry Transformation Maps (ITMs)-Overview." Last modified 9 March 2021. https://www.mti.gov.sg/ITMs/Overview.

Mirza, Hafiz. 1986. *Multinationals and the Growth of the Singapore Economy.* New York, NY: St Martin's Press.

Miscovich, Peter. 2017. "The Future is Automated. Here's How We Can Prepare for It." World Economic Forum. Last modified 12 January 2017. https://www.weforum.org/agenda/2017/01/the-future-is-automated-heres-how-we-can-prepare-for-it/.

Mittelstadt, Brent Daniel, Patrick Allo, Mariarosaria Taddeo, Sandra Wachter, and Luciano Floridi. 2016. "The Ethics of Algorithms: Mapping the Debate." *Big Data & Society* 3 (2). doi: 10.1177/2053951716679679.

Mock, Annika. 2017. "Poll: 2 in 5 Millennials Wary of Not Being in Office." *The Straits Times,* 31 March 2017. https://www.straitstimes.com/singapore /manpower/poll-2-in-5-millennials-wary-of-not-being-in-office.

Mokhtar, Faris. 2018. "NUS to Allow Non-alumni to Take Modules, Says New President Tan Eng Chye." *Today Online,* 5 January 2018. https://www .todayonline.com/singapore/nus-allow-non-alumni-take-modules-says-new-president-tan-eng-chye.

Mokyr, Joel, Chris Vickers, and Nicolas L. Ziebarth. 2015. "The History of Technological Anxiety and the Future of Economic Growth: Is This Time Different?" *Journal of Economic Perspectives* 29, no. 3: 31–50.

Molz, Jennie Germann. 2013. "Social Networking Technologies and the Moral Economy of Alternative Tourism: The Case of Couchsurfing.Org." *Annals of Tourism Research* 43: 210–30. doi: 10.1016/j.annals.2013.08.001.

Moreno, Johan. 2019. "25% of Google Duplex Calls Are Placed by Humans, But Likely Not for Long." *Forbes,* 28 May 2019. https://www.forbes.com /sites/johanmoreno/2019/05/28/25-of-google-duplex-calls-are-placed-by-humans-but-likely-not-for-long/#6c42ba8b627c.

Mühleisen, Martin. 2018. "The Long and Short of the Digital Revolution." *Finance and Development* 55, no. 2: 4–8. https://www.researchgate.net /publication/329515181_The_Long_and_Short_of_The_Digital _Revolution.

Myers, Andrew. 2013. "Stanford Scientists Develop New Type of Solar Struc-
     ture That Cools Buildings in Full Sunlight." *Stanford News,* 15 April 2013.
     https://news.stanford.edu/news/2013/april/fan-solar-cooling-041513.html.

Myers, Chris. 2016. "Why Are Millennials So Hard to Manage? The Modern
     Workplace Might Be to Blame." *Forbes,* 6 July 2016. https://www.forbes
     .com/sites/chrismyers/2016/07/06/why-are-millennials-so-hard-to-manage-
     the-modern-workplace-might-be-to-blame/#7d24bd785f95.

Myers, Karen K., and Kamyab Sadaghiani. 2010. "Millennials in The Work-
     place: A Communication Perspective on Millennials' Organizational
     Relationships and Performance." *Journal of Business and Psychology* 25, no.
     2: 225–38. doi; 10.1007/s10869-010-9172-7.

Nanyang Technological University. 2016. "Overseas Entrepreneurship Pro-
     gramme." Last modified 18 August 2020. http://www.ntc.ntu.edu.sg
     /Programmes/oep/Pages/Home.aspx.

– 2018. "Nanyang Technopreneurship Center." Last modified 28 September
     2020. http://www.ntc.ntu.edu.sg/Pages/Home.aspx.

National Heritage Board. 2019. "National Pledge." Last modified 16 August
     2019. https://www.nhb.gov.sg/what-we-do/our-work/community-
     engagement/education/resources/national-symbols/national-pledge.

National Research Foundation. 2018. "Virtual Singapore." Prime Minister's
     Office Singapore. Last modified 20 February 2021. https://www.nrf.gov.sg
     /programmes/virtual-singapore.

National Trades Union Congress (NTUC). n.d-a. "Building a Career."
     Accessed 13 April 2020. https://www.ntuc.org.sg/wps/portal/up2/home
     /work/buildingacareer.

– n.d-b. "NTUC & Tripartism." Accessed 8 May 2020. https://www.ntuc.org
     .sg/wps/portal/up2/home/aboutntuc/whoweare/tripartism.

– n.d-c. "About NTUC: Who We Are." Accessed 8 May 2020. https://www
     .ntuc.org.sg/wps/portal/up2/home/aboutntuc.

NTUitive. 2016. "Overseas Entrepreneurship Programme." Last modified
     2016. https://web.archive.org/web/20160826164639/http:/www.ntuitive
     .sg/overseas-entrepreneurship-programme.html.

National University of Singapore. n.d.-a. "Block 71 Singapore: History."
     Accessed 18 July 2020. https://singapore.block71.co/about-us/what-we-do.

– n.d.-b. "NUS Overseas Colleges." Accessed 13 April 2020. https://enterprise
     .nus.edu.sg/education-programmes/nus-overseas-colleges/programmes/.

NUS News. 2016a. "NUS Launches School of Continuing and Lifelong Edu-
     cation." Last modified 17 June 2016. https://news.nus.edu.sg/nus-
     launches-school-of-continuing-and-lifelong-education/.

– 2016b. "SCALE-ing New Heights in Lifelong Education." Last modified 17 June 2016. https://news.nus.edu.sg/highlights/scale-ing-new-heights-life-long-education.

– 2016c. "Consortia for Cybersecurity, Synthetic Biology Launched." Last modified 21 September 2016. https://news.nus.edu.sg/consortia-for-cybersecurity-synthetic-biology-launched/.

– 2017. "NUS Introduces Three New Part-Time Degree Programmes in Business Analytics, Cybersecurity, And Software Engineering." Last modified 23 May 2017. https://news.nus.edu.sg/press-releases/nus-introduces-three-new-part-time-degree-programmes-business-analytics.

Ng, Chee Meng. 2017. "MOE FY 2017 Committee of Supply Debate Speech by Minister of Education (Schools) Ng Chee Meng." *Ministry of Education*. Last modified September 29 2020. https://www.moe.gov.sg/news/speeches/moe-fy-2017-committee-of-supply-debate-speech-by-minister-of-education-schools-ng-chee-meng.

Ng, Kelly. 2015. "Singapore Feeling Impact of Rapidly Ageing Population." *Today Online*, 1 July 2015. https://www.todayonline.com/singapore/singapore-feeling-impact-rapidly-ageing-population.

Nielsen. 2015. *Global Generational Lifestyles: How We Live, Eat, Play, Work and Save for Our Futures*. United States: Nielson. https://w ww.nielsen.com/wp-content/uploads/sites/3/2019/04/global-generational-report-november.pdf.

Nijhof, Andre, H. F. and Ronald Jeurissen. 2010. "The Glass Ceiling of Corporate Social Responsibility." *International Journal of Sociology and Social Policy* 30, nos.11/12: 618–31. doi: 10.1108/01443331011085222.

Ochen. 2017. "Transcript of Simon Sinek Millennials in the Workplace Interview." Last modified 4 January 2017. https://ochen.com/transcript-of-simon-sineks-millennials-in-the-workplace-interview/.

Oltermann, Philip. 2016. "State Handouts for All? Europe Set to Pilot Universal Basic Incomes." *The Guardian*, 2 June 2016. https://www.theguardian.com/world/2016/jun/02/state-handouts-for-all-europe-set-to-pilot-universal-basic-incomes.

Ong, Justin. 2020. "NUS' Big Push For Interdisciplinary Learning: Timely Change But There'll Be Practical Challenges, Experts Say." *Today Online*. Last modified on 15 September 2020. https://www.todayonline.com/nlisingapore/big-push-interdisciplinary-learning-nus-timely-change-therell-be-practical-challenges.

Ong, Ye Kung. 2016a. "Speech by Mr. Ong Ye Kung, Minister for Education (Higher Education and Skills) At the Adult Learning Symposium 2016 3

November 2016, Sands Expo and Convention Centre, 9.00am." Skills-Future and Workforce Singapore. Accessed 28 May 2020. https://www.ssg-wsg.gov.sg/speeches/3_Nov_2016.html.

— 2016b. "Opening Address by Mr. Ong Ye Kung, Minister for Education (Higher Education and Skills) at the Lifelong Learning Festival 2016, 12 November 2016, Lifelong Learning Institute, 11.00 Am." SkillsFuture and Workforce Singapore. Accessed 28 May 2020. https://www.ssg-wsg.gov.sg/speeches/12_Nov_2016.html.

Organization for Economic Co-operation and Development (OECD). 2012. *Innovation for Development*. Paris, France: OECD. http://www.oecd.org/innovation/inno/50586251.pdf.

Oxford Economics. 2015a. *Workforce 2020: The Looming Talent Crisis*. United Kingdom: Oxford Economics. https://www.oxfordeconomics.com/recent-releases/workforce-2020-the-looming-talent-crisis.

— 2015b. SAP *Workforce 2020: A Millennial Misunderstanding*. United Kingdom: Oxford Economics. http://www.sapevents.edgesuite.net/previewhub/africa-hr-solutions/pdfs/downloadasset.2015-01-jan-13-15.oxford-research-think-pieces—a-millennial-misunderstanding-british-english-pdf.bypassReg.pdf.

Ozanne, Julie, and Lucie K. Ozanne. 2011. "Innovative Community Exchange Systems: Grassroots Social Experiments in Sustainability." *Advances in Consumer Research* 39: 65–9.

Paquette, Danielle. 2017. "Half of Millennials Could Be Competing with Robots for Jobs." *The Washington Post*, 1 May 2017. https://www.washingtonpost.com/news/wonk/wp/2017/05/01/millennials-arent-robot-proof/.

Parker, Kim, and Ruth Igielnik. 2020. "On the Cusp of Adulthood and Facing an Uncertain Future: What We Know about Gen Z So Far." Pew Research Center. Last modified 24 May 2020. https://www.pewsocialtrends.org/essay/on-the-cusp-of-adulthood-and-facing-an-uncertain-future-what-we-know-about-gen-z-so-far/.

Patterson, Orlando. 2014. "Making Sense of Culture." *Annual Review of Sociology* 40: 1–30. doi: 10.1146/annurev-soc-071913-043123.

Pek, Sara. 2017. "Economic Development Board." Accessed 21 September 2017. Singapore Infopedia. https://eresources.nlb.gov.sg/infopedia/articles/SIP_2018-01-08_135544.html.

Pew Research Center. 2010. *Millennials: Confident. Connected. Open to Change. Millennials: Generation Next*. United States: Pew Research Center. https://www.pewresearch.org/wp-content/uploads/sites/3/2010/10/millennials-confident-connected-open-to-change.pdf.

— 2014. "Millennials in Adulthood: Detached from Institutions, Networked

with Friends." Last modified 7 March 2014. https://www.pewsocialtrends
.org/2014/03/07/millennials-in-adulthood/.

– 2016. "The State of American Jobs." Last modified 6 October 2016.
https://www.pewsocialtrends.org/2016/10/06/the-state-of-american-jobs/.

Poon, Chew-Leng, Karen W.L. Lam, Melvin Chan, Melvin Chng, Dennis
Kwek, and Sean Tan. 2017. "Preparing Students for the Twenty-First Cen-
tury: A Snapshot of Singapore's Approach." In *Educating for the 21st Cen-
tury: Perspectives, Policies and Practices from Around the World*, edited by
Susanne S. Choo, Deb Sawch, Alison Villanueva, and Ruth Vinz, 225–41.
Singapore: Springer.

Poon, King Wang, Hyowon Lee, Wee Kiat Lim, Rajesh Elara Mohan,
Youngjin (Marie) Chae, Gayathri Balasubramanian, Arron Wai Keet Yong,
and Raymond Wei Wen Yeong. 2017. *Living Digital 2040: Future of Work,
Education, and Healthcare*. Singapore: World Scientific Publishing Co.

Portes, Alejandro. 1998. "Social Capital: Its Origins and Applications in
Modern Sociology." *Annual Review of Sociology* 24 (1): 1–24. doi:
10.1146/annurev.soc.24.1.1.

PricewaterhouseCoopers (PwC). 2018. *Workforce of the Future: The Competing
Forces Shaping 2030*. United States: PwC. https://www.pwc.com/gx/en
/services/people-organisation/workforce-of-the-future/workforce-of-the-
future-the-competing-forces-shaping-2030-pwc.pdf.

Prime Minister's Office Singapore. n.d. "Mr. Tharman Shanmugaratnam."
Accessed 12 August 2020. https://www.pmo.gov.sg/cabinet/Mr-Tharman-
Shanmugaratnam.

Pugh, Allison J. 2015a. *The Tumbleweed Society: Working and Caring in an Age
of Insecurity*. Oxford: Oxford University Press.

– 2015b. "Your Job Will Never Love You: Stress and Anxiety in our Frightening New Job World." *Salon*. Last modified 27 July 2015. https://www
.salon.com/2015/07/26/your_job_will_never_love_you_stress_and_anxiety
_in_our_frightening_new_job_world/.

– 2017. "What Happens at Home When People Can't Depend on Stable
Work." *Harvard Business Review*. Last modified 4 April 2017. https://hbr.org
/2017/04/what-happens-at-home-when-people-cant-depend-on-stable-work.

Putnam, Robert D. 2000. *Bowling Alone: The Collapse and Revival of American Community*. New York, NY: Simon and Schuster.

– 2001. "Social Capital: Measurement and Consequences." *Canadian Journal
of Policy Research* 2, no. 1: 41–51. https://www.jstor.org/stable/4532503.

– 2007. "E Pluribus Unum: Diversity and Community in the Twenty-first
Century: The 2006 Johan Skytte Prize Lecture." *Scandinavian Political
Studies* 30, no. 2: 137–74. doi: 10.1111/j.1467-9477.2007.00176.x.

Raghunath, Nilanjan. 2019. "Automation versus Nationalism: Challenges to the Future of Work in the Software Industry." In *The SAGE Handbook of Media and Migration*, edited by Kevin Smets, Koen Leurs, Myria Georgiou, Saskia Witteborn and Radhika Gajjala, 477–88. London: SAGE.

Raghunath, Nilanjan, and Tony Tan. 2020a. "Covid-19 and Its Impact on Remote Work." [Blog]. Centre on Migration, Policy, and Society (COMPAS). Last modified 20 May 2020. https://www.compas.ox.ac.uk/2020/covid-19-and-its-impact-on-remote-work/.

‒ 2020b. "COVID-19 and Challenges to the Future of Work." [Blog]. Centre on Migration, Policy, and Society (COMPAS). Last modified 21 May 2020. https://www.compas.ox.ac.uk/2020/covid-19-and-challenges-to-the-future-of-work/.

Rainie, Lei, and Barry Wellman. 2012. *Networked: The New Social Operating System*. Cambridge, MA: MIT Press.

Ramaswamy, Srinivasan, and Hemant Joshi. 2009. "Automation and Ethics." In *Springer Handbook of Automation*, edited by Shimon Y. Nof, 809–33. Berlin, Germany: Springer. doi: 10.1007/978-3-540-78831-7_47.

Randstad. 2016. *Gen Z and Millennials Collide at Work*. United States: Randstad.

Rapoza, Kenneth. 2013. "Top Ten Risks Businesses Fear Today." *Forbes*, 23 April 2013. https://www.forbes.com/sites/kenrapoza/2013/04/23/top-ten-risks-businesses-fear-today/#177dc088682f.

Reeves, Martin, Kevin Whitaker, and Christian Ketels. 2019. "Companies Need to Prepare for the Next Economic Downturn." *Harvard Business Review*, 2 April 2019. https://hbr.org/2019/04/companies-need-to-prepare-for-the-next-economic-downturn.

Reynolds, Isabel. 2017. "Japan's Shrinking Population." *Bloomberg*, 17 May 2017. https://www.bloomberg.com/quicktake/japan-s-shrinking-population.

Ricardo, David. 1821. "On the Principles of Political Economy and Taxation." In *Works and Correspondence of David Ricardo* (1951), edited by Piero Sraffa, Volume I. Cambridge: Cambridge University Press.

Rigoni, Brandon, and Amy Adkins. 2016. "What Millennials Want from a New Job." *Harvard Business Review*, 11 May 2016. https://hbr.org/2016/05/what-millennials-want-from-a-new-job.

Robotic Industries Association. 2016. "North American Robotics Market Sets New Records in 2015." Robotics Online. Last modified 10 February 2016. https://www.robotics.org/content-detail.cfm/Industrial-Robotics-News/North-American-Robotics-Market-Sets-New-Records-in-2015/content_id/5951.

Rosa, Eugene A., Ortwin Renn, and Aaron M. McCright. 2013. *The Risk Society Revisited: Social Theory and Risk Governance*. Philadelphia, PA: Temple University Press.

Russell, Helen, Philip J. O'Connell, and Frances McGinnity. 2009. "The Impact of Flexible Working Arrangements on Work-life Conflict and Work Pressure in Ireland." *Gender, Work and Organization* 16, no. 1: 73–97. doi: 10.1111/j.1468-0432.2008.00431.x.

Sawhney, Mohanbir. 2018. "As Robots Threaten More Jobs, Human Skills Will Save Us." *Forbes*. Last modified 10 March 2018. https://www.forbes.com/sites/mohanbirsawhney/2018/03/10/as-robots-threaten-more-jobs-human-skills-will-save-us/#3d25b92e3fce.

Schaltegger, Christoph A., and Benno Torgler. 2010. "Work Ethic, Protestantism, and Human Capital." *Economics Letters* 107, no. 2: 99–101. doi; 10.1016/j.econlet.2009.12.037.

Schneider, Louis. 1978. "On Human Nature, Economy, and Society." Review of *The Passions and the Interests: Political Arguments for Capitalism before its Triumph*, by Albert O. Hirschman. *Contemporary Sociology* 7, no.4: 400–02. doi: 10.2307/2064317.

Schor, Juliet. B, Shehzad Nadeem, Edward T. Walker, Caroline W. Lee, Paolo Parigi, and Karen Cook. 2015. "On the Sharing Economy." *Contexts* 14, no.1: 14–15. https://contexts.org/articles/on-the-sharing-economy/.

Schwab, Klaus. 2016. "The Fourth Industrial Revolution: What It Means, What to Do." World Economic Forum. Last modified 14 January 2016. https://www.weforum.org/agenda/2016/01/the-fourth-industrial-revolution-what-it-means-and-how-to-respond./

Seng, Lim Tin, and Eugene Tan. 2015. "Shared Values." Last modified 13 July 2015. https://eresources.nlb.gov.sg/infopedia/articles/SIP_542_2004-12-18.html.

Sennett, Richard. 2007. *The Culture of the New Capitalism*. New Haven, CT: Yale University Press. doi: 10.1086/599148.

Seow, Joanna. 2016. "President, Pope Discuss Inter Faith Harmony." *The Straits Times,* 30 May 2016. https://www.straitstimes.com/world/president-pope-discuss-inter-faith-harmony.

– 2017. "Wide Array of Courses on Offer." *The Straits Times,* 20 May 2017. https://www.straitstimes.com/singapore/wide-array-of-courses-on-offer.

Shamir, Ronen. 2004. "The De-Radicalization of Corporate Social Responsibility." *Critical Sociology* 30, no. 3: 669–89. doi: 10.1163/1569163042119831.

Shanmugaratnam, Tharman. 2014. 2014. "Speech by Mr. Tharman Shanmugaratnam, Deputy Prime Minister and Minister for Finance, at the Official Opening of the Lifelong Learning Institute." Ministry of Finance. Last modified 17 September 2014. https://www.mof.gov.sg/news-publications/speeches/Speech-by-Mr-Tharman-Shanmugaratnam-Deputy-Prime-Minister-and-Minister-for-Finance-at-the-Official-Opening-of-the-Lifelong-Learning-Institute.

– 2016a. "DPM Tharman Shanmugaratnam at the Launch of the SkillsFuture Credit Inaugural Roadshow on 9 January 2016." *Prime Minister's Office Singapore*. Last modified 9 January 2016. https://www.pmo.gov.sg /Newsroom/dpm-tharman-shanmugaratnam-launch-skillsfuture-credit-inaugural-roadshow-9-january-2016.

– 2016b. "DPM Tharman Shanmugaratnam at the Switzerland-Singapore Business Forum: SkillsFuture – Developing a Future Ready Workforce." *Prime Minister's Office Singapore*. Last modified 12 July 2016. https://www .pmo.gov.sg/Newsroom/dpm-tharman-shanmugaratnam-switzerland-singapore-business-forum-skillsfuture-developing.

– 2017. "DPM Tharman Shanmugaratnam at ITE's 25th Anniversary Celebrations." *Prime Minister's Office Singapore*. Last modified 26 May 2017. https://www.pmo.gov.sg/Newsroom/dpm-tharman-shanmugaratnam-ites-25th-anniversary-celebrations.

Sheldon, Peter, Bernard Gan, and David Morgan. 2015. "Making Singapore's Tripartism Work (Faster): The Formation of the Singapore National Employers' Federation in 1980." *Business History* 57, no. 3: 438–60. doi: 10.1080/00076791.2014.983484.

Shestakofsky, Benjamin. 2017. "Working Algorithms: Software Automation and the Future of Work." *Work and Occupation* 44, no. 4: 376–423. doi: 10.1177/0730888417726119.

Siebel, Tom, Anne-Marie Slaighter, Jeff Weld, Sadia Zahidi, Diana Farrell, Katie George, James Manyika, and Michael Chui. 2017. "The Digital Future of Work: Policy Implications of Automation." Last modified 21 July 2017. https://www.mckinsey.com/featured-insights/future-of-work/the-digital-future-of-work-policy-implications-of-automation.

Siemens. n.d. "About Us." Accessed 4 June 2019. https://new.siemens.com /global/en/company/about.html.

Sim, Cheryl. 2014. "School Ranking." Last modified 7 September 2014. *Singapore Infopedia*. https://eresources.nlb.gov.sg/infopedia/articles/SIP _512_2005-01-03.html.

Sim, Royston. 2017a. "Committee on the Future Economy Outlines 7 Strategies to Take Singapore Forward." *The Straits Times*, 9 February 2017. https://www.straitstimes.com/singapore/committee-on-the-future-economy-outlines-7-strategies-to-take-singapore-forward.

– 2017b. "Siemens Digitalisation Hub to Help Boost Smart Nation Effort." *The Straits Times*, 12 July 2017. https://www.straitstimes.com/business /companies-markets/siemens-digitalisation-hub-to-help-boost-smart-nation-effort.

Sin, Yuen. 2016. "Young Singaporeans 'More Open to Entrepreneurship." *The Straits Times*, 14 June 2016. https://www.straitstimes.com/singapore /young-singaporeans-more-open-to-entrepreneurship.

– 2018. "Govt. Aid Alone Not Enough to Raise Birth Rate: Minister." *The Straits Times*, 2 March 2018. https://www.straitstimes.com/singapore/govt-aid-alone-not-enough-to-raise-birth-rate-minister.

Singapore University of Technology and Design. 2010. "Singapore University of Technology and Design Welcomes Applications for Its First Intake." Last modified 19 March 2010. https://www.nas.gov.sg/archives online/data/pdfdoc/20100326002/press_release_sutd_admission.pdf.

– 2016. "ST Electronics and SUTD Launch S$44.3M Cyber Security Laboratory." Last modified 13 May 2016. https://www.sutd.edu.sg/About-Us/News-and-Events/Press-Releases/2016/5/ST-Electronics-and-SUTD-launch-S$44-3M-Cyber-Secur.

– n.d.-a. "About Us." Last modified 19 May 2020. https://www.sutd.edu.sg /About-Us.

– n.d.-b. "SUTD Academy." Last modified 19 May 2020. https://www.sutd .edu.sg/Education/Academy.

– n.d.-c. "Unique Academic Structure." Last modified 19 May 2020. https://www.sutd.edu.sg/Education/Unique-Academic-Structure.

Sinnakaruppan, R. 2017. "Why Singapore's Education System Needs an Overhaul." *Today Online*, 27 March 2017. https://www.todayonline .com/daily-focus/education/why-spores-education-system-needs-overhaul.

Sinniah, Viva. 2017. "Singapore Graduates Facing a Creativity Gap." *Singapore Business Review*, 17 July 2017. https://sbr.com.sg/hr-education /commentary/singapore-graduates-facing-creativity-gap.

SkillsFuture SG. 2017. "Steady Progress in Implementation of SkillsFuture Credit." Last modified 8 January 2017. https://www.skillsfuture.sg/News AndUpdates/DetailPage/c68e69e5-bf1f-4cb6-92be-8b60183b9c56.

– n.d.-a. "About SkillsFuture." Accessed 13 July 2019. https://www.skillsfuture .sg/AboutSkillsFuture.

SkillsFuture SG and Workforce Singapore. n.d. "For Training Providers." Last modified 14 November 2020. https://www.ssg-wsg.gov.sg/for-training-providers/initiatives-for-providers.html.

Smart Cities World. 2021. "Collaboration to Help Shape the Future of Smarter Living in Singapore." Last modified 12 January 2021.

https://www.smartcitiesworld.net/news/news/collaboration-to-help-shape-the-future-of-smarter-living-in-singapore-6000.

Smart Nation Singapore. n.d. "Smart Nation." Accessed 13 July 2019. https://www.smartnation.gov.sg/.

Smith, James P., and Barry Edmonston. 1997. *The New Americans: Economic, Demographic, and Fiscal Effects of Immigration*. Washington, DC: National Academy Press.

Smola, Karen W., and Charlotte D. Sutton. 2002. "Generational Differences: Revisiting Generational Work Values for the New Millennium." *Journal of Organizational Behaviour* 23, no. 4: 363–82. doi: 10.1002/job.147.

Soh, Tze Min. 2012. "The Future of Tripartism in Singapore: Concertation or Dissonance?" *Ethos*, no. 11 (August): 10–18. https://www.csc.gov.sg/articles/the-future-of-tripartism-in-singapore-concertation-or-dissonance.

Sondergaard, Peter. 2015a. "Wake Up to the Algorithm Economy." *Smarter with Gartner*. Last modified 5 August 2015. https://www.gartner.com/smarter withgartner/wake-up-to-the-algorithm-economy/.

– 2015b. "Big Data Fades to the Algorithm Economy." *Forbes*, 14 August 2015. https://www.forbes.com/sites/gartnergroup/2015/08/14/big-data-fades-to-the-algorithm-economy/#71fe20ca51a3.

SPRING Singapore. n.d. Last modified 28 October 2020. https://www.enterprisesg.gov.sg/about-us/overview.

– 2015. "Setting the Standard Worldwide: Intelligent City, Smart Nation." 3 August 2015. https://web.archive.org/web/20160305103931/https://www.spring.gov.sg/Inspiring-Success/Enterprise-Stories/Page/Setting-the-standard-worldwide-intelligent-city-Smart-Nation.aspx.

Stiegler, Bernard. 2016. *Automatic Society*. Translated by D. Ross. London: Polity Press.

Steinhage, Anna, Dan Cable, and Duncan Wardley. 2017. "The Pros and Cons of Competition Among Employees." *Harvard Business Review*, 20 March 2017. https://hbr.org/2017/03/the-pros-and-cons-of-competition-among-employees.

The Straits Times. 2020. "Up Goes the Flag." 17 September 2020. https://www.straitstimes.com/world/united-states/removal-of-flag-honouring-veterans-from-white-house-sparks-anger.

– 1963. "Birth of a Nation." 10 July 1963, 8. Retrieved from NewspaperSG. https://eresources.nlb.gov.sg/newspapers/Digitised/Article/straitstimes196 30710-1.2.52.1

Strategy Group Singapore. 2017. "Key Findings from Marriage and Parent-hood Survey 2016." Last modified 8 July 2017. https://www.strategygroup

.gov.sg/media-centre/press-releases/article/details/key-findings-from-marriage-and-parenthood-survey-2016.

Sundararajan, Arun. 2016. *The Sharing Economy: The End of Employment and the Rise of Crowd-Based Capitalism*. Cambridge, MA: MIT Press.

Tan, Charlene. 2012. "'Our Shared Values' in Singapore: A Confucian Perspective." *Educational Theory* 62, no. 4: 449–63. doi: 10.1111/j.1741-5446.2012.00456.x.

Tan, Charlene, and Chee Soon Tan. 2014. "Fostering Social Cohesion and Cultural Sustainability: Character and Citizenship Education in Singapore." *Diaspora, Indigenous, and Minority Education* 8, no. 4:191–206. doi: 10.1080/15595692.2014.952404.

Tan, Eng Chye. 2020. "Universities Need to Tear Down Subject Silos." *The Straits Times*. Last modified 10 September 2020. http://www.nus.edu.sg/newshub/news/2020/2020-09/2020-09-10/UNIVERSITIES-st-10sep-pA21.pdf.

Tan, Lynette. 2020. "Change Mindset towards Skills Training in Covid-19 and Beyond: SkillsFuture Forum 2020 Panel." *The Business Times*, 20 July 2020. https://www.businesstimes.com.sg/companies-markets/skillsfuture-forum-2020/change-mindset-towards-skills-training-in-covid-19-and.

Tan, Lay Yuen. 1997. "Maria Hertogh Riots." *Singapore Infopedia*, 29 September 1997. https://web.archive.org/web/20090228164120/http://infopedia.nl.sg/articles/SIP_83_2005-02-02.html

Tan, Min-Liang. 2017. Twitter Post. 23 August 2017. 12.38pm. https://twitter.com/minliangtan/status/900215622893785089?s=20.

Tan, Tai Yong. 2008. *Creating "Greater Malaysia": Decolonization and the Politics of Merger*. Singapore: Institute of Southeast Asian Studies.

Tan, Weizhen. 2017. "The Big Read: Speed Bumps Hinder Singapore's Smart Nation Drive." *Today Online*, 14 April 2017. https://www.todayonline.com/singapore/big-read-speed-bumps-hinder-singapores-smart-nation-drive.

Tang, See Kit. 2019. "Singapore Rolls Out National Strategy on Artificial Intelligence for 'Impactful' Social, Economic Benefits." *Channel News Asia*. 13 November 2019. https://www.channelnewsasia.com/news/singapore/singapore-national-strategy-ai-economic-benefits-heng-swee-keat-12089082.

Target. 2018. "Target's Techstars and Takeoff Accelerator Programs Now Accepting Applications." Last modified 2 March 2018. https://corporate.target.com/article/2018/03/techstars-takeoff-applications-open.

Taylor, Matthew. 2018. "Millennials Are Killing Capitalism – and That's a Good Thing." *WIRED Magazine*, 13 January 2018. https://www.wired.co.uk

/article/millennials-kill-materialism-matthew-taylor-experience-
economy.

Teo, Josephine. 2019. "Keynote Address at Economic Society of Singapore
Annual Dinner 2019." Ministry of Manpower. Last modified 22 August
2019. https://www.mom.gov.sg/newsroom/speeches/2019/0822-keynote-
address-by-minister-for-manpower-at-the-economic-society-of-singapore-
annual-dinner.

Teo, Terry-Anne, Nur Diyanah Binte Anwar, Norman Vasu, and Pravin
Prakash. 2018. *Singaporean Youth and Socioeconomic Mobility*. Singapore:
Nanyang Technological University. https://www.rsis.edu.sg/rsis-publication
/cens/singaporean-youth-and-socio-economic-mobility/.

Teo, Youyenn. 2018. *This Is What Inequality Looks Like*. Singapore: Ethos
Books.

Ter Bogt, Tom, Quinten Raaijmakers, and Frits van Wel. 2005. "Socialization
and Development of the Work Ethic among Adolescents and Young
Adults." *Journal of Vocational Behaviour* 66, no. 3: 420–37. doi: 10.1016
/j.jvb.2003.12.003.

Tham, Irene. 2019. "Singapore Tops List of 105 Cities Most Ready for AI
Disruption, New Index Shows." *The Straits Times*, 27 September 2019.
https://www.straitstimes.com/tech/singapore-tops-list-of-cities-most-ready-
for-ai-disruption.

Thierer, Adam. 2012. "Why Do We Always Sell the Next Generation Short?"
Forbes, 8 January 2012. https://www.forbes.com/sites/adamthierer/2012
/01/08/why-do-we-always-sell-the-next-generation-short/#2b9ef4f12d75.

Thompson, Charles, and Jane-Brodie Gregory. 2012. "Managing Millennials:
A Framework for Improving Attraction, Motivation, and Retention." *Psy-
chologist-Manager Journal* 15, no. 4: 237–46. doi: 10.1080/10887156
.2012.730444.

Today. 2016. "NUS Enterprise to Support Start-ups in Overseas Expansion."
Today, 30 September 2016, https:// www.todayonline.com/singapore/nus-
enterprise-support-start-ups-overseas-expansion.

Toh, Elgin. 2013. "All Get a Shot at Success." *The Straits Times*, 27 April 2013.
https://www.nie.edu.sg/about-us/news-events/news/news-detail/all-get-a-
shot-at-success.

Totty, Michael. 2017. "The Rise of the Smart City." *The Wall Street Journal*, 16
April 2017. https://www.wsj.com/articles/the-rise-of-the-smart-city-
1492395120.

Turco, Catherine. 2016. *The Conversational Firm: Rethinking Bureaucracy in
the Age of Social Media*. New York: Columbia University Press.

Twenge, Jean M., Stacy M. Campbell, Brian J. Hoffman, and Charles E. Lance. 2010. "Generational Differences in Work Values: Leisure and Extrinsic Values Increasing, Social and Intrinsic Values Decreasing." *Journal of Management* 36, no. 5: 1117–42. doi: 10.1177/0149206309352246.

United Nations Department of Economic and Social Affairs (UNDESA). 2017. "Will Robots and AI Cause Mass Unemployment? Not Necessarily, But They Do Bring Other Threats." Last modified 13 September 2017. https://www.un.org/development/desa/en/news/policy/will-robots-and-ai-cause-mass-unemployment-not-necessarily-but-they-do-bring-other-threats.html.

Urry, John. 2000. *Sociology Beyond Societies: Mobilities for the Twenty-first Century*. London: Routledge.

Vallas, Steven P., and Andrea L. Hill. 2018. "Reconfiguring Worker Subjectivity: Career Advice Literature and the "Branding" of the Worker's Self." *Sociological Forum* 33, no. 2: 287–309. doi: 10.1111/socf.12418.

Vallas, Steven P., and Christopher Prener. 2012. "Dualism, Job Polarization, and the Social Construction of Precarious Work." *Work and Occupations* 39, no. 4: 331–53. doi: 10.1177/0730888412456027.

Van Ness, Raymond K., Kimberly Melinsky, Cheryl L. Buff, and Charles F. Seifert. 2010. "Work Ethic: Do New Employees Mean New Work Values?" *Journal of Managerial Issues* 22, no. 1: 10–34. https://www.jstor.org/stable/25822513.

Vaswani, Karishma. 2017. "Tomorrow's Cities: Singapore's Plans for a Smart Nation." *BBC News*, 21 April 2017. https://www.bbc.com/news/technology-39641262.

Veblen, Thorstein. 1921. *The Engineers and the Price System*. New Brunswick: Transaction Books.

Walsh, Toby. 2017. "Will Robots Bring About the End of Work?" *The Guardian*, 1 October 2017. https://www.theguardian.com/science/political-science/2017/oct/01/will-robots-bring-about-the-end-of-work.

Warner, Mark, and Mitch Daniels. 2015. "The Future of Work." Aspen Institute. Last modified 16 December 2015. https://www.aspeninstitute.org/blog-posts/future-work/.

Watts, Jake Maxwell, and Newley Purnell. 2016. "Singapore Is Taking the 'Smart City' to a Whole New Level." *The Wall Street Journal*, 24 April 2016. https://www.wsj.com/articles/singapore-is-taking-the-smart-city-to-a-whole-new-level-1461550026.

Weber, Max. 1920/. *Theory of Social and Economic Organization*. New York, NY: Oxford University Press, 1947.

– 1922. *Economy and Society*. Berkeley, CA: University of California Press, 1978.

– 1904. *The Protestant Ethic and the Spirit of Capitalism* (2nd ed.). Los Angeles, CA: Roxbury Publishing Company, 1998.

Weeks, Kelly Pledger. 2017. "Every Generation Wants Meaningful Work – but Thinks Other Age Groups Are in It for the Money." *Harvard Business Review*, 31 July 2017. https://hbr.org/2017/07/every-generation-wants-meaningful-work-but-thinks-other-age-groups-are-in-it-for-the-money.

Weil, David. 2014. *The Fissured Workplace: Why Work Became So Bad for So Many and What Can Be Done to Improve It*. Cambridge: Harvard University Press.

Weinbaum, Cortney, Richard S. Girven, and Jenny Oberholtzer. 2016. *The Millennial Generation: Implications for the Intelligence and Policy Communities*. Santa Monica, CA: RAND Corporation. https://www.rand.org/pubs/research_reports/RR1306.html.

The White House Council of Economic Advisors. 2014. *15 Economic Facts About Millennials*. United States: Council of Economic Advisers. https://obamawhitehouse.archives.gov/sites/default/files/docs/millennials_report.pdf.

Wilson, Bill. 2017. "What Is the 'Gig' Economy." *BBC*, 10 February 2017. https://www.bbc.co.uk/news/business-38930048.

Wimmer, Jeffrey, and Thorsten Quandt. 2006. "Living in the Risk Society: An Interview with Ulrich Beck." *Journalism Studies* 7, no. 2: 336–47. doi: 10.1080/14616700600645461.

Wong, Pei Ting. 2017. "Heng Swee Keat Will Head Council to Transform Singapore's Economy." *Today*. 1 May 2017. https://www.todayonline.com/business/heng-swee-keat-heads-future-economy-council.

Woo, Wei-Ling 2016. "Rewriting the Singapore Story." *Asian American Writers' Workshop*, 28 September 2016. https://aaww.org/rewriting-singapore-story/.

Woolley, Anita Williams, Ishani Aggarwal, and Thomas W. Malone. 2015. "Collective Intelligence and Group Performance." *Current Directions in Psychological Science* 24, no. 6: 420–4. doi: 10.1177/0963721415599543.

World Economic Forum. 2018. *Agile Governance: Reimagining Policy-making in the Fourth Industrial Revolution*. World Economic Forum. Last modified 24 April 2018. https://www.weforum.org/whitepapers/agile-governance-reimagining-policy-making-in-the-fourth-industrial-revolution.

World Economic Forum, and Futurity. 2020. "How 2 out of Every 5 Jobs Lost During COVID-19 May Not Come Back." Last modified 25 May 2020. World Economic Forum. https://www.weforum.org/agenda/2020/05/42-of-jobs-lost-during-covid-19-may-not-come-back.

Wu, Irene. 2018. "Developing 21st Century Skills in Asia Through Design Thinking." *Think: The Head Foundation Digest* (April): 9–10. https://www.dropbox.com/s/uk3podlzf8z77d1/THink-APR-2018-ebook.pdf?dl=0.

Wyckoff, Andy. 2017. "Re-booting Government as a Bridge to the Digital Age." OECD Volume 1. Last modified 25 July 2017. http://www.oecd.org/governance/re-booting-government-as-a-bridge-to-the-digital-age.htm.

Yeoh, Francis. 2017. "Commentary: Helping Start-ups and Entrepreneurs, the 'New Heroes' of Singapore, Succeed." Last modified 1 October 2017. https://news.nus.edu.sg/sites/default/files/resources/news/2017/2017-10/2017-10-01/ENTREPRENEURS-cnaonline-1oct.pdf.

Young, Alwyn. 1992. "A Tale of Two Cities: Factor Accumulation and Technical Change in Hong Kong and Singapore." In *NBER Macroeconomics Annual* 7: 13–5nom4.

Zhi, Wei, and Kartini Saparudin. 2014. "National Pledge." Last modified 1 August 2014. https://eresources.nlb.gov.sg/infopedia/articles/SIP_84_2004-12-13.html.

Zuboff, Shoshana. 1988. *In the Age of The Smart Machine: The Future of Work and Power*. New York, NY: Basic Books.

– 2015. "Big Other: Surveillance Capitalism and the Prospects of an Information Civilization." *Journal of Information Technology*, 30, no. 1: 75–89. doi:10.1057/jit.2015.

Zuckerman, Ezra W. 2010. "Speaking with One Voice: A 'Stanford School' Approach to Organizational Hierarchy." In *Stanford's Organization Theory Renaissance, 1970–2000 (Research in the Sociology of Organizations, Volume 28)*, edited by Claudia Bird Schoonhoven and Frank Dobbin, 289–307. Bingley: Emerald Group Publishing Limited.

Index

References to figures are indicated with the letter *f*.